THE PEOPLE'S PARTY IN TEXAS
A Study in Third Party Politics

By Roscoe C. Martin

PUBLISHED IN COOPERATION WITH

THE TEXAS STATE HISTORICAL ASSOCIATION

UNIVERSITY OF TEXAS PRESS, AUSTIN & LONDON

Standard Book Number 292–70033–4
Originally published by The University of Texas as
University of Texas Bulletin No. 3308, February 22, 1933
University of Texas Press Reprint, 1970
Printed in the United States of America

To
M. E. M.

PREFACE

It is possible to study the American political party in and from the capital city of the nation, but this will give a very incomplete picture of what is happening. A thorough understanding of the American party system cannot be obtained until the party is studied in the setting of the individual states in which it functions.

The party in the state may be less dramatic in its setting and operations, but the basic factors in the American political process are revealed through such examination more clearly than elsewhere. The social composition of the party, its organization and leadership, its techniques of organization and propaganda, the function of the political association in the community of which it is a part—all these are shown through an intensive study of the party activity in a limited area and period. Further, it is from a series of detailed studies of this type that there may finally be assembled the data from which a truer understanding of the party and sounder interpretations of its meaning both in American life and in modern democracy may be made.

The study of the Populist Party in Texas is one of the indispensable contributions to the knowledge of the American party and the American political process. With great care and patience, Dr. Martin has examined the available data regarding the political operations of this organization at an interesting moment in our national life, and has pieced the materials together to make a view of this episode. His monograph not only throws much needed light on the local history of Texas, but it also helps to illuminate our knowledge of the radical movement of the 1890's throughout the whole country, and indeed of the growth of the "insurgent" movements in the more general sense. This painstaking inquiry into the detailed operations of a special party association in a special period is a contribution to political science which no student of American politics can afford to ignore.

CHARLES E. MERRIAM.

Chicago, Illinois,
February 13, 1933.

The author takes this means of acknowledging his indebtedness to his friends throughout Texas, whose coöperation in gathering the data for this work has been invaluable; to Professors Charles E. Merriam and Harold F. Gosnell of the University of Chicago, whose suggestions have been of very material assistance; and to the Bureau of Research in the Social Sciences of The University of Texas, whose financial aid made possible a thorough investigation of the subject.

ROSCOE C. MARTIN.

Austin, Texas.

TABLE OF CONTENTS

LIST OF TABLES

LIST OF MAPS

LIST OF CHARTS

INTRODUCTION

The UNITED STATES is looked upon by students as being, along with Great Britain, the foremost exemplar of the two-party system among the world's democracies of the present day. Like its progenitor, however, its record as a two-party nation is not without fault. Its old parties have been beset from time to time by no less than half a dozen third and minor parties of some consequence, one of which, the present Republican Party, rose from obscurity to preëminence through the channel of third party politics. The third party therefore has been a factor of considerable significance in our national history despite the two-party tradition, for more than one such party has risen to exercise a large influence on the course of our affairs, either by direct participation in politics or by unceasing adherence to a program which ultimately has triumphed.

Not least among the third parties we have known in this country was the People's Party, which wielded a powerful influence during the last decade of the nineteenth century, especially in the states of the West and the South. Contemplation of that party leads naturally to the same questions as those which arise with reference to other similar parties. What were the conditions from which grew the movement of protest heading in the new party? Whence came the party, what classes did it draw upon for its strength, and what was the program with which it attracted the dissident elements? What were the achievements, direct and indirect, of the third party? In addition to these time-honored questions which usually have received attention from historians in the past and which may be considered still as being of very great importance, the student of politics lists a number of queries which reveal his interest in the minor party as an intriguing and significant phenomenon in the political life of the country. He desires to know, among other things, what types of men gravitated to the front as leaders of the third party, what was the organization of the party, what were the various forms of propaganda and campaign technique employed to further its cause, and what was the reception accorded it by the established parties. In short, he considers the third party as a manifestation of political behavior and seeks to explain it in intelligible terms. In so doing, he does not ignore or underestimate the value of the traditional content of studies of minor party movements, but he does subordinate the chronicling of his subject to analysis and interpretation.

If the political scientist of the present day parts ways with the chronicler in the matter of content, he also departs from the beaten path in his method of approach. Time was, in the not far distant past, when a formidable study of a third party might be made without stirring from one's library, and indeed many worth while studies have followed investigations of a purely formal character. The latter day student is not content, however, merely to read and digest. This he must do, to be sure, but it is only part of his preparation, and, if the truth be told, a minor part, for it but fits him for the minute and objective research which alone will eventuate in a clear understanding of his problem.

The study which follows is the result of an investigation in the field of the new politics. The first point of departure is to be noted in the territorial scope of the work. The author, concluding that such a study as he purposed to make could not be conducted satisfactorily for the whole country or even for a section, as the Southwest, has limited his investigation to the State of Texas, in the belief that intensiveness is to be preferred over extensiveness. The findings will lead, it is hoped, to certain conclusions which will prove of general applicability where third parties are concerned.

A second point of departure in method may be seen in the approach to the problem. The author first familiarized himself with the general facts of an historical nature pertaining to the party and its predecessors by an extensive course of general reading, following which he made use at length of the *Register of State and County Officers* in the office of the Secretary of State in Austin. Intensive examination of those records indicated that, for the purposes of the proposed study, one section of the State, namely that lying west of a line drawn through Taylor and Kimble counties, might be ignored largely as being so sparsely settled as to be of little consequence in the days of Populism. It seemed further to warrant the division of the remaining counties of the State into five categories which were, briefly: first, that comprising those counties which "went Populist" for Governor in three or more elections; second, that whose counties went Populist in one or two elections, but which returned a heavy Populist vote several times;

third, that whose counties, normally Democratic in their vote, successfully repulsed the Populist onslaughts; fourth, that whose counties either were normally Republican or polled a large Republican vote; and fifth, that including counties which over a period of years appeared to have no preferences in politics but were opportunist in their vote. The first category included only fifteen counties and the fourth and fifth, only half a dozen each, so that it appeared practicable to study substantially all of the counties listed in the three. The second and third, however, included perhaps a hundred counties, which had to be narrowed down to not more than fifteen in each class if the investigation was to be pursued with thoroughness. The author proceeded thereupon to select for study certain significant counties from each group, having regard for factors of geographical location, type of agricultural area, racial origins of the populations, and the vote (both by comparison and by contrast) of the surrounding counties. The final result was a list of some sixty counties, arranged into the five categories abovementioned and distributed throughout the State in such a way as to present a complete picture, by representation, of the political, social and economic, and racial complexions of its people.

The author then fared forth to investigate the districts selected for study, visiting virtually every county listed and making an intensive examination into the political background of each. The sources relied upon chiefly were personal interviews, election records, and local newspapers. Of the first, the author had audiences in sixty-four counties with some 250 men from every walk of life and every political party, including a generous number of former Populists. Concerning the second, it was discovered that the county's election records sometimes are not kept at all and frequently are poorly kept, yet the election returns for the Populist era were found and used in no less than forty counties in widely separated sections of the State. With regard to the third, the author learned that local editors lose their entire plants, including their files, by fire every few years and that they themselves come and go with amazing fluidity, yet the files, partial or complete, of some thirty weekly newspapers were discovered and examined.

By these means has the author attempted to avoid the taint of scholasticism. He has of course made use of the standard references, including half a dozen of the daily newspapers of the

State of the time of the People's Party, but he has sought to escape the sterile generalizations for which the dailies afford such an excellent basis. Rather he has endeavored to make the study intensely practical by carrying the investigation to the level of the county and even the voting precinct. He has, in short, dealt with the problem of the People's Party by employing an objective method; and while such significance as may be conceded to the following essay may be supposed to derive largely from content, it should not escape notice that the study parts ways with the usual work on state politics in the matter of method.

CHAPTER I

THE FIELD OF ACTION: POLITICAL AND ECONOMIC BACKGROUND

IT HAS long been recognized that the "Great Game of Politics" is one whose rules are determined largely by the conditions under which the game is played. Thus industrial Massachusetts may be expected to adopt a point of view with regard to politics somewhat, if not wholly, different from that of agricultural Louisiana; urban New York quite naturally views public affairs with eyes different from those of rural Georgia; Illinois' aristocratic citizenry of the "North Shore" differs in politics from coal-mining, day-laboring West Virginia in training, temperament, and interests; and traditionally Democratic Alabama finds little in common with the Republican strongholds of Pennsylvania. In short, politics cannot be separated from its surroundings and studied with any degree of intelligence, nor can political parties be lifted from the environment in which they developed and operated without the loss of that vital something which leads to a real understanding of their nature and significance.

What is true of politics and political parties in general is no less true of the People's Party in Texas. One cannot take that party from the place of its nativity and subject it to a laboratory analysis with any degree of success, for it was inextricably interwoven with the political, social, and economic fabric of the State; and it can no more be understood considered separately than can an intricate figure cut from a piece of tapestry in whose pattern it forms a basic design. There is also the further fact that the People's Party was not an event but rather part of a process, and the process of which it was in some sense the culmination had its beginning during the days of Reconstruction. Hence it appears advantageous, nay necessary, to analyze the situation and to summarize briefly on the conditions which were precedent to the political rebellion of the nineties. This may be done most readily and most pointedly by treating of (1) Texas as a field of action for political parties; (2) the grievances of the farmers; (3) the "agrarian crusade;" and (4) the situation at the beginning of the rebellion, i.e., in 1890.

I

Since Reconstruction days, Texas has been essentially a one-party state. Circumstances conspired almost inevitably to array her on the side of the Old South in the titanic struggle called the Civil War. Hence, when the conflict was over, the State was subjected to the usual military and semi-military regimes of the Reconstruction era; and it was not until 1873, when the Democratic Party under Richard Coke decisively defeated the Republicans under E. J. Davis, that "popular" government was restored. Since that time, notwithstanding the recurrent challenges of various minor parties, the Democrats have controlled politics in Texas almost without interference of a serious nature.

Here then is the first factor of importance to be borne in mind when taking account of the State of Texas as a field of battle for political parties. The ground has not proved fertile, for while many opposition parties have come into existence none has been successful. This fact may be explained in a variety of terms, but none is so simple nor yet so logical as that which places in front rank the Confederate tradition. The Republican Party was the party of union; the Democratic, the party of secession—and Texas had been a Confederate state, many of her favorite sons high in the councils of the Confederacy. The Democratic Party was looked upon, rightly or wrongly, as the defender of all that was dearest to the hearts of Texans, and those not members of that party were regarded virtually as traitors to the State. It is true that as time passed the virulence of this doctrine grew less; but it is also true, as we shall have occasion to note, that to the very end of the era of political unrest the "bloody shirt" specter rose frequently to bring about the downfall of those who would overthrow the Democratic Party.

A second factor which distinguishes Texas as a field of action for political parties is its essentially agrarian complex. The farmers have always spoken with a weighty voice in the politics of the State, and during the days of the agrarian crusade their influence was especially great. In 1870 approximately 70 per cent of all persons gainfully employed in Texas were engaged in agricultural pursuits, as farm laborers, farmers proper, planters and overseers of plantations, apiarists, stockmen, dairymen, etc.[1] By 1900 the relative numbers of those employed in agriculture had shrunk somewhat, but they still included 65 per cent of the State's working population.[2] The figures are not to be taken literally as being indicative of the strength of the farmers as a class, although they are suggestive of the preponderantly agricultural character of the State from the end of the War to 1900.

The predominance of the agrarian classes in Texas during the last quarter of the last century is a factor of large importance in evaluating the State as a party battleground. It has been said that the agricultural classes exercise a power in politics far greater than that to which their numerical strength would entitle them, and a persuasive argument may be adduced in behalf of this proposition.[3] It is not necessary that this thesis be accepted, however, to explain the influence of the farmers in Texas politics in times past, for the simple fact is, they have controlled through sheer force of numbers. The farmers therefore have been recognized as a class, or rather as *the* class, to be reckoned with, and serious consideration necessarily has been given to the desires of that class.[4]

II

The significance of the above brief analysis becomes apparent when attention is directed to the nation-wide movement of agrarian unrest which swept the United States during the last quarter of the last century. That movement, evidenced in a series of waves of discontent, counted the farmers of the State of Texas among its staunchest supporters, and its every phase found a local counterpart in this State. Thus the farmers of Texas found themselves constantly embroiled in the activities of organizations designed to

---

[1] *Ninth Census of the United States*, I, 671.

[2] *Twelfth Census*, XI, Part II, 541.

[3] Arthur N. Holcombe, *The Political Parties of Today* (New York, 1924), Chap. III.

[4] A third feature which characterized the State as a field of action for political parties was the racial diversity of her people. The author has discussed this factor in Chapter IV.

bring relief to the agricultural classes, and they carried their share and more of the burdens of those organizations. It is no more than just that we examine the ills complained of by the farmer before turning to a brief analysis and evaluation of the various phases of the movement itself, as it is no less than necessary if we are to grasp the significance of the agrarian crusade.

The conditions making for agrarian discontent in Texas, though peculiar in part to the State, were not greatly different from those which motivated the farmers in other of the southern states, and in the Middle- and Northwest. Specifically, the citizen of the State, and hence the farmer, had to deal first with the political situation which obtained after the War. The administration of the Radical Republican Governor E. J. Davis was nothing less than a semi-military regime, and the people seized the first opportunity to rid themselves of the undesirable Governor by electing Richard Coke to the office. The inauguration of Coke marked the end, formally at least, of Reconstruction in Texas, and the State supposedly was rehabilitated politically by 1876. Nevertheless, the experiences of the decade from the end of the War to that time were indelibly stamped on the minds of its people, and the rule of the Radicals embittered them for many years to come. And indeed, if the whole truth be told, Reconstruction, applying the term to local jurisdictions, was not an accomplished fact in some sections of the State much if any before the end of the century. The citizens of Texas then found themselves forced to deal with problems of a political nature, involving among other questions that concerning the status of the negro, the seriousness of which can hardly be over-stated.

A second group of problems confronting the people of Texas immediately following the War were those pertaining to agriculture. The returning soldier-farmer expected to and did find his interests demoralized by the conditions inevitably following in the wake of the War, and he set about at once to effect a recovery. Even when agriculture had recovered somewhat from the effects of the War, however, there were conditions prevailing which made for discontent among the farmers. For example, when the price of agricultural produce remained stationary from year to year, or worse, declined, so that the debtor farmer found himself meeting his obligations with appreciated money, a heated protest arose from all parts of the

State. Again, the labor problem was one affecting primarily the agriculturists: and when the negro quitted the farm and refused to work either on shares or for wages, a situation was created in which the larger farmer was vitally concerned. Yet again, the credit system in vogue in the State bound the farmer over to his creditor, who was often the merchant with whom he traded, and obligated him to plant the crop stipulated by the terms of his contract. Each year saw him deeper and deeper in debt until at last the creditor was forced to foreclose on the farm, retaining its former owner as tenant or selling it to satisfy his claims. Nor was the credit system alone responsible, in the eyes of the farmer, for the process by which he was gradually and systematically reduced to a state which he chose to consider but little better than that of peonage, for there was the mortgage evil which was the subject of bitter complaint on his part. Still another problem in connection with agriculture arose from the general adherence to the one-crop system. Cotton, the "money" crop of the farmer, was cultivated almost to the exclusion of other staples, and the strange spectacle was seen of the farmer's buying imported supplies that might much more easily have been produced on his own farm. The movement for diversification of crops began in the seventies, but to the present day it remains next to impossible to convince the farmer of the folly of his homage to "King Cotton." A fifth problem confronting the agriculturist was that of marketing his produce after he had grown it. The middleman stood ready to assist him, providing he would sell at a price which would guarantee a substantial return to the benefactor; and if the ingenious farmer was able to pass the middleman in safety, there were numerous marketing monopolies ready and eager to handle his produce—at his expense. The difficulty of marketing his produce at any price, together with the knowledge that its value would multiply some three or four times after leaving his hands, caused the farmer to cry out against monopolies and to demand government regulation of all concerns which appeared to combine against him.

Inseparable from the problem of marketing agricultural produce went that of transportation, which resolved itself into the problem of dealing with the railroads. What should be the policy of the Government in the construction of railway lines? Should financial aid be granted the railway companies; should the State give aid in the form of grants of the public domain; or should the companies be forced to rely on their own resources? Again, once their lines were in operation, their monopolistic character was almost universally recognized, and it was insisted that freight and passenger rates could not be allowed to go unregulated; but what form should the needed regulation take? These were questions which arose with regard to railway transportation, and each of them demanded prompt and firm action. Hesitancy on the part of the Government, solutions worked out which later proved unpopular, the apparent inability of the Legislature to cope with the railroads—all of these were causes for agrarian discontent during the last quarter of the nineteenth century.

After the question of railroad construction and regulation came a number of problems pertaining to public finance for which no satisfactory solution had been found. First among these may be listed the currency question, on which the farmers took a decided stand for free silver and more paper money, agitation for which did not cease until the voices of their spokesmen were finally stilled. Second may be noted the problem of taxation. Taxes weighed more heavily on the agricultural than on other classes, or so it seemed to the farmer. Certain it was that the produce tax was undesirable, and indeed the whole theory of the general property tax was attacked and numerous and varied substitutes suggested. A third problem was that arising from the tariff policy of the United States Government. The farmers objected to protection, arguing that the protective principle favored other and smaller classes while it ignored the interests of the great masses of agriculturists. In all of these fields, which involved questions of the financial policy of the Government, state and national, the farmers took a hand, demanding concessions here and making recommendations there and at all times keeping the Legislature and the world at large informed of their desires and wishes, whatever the question at hand.

Such were the conditions, in brief, in Texas at the beginning of the period under consideration. The political situation, the position of agriculture, transportation, Government finance—these problems with their various ramifications made for agrarian unrest and caused the farmer to take under advisement ways and means of bettering

existing condition. Conditions did not of course remain un-
changed throughout the period; on the contrary, they were in a
state of constant flux and change. Whatever the situation at any
given time, however, the farmer was convinced of one thing, namely,
that he received justice at the hands of none. And as the century
drew to a close, his conviction became more and more firm until
he was constrained, as he viewed it, to resort to drastic measures
to relieve himself of an intolerable situation. Meanwhile, however,
while the state of mind which led eventually to the formation of
the People's Party was in process of evolution, the rising tide of
discontent was to be seen in the development of those organizations
which had their climax in the stirring campaigns of the nineties.[5]

III

The agrarian crusade in Texas may be divided into two distinct
periods. The first period was characterized by the rise and decline
of the Granger movement and the taking over of the currency
issue by the Greenback Party. It came to an end in the middle
eighties when the Greenback Party, which had supplanted the
Grange as the representative of the farmers, passed out of politics
in Texas, dying a natural death after the campaign of 1884. The
second period was ushered in with the establishment, in the late
eighties, of the State Farmers' Alliance, which became the champion
of the cause of the farmer just as the Grange had been ten years
before. The Alliance gave way, in the early nineties, to the People's
Party, which gave political expression to the principles of the
Alliance and which conducted several campaigns for state offices as
the representative of the agricultural and laboring classes. Toward
the end of the century, the People's Party passed on, as had the

---

[5]No attempt has been made in this section to evaluate the fairness of the
complaints brought by the farmers. Had such an effort been made along
objective lines, it is hardly to be doubted that reasonable explanations largely
foreign to the world of politics would have been found for most of the
phenomena against which the farmers raised their voices. It is not, however,
within the province of the present discussion either to justify or to condemn
the charges brought. It is quite enough, for our purposes, if we summarize
and explain briefly the attitude of the agriculturists without regard to considerations of rightness and justness.

Greenback Party before it; and its passing marked the end of the agrarian movement.

The Grange was an organization of farmers founded in 1867–68 under the leadership of a small group of Government clerks in Washington. From there the order spread in every direction, reaching Texas with the founding, in 1873, of a subordinate Grange in Bell County. In the latter part of that year the State Grange was established, and by 1875–76 the order had come to be a power in the State. Its growth continued until, in 1877, it boasted a membership of some 45,000. A decline set in during that year and the next, and within a short time the order had lost so heavily as to have become impotent as a state organization.

The objects of the Grange—to secure for its members a fuller home life, more social intercourse, and the advantages of coöperative dealing with the business world—did not include participation, either direct or indirect, in politics; and from 1874 to 1878, when the Grange was at its height in Texas, the leaders of the organization accepted at its face value the principle of nonpartisanship and strove steadily to gain the ends outlined in the first declaration of principles. The order nevertheless enjoyed considerable political influence, even while protesting its innocence of all political designs, through its petitions and memorials to the State Legislature which, in view of the numerical strength of the petitioner, was constrained frequently to take favorable action on its requests.[6]

The Greenback Party, which followed the Grange as the representative of the agricultural classes, based its existence on the demand for an inflated currency. The Grange had taken cognizance of the currency question in numerous memorials and petitions for more money; and it was no more than natural that when that order had run its course, its members should drift into the newly organized Greenback Party, which offered at once a haven of refuge for the inflationist Grangers and a hope of achievement in a field in which the old order had failed. The new party thus succeeded to the position previously occupied by the Grange and became the

---

[6] See the author's article, "The Grange as a Political Factor in Texas," in *The Southwestern Political and Social Science Quarterly*, VI (March, 1926), 363–384.

organ through which the farmer voiced his complaints and sought concessions.

The Greenback movement reached Texas in 1878, when a state convention of Greenbackers met. In that year, and for several years thereafter, the party was very active in state politics. Candidates were put in the field for state offices in the elections of 1878, 1882, and 1884, and a few members of the State Legislature and one Congressman were elected as Greenbackers.[7] The party achieved only a modicum of success, and by 1884 it had demonstrated its impotence to deal with the currency problem which became less acute with the return of comparative prosperity in the early eighties. Hence the movement fell apart; the Greenbackers returned to the Democratic and the Republican parties, whence they came; and Greenbackism passed out of state politics a few years after the movement had become moribund nationally.[8]

The second period of the agrarian crusade in Texas was characterized by the rise of the Farmers' Alliance and the taking over of its principles, in the early nineties, by the People's Party. The Alliance had its origin in Texas in 1874 or 1875; and while the original organization disintegrated in 1879, a second Alliance was founded in the same year by an officer of the first. The organization grew and prospered, though it experienced varying fortunes, and eventually it established itself firmly as an order to be considered in any project which called for popular support. In 1887,

---

[7]The votes of the candidates of the various parties for Governor for the years noted may be seen from the following table:

	1878	1880	1882	1884
Democratic	158,933	166,101	150,891	212,234
Republican	23,402	64,382		25,557
Greenback	55,002	33,721	102,501*	88,450*

*This candidate ran as an Independent-Greenbacker, but his sympathies were so definitely with the Greenbackers that he was reckoned the candidate of their party.

The party elected ten representatives to the lower house of the Legislature in 1878, and three in 1880. A scattering few legislators called themselves independents after the elections of 1882, but of confessed Greenbackers in the legislative body there was none.

George W. Jones, of Bastrop, was elected to the national House of Representatives in 1878 as a Democrat and was reëlected in 1880 as a Greenbacker. He was not a candidate for reëlection in 1882.

[8]See the author's article, "The Greenback Party in Texas," in *Southwestern Historical Quarterly*, XXX (Jan., 1927), 161–178.

Dr. C. W. Macune, leader of the Alliance in Texas, organized the National Alliance, which, by a process of amalgamation and consolidation, attained a strength within the next four years variously estimated at from one to three million members.[9] During the same years, a similar organization was in process of development in the midwestern states, and but for some differences which appear not to have been serious the two might have combined. As it was, the northern and the southern Alliances pursued separate courses, though their paths paralleled so closely that it was not difficult for them to coöperate in the end in support of a newer and mightier movement for the emancipation of the farmer.[10]

The Farmers' Alliance (for it is not necessary for our purposes that the two orders be kept distinct), like the Grange, proposed to obtain political remedies for the ills of the farmer without actually entering the field of politics as an organization. This it did by preparing a list of desirable reforms, as the Grange had done, calling them, however, *demands* instead of *petitions*. By means of these demands, the Alliance was able to bring about the passage by the Legislature of certain reform measures and to secure certain concessions for the farmers in the platform of the Democratic Party. It was in these ways that the Farmers' Alliance made its influence felt politically, although from time to time members of the order announced their candidacies, waged active campaigns, and got themselves elected to public office. The Alliance is remembered primarily, then, for the influence it wielded by reason of its demands and the pressure which it brought to bear on public officials, and not for active participation in politics by its members.

IV

The approach of the year 1890 found the farmer in a position no more favorable than that which he had occupied fifteen years earlier, and indeed in many respects his lot was worse than it had

---

[9]John D. Hicks, *The Populist Revolt* (Minneapolis, 1931), pp. 112–113. Technically, the order was called the Farmers' and Laborers' Union of America; in practice it operated under the name of National Alliance, or simply the Alliance.

[10]The northern Alliance boasted a membership in 1890 of about 1,000,000. *Ibid.*, p. 103.

For the rise of the Alliance, see *ibid.*, Chap. IV.

been previously. To be sure he had been the recipient of legislative favors in the form of sympathetic statutes from time to time, and the Democratic Party had taken cognizance of his demands now and again, but to substantial economic benefits and advantages he was still almost a total stranger. He was a victim of the appreciating dollar, whose value rose steadily to the end of the century, and of the consequent diminishing price level for agricultural products, and especially for cotton. Reducing these facts to the terminology of the farmer, it appeared that the less money he had, the more he had need for, and if this elementary fact be kept in mind it will be a simple matter to explain his demand for more money at the hands of the Government. The system of taxation likewise continued to annoy him as it had during the days of the Grange, as did also the whole problem of monopolies and their regulation. In short, the conditions of which he had complained for almost two decades remained with him, apparently unalleviated by the passing of time.

Notwithstanding these facts, the situation was not entirely hopeless, thanks largely to the Farmers' Alliance. That organization in the late eighties named a special committee to promote the welfare of its members before the Legislature; outside that body it continued with its usual energy to advocate what it considered to be the interests of the agricultural classes. Partly as a result of the agitation of the Alliance, the state platform of the Democratic Party for 1888 pronounced in favor of railway and trust regulation. In 1889 the law-making body turned its attention to the trust problem, passing a law designed to meet the demand of the convention of the preceding year. No action was taken on the problem of the railways, however, and the Alliance and various other organizations of a like nature continued to agitate the matter of railroad regulation until in 1890 the Democrats were forced to take definite action in the direction of granting the demands made of their party. This they did by nominating for Governor James Stephen Hogg, Attorney-General under the preceding administration, who had declared for the railroad commission, and by drafting a platform which granted much to the Alliance and its sympathizers. It is particularly worthy of note that the platform demanded the abolition of the national banking system and called for the free and unlimited coinage of silver. The Alliance, considering that it had won a notable victory with the adoption by the Democratic Party of these several principles, expressed its gratification by endorsing Hogg and the commission. That candidate won in the elections by an overwhelming majority, and in the spring of 1891 the Legislature passed an act which provided for a commission with the power to regulate the railroads of the State. The passage of the commission act was accounted the crowning achievement of the Alliance to that time. Its leaders felt that, although the dominant party had not accepted their subtreasury scheme, it had attempted to meet them half way by adopting other important features of the Alliance program. Hence, while they were not universally convinced of the good faith of that party, they were willing to give the new Governor a chance.

The truth of the matter was, the farmer derived considerable comfort from the candidacy and the campaign successes of Governor Hogg. Previous candidates for high office had professed an interest in his welfare, but he had learned not to place too great faith in their promises. Here, however, was a man of the people: here was a man who spoke a language all might understand, who removed his coat when he made a public address and threw his suspenders off from his shoulders, letting them dangle about his knees, who drank out of the water pitcher provided for him "like a horse," as one of his disillusioned followers put it later, and who came out unequivocally for the railroad commission. After all, it was the commission that mattered, and it was the commission that put the Democratic Party to test. Thus it was that the Governor took office under conditions which were at once auspicious and perilous: the people of the State had united to elect him, but he was for all that on trial in the mind of a goodly portion of the electorate and so was the cynosure of all eyes.

He had been in office no more than a few months when leaders of the Alliance began to give evidence of their disappointment in the new administration. The Democrats, they charged, now refused to carry out the spirit of the Alliance program. Petitions presented by spokesmen of the farmers were ignored, and the Governor refused to name to the new commission a trusted leader of the Alliance whose appointment had been urged by petition. The Governor stated that he had never seen the petition and that he therefore had not been aware of the desires of the Alliance in the matter. A prominent Alliance man replied that he personally had carried the document in question to the office of the chief executive; and when both the Governor and the confessed bearer of the petition maintained their positions, a delicate situation arose. From the state of mind induced among the leaders of the Alliance by this incident, it was easy to proceed to the point where the commission itself was looked upon with suspicion and distrust and to conclude finally, when no marked change for the better followed its institution, that the thing had failed to accomplish the ends sought. In short, the Alliance men chose to consider that they had been betrayed by the Governor and the Democratic Party of Texas.

Nor were the local spokesmen of the Democracy solely at fault in the minds of their agrarian constituents. The Democratic Party was, after all, a national organization, and the voter in this State had learned long since to pin great faith in the jealous guardianship of his interests by its leaders. It appeared to him now, however, that those very leaders in whom he had reposed the greatest confidence were determined to ignore him in his day of distress. There were, to be sure, the usual expressions of sympathy from high Democratic sources, but nothing tangible came of them prior to 1892. In that year the party was placed on final trial by the election of Cleveland to the Presidency. Had the nation prospered under the new administration, the rumblings of discontent probably would have died away in their incipiency; but instead of prosperity the Democrats seemed to bring with them conditions which steadily became worse. Further, as if the burdens were not already sufficiently grievous, the President himself completed the disillusionment of the southern and the western farmer by his "betrayal" of the cause of free silver.[11] Thereafter, it was patent to the discontented workingman, no favorable action was to be expected from the Democratic Party; for the national party was as little concerned in his welfare as was the state party. In his extremity, he concluded to seek redress for grievances where it could be had most readily and most effectively.

He was abetted in this resolve by a somewhat changed point of view on the part of the people, or considerable groups of them, regarding political parties. Fifteen years before, a native Texan

---

[11] See *ibid.*, pp. 311 ff.

was a Democrat by force of circumstances; in some communities he was literally forced to conform if he would maintain his position in society. The Confederate tradition had at least two aspects, however, and if on the one hand it led Southerners to mobilize in the ranks of the party of secession, on the other it counselled, nay encouraged, rebellion against tyrannical authority. Further, in 1890 the War was twenty-five years in the past, and even the memories of Reconstruction had become somewhat dulled. This is not to say that the "bloody shirt" had lost its effectiveness as an argument: it is rather to state only that, if it was not yet polite, it was at least no longer dangerous to question the dominant party. Hence there was occasionally some criticism here and there of the blind and straight-ticket voter and considerable comment, some of it savoring of bitterness, about "brass collar" Democracy. These murmurings, feeble and indistinct at first, increased in volume and intensity with the passing of time. Each succeeding movement of disaffected citizens left the dominant party a little more vulnerable, providing, as each did, precedent for protest against the alleged highhanded tactics and uncompromising attitude of its leaders. It came to be understood that no catastrophe would follow if the Democratic Party were challenged at the polls and that the need for united support of the policies of that party, if indeed such need had ever existed, had largely disappeared. With the frequent if not the general acceptance of these ideas, the Alliance perceived that it no longer needed to play the role of the humble petitioner but that a more exalted position for it gradually was assuming form.

It was out of the conditions above described that the People's Party evolved in the way presently to be seen. The agricultural classes had certain grievances which they thought entitled them to a hearing. Nevertheless their situation did not improve perceptibly but on the other hand seemed gradually to grow worse, and this in the face of constant efforts on their part to gain redress at the hands of the Governor and the Legislature. It mattered little to them that their ills were in good part the result of national economic maladjustments and therefore largely beyond the point where legislative assistance would avail to effect a recovery. Farmers either did not consider this fact or did not understand it—perhaps they

did not even wish to understand it. They wanted relief, and that
without delay, and they sought it by direct approach to the authority
most accessible. That authority was found in the public officials,
which as the farmers viewed it was quite logical inasmuch as they
invariably connected "hard times" with political malpractices or
official neglect. It was a source of never-ending wonder to the
agriculturists that the classes of society by all odds the largest and
most important should be sorely neglected by their public servants,
and they proposed, by coöperating among themselves, to inquire
into the causes of and put an end to this perplexing situation. They
had made more than one honest effort to obtain redress at the hands
of the Democratic Party, which however, they had convinced themselves, had served but poorly and mayhap not even honestly the
interests of its agrarian constituents. But if the thing could not be
done indirectly, then perhaps it might be accomplished by direct
attack upon the offices themselves. And if consideration of this
alternative brought them face to face with the tradition of party
loyalty, it revealed at the same time a precedent for independent
action. The farmers of Texas, therefore, were not wholly unpre-
pared, when the opportunity presented, to go into the People's
Party and to seek there the justice which they considered had been
denied them in the party of their fathers.

CHAPTER II

THE PEOPLE'S PARTY AND ITS PROGRAM FOR RELIEF

I

IT CANNOT be said of the People's Party that it was organized at any particular time or on any given date. The evils which led to the political rebellion called the Populist movement were in process of development for two decades, and their effects were cumulative. The farmer, of course, realized early that his condition was not satisfactory, but for long he was loath to resort to drastic remedial measures, preferring to seek redress by pacific means. Hence for many years the spirit of unrest was allowed to ferment with no strong hand turned to the removal of its causes, while the farmer experimented with various agencies designed to improve his condition. Indeed, as is frequently the case with significant social and political upheavals, the symptoms of disaffection were not recognized in their incipiency. They were present nevertheless for several years before the first state convention of the People's Party was called, and this fact explains the statement that the person who begins with the so-called organization of that party in Texas in truth understands little of its origin but sees merely the result of a process set in motion years before.[1]

Mutterings of that discontent which came to the surface as the People's Party were heard locally in divers sections of the State as early as 1885–86. At that time, it will be recalled, the farmers relied heavily on the Alliance for assistance, and that organization responded to the best of its ability. Where political action seemed advisable, however, the Alliance apparently was helpless; for it was avowedly a non-partisan order, and it elected so to remain— ostensibly, at least. The farmers then found themselves without an agent through which they could speak and act effectively in the

---

[1]It must be borne in mind constantly that the People's Party was but one phase of a larger agrarian movement and that, far from being purely local in character, that movement swept the whole country during the last three decades of the nineteenth century. See *supra*, Chap. I. See also Solon J. Buck, *The Agrarian Crusade* (New Haven, 1920), and Hicks, *op. cit.*

field of politics; yet it was precisely in that field, they were convinced, that a spokesman was most needed. The answer to the dilemma assumed form gradually and hesitantly, yet eventually it appeared to be plain: let them organize, and seek the advantages in politics which their Alliance offered them already in the social and economic worlds.

Exactly where the first Populist local organization was effected cannot be said definitely, for the answer to that question hinges on the precision with which the term *People's Party* is defined. It appears, however, that it was in Comanche County that the malcontents first broke through the lines of the Democracy and assumed control. The government of that county had fallen into the hands of a "ring" of local politicians whose long tenure of power had given them almost proprietary interests in their offices. In 1886 a movement was set on foot, sponsored tacitly if not openly by the Farmers' Alliance and led by Thomas Gaines, to purge the county offices of their traditional incumbents; a full "Farmers' Democratic" or "People's" ticket was nominated, and a system of schoolhouse clubs was set up from which to launch the campaign in its behalf. To the consternation of the Democrats, who were non-plussed by the suddenness and fury of the attack, the entire People's ticket was successful.[2] After the campaign of '86, the Citizen's Party experienced the usual successes and reverses. It never failed, however, to preserve its identity and its organization; and when the movement had spread and become the People's Party of Texas, that party found its staunchest supporters and at least one of its ablest leaders among those who as backers of the People's ticket first carried the banner of reform to a large measure of local success.

Almost simultaneously with the outbreak in Comanche County a similar movement got under way in Erath County, immediately to the north, and under substantially similar conditions. Favored by

---

[2]The information on which is based the above summary of the Citizens' Party in Comanche County comes from *The Comanche Vanguard,* of the issues of July 12 through Sept. 13, 1913 (in the Library of The University of Texas, Austin, Texas). The *Vanguard* at that time was edited by Judge Lyman B. Russell, an old-time lawyer and newspaper man of Comanche. Judge Russell's love for history prompted him to write and publish serially the complete story of what he called "The Ten Years' War," an interesting account of the People's Party in Comanche County.

the support of an unusually strong Alliance organization and exceptionally able local leaders,[3] the new independent party swept the old politicians from power in the elections of '86 and gained control of the county. The organization perfected during the campaign of that year carried over into succeeding years, and in 1892 the independent party of Erath County became bodily the local unit of the People's Party.[4]

Proof that the independent movement in Comanche and Erath counties was not the result wholly of purely local conditions may be found in the fact that in the same year in which the non-conformists assumed control in those counties a group of dissenters who called themselves Nonpartisans organized in Fort Worth, Tarrant County, put candidates in the field for both municipal and county offices, and captured for themselves the Mayor's office and a place in the State Legislature. They reëlected their Mayor in 1888, though their other candidates were defeated, and in 1890 their last representative failed of reëlection. The spirit of revolt had taken deep root, however, and it came to the surface again in 1892 with the appearance of the People's Party, which was regarded by contemporary observers as nothing more than the continuation under a new name of the old Nonpartisan movement.[5]

During the years immediately following 1886, the independent movement made its appearance in divers sections of the State. Thus in 1888 dissatisfied farmers organized a "Nonpartisan Party" in Lampasas County, the home of the Alliance, and nominated candidates for county offices;[6] in Robertson County a "new political party" appeared and made arrangements to nominate a county

---

[3]As in Comanche County, the rank and file of the discontented were farmers, and their leaders were high in the councils of the Alliance. Among these leaders was Evan Jones, for many years President of the State Alliance and an able and universally respected man.

[4]*The Dublin Progress,* Sept. 25, 1896 (in the office of the *Progress,* Dublin, Texas).

[5]*Fort Worth Daily Gazette,* Feb. 12, 1893 (in the State Library, Austin, Texas). The *Gazette* remarked, with reference to the People's Party advocates with whom it was acquainted, that "They were not Populists (in 1886), but went under some other alias, though the odor was the same."

[6]*The Lampasas Leader,* Oct. 6, 27, 1888 (in the office of the *Leader,* Lampasas, Texas).

ticket;[7] and in Navarro County the reformers nominated candidates on what the *Southern Mercury* later was pleased to call the "first People's Party ticket."[8] Yet again, in Red River County, in the northeastern part of the State, an organization was perfected in 1888 under the leadership of Dr. Pat B. Clark, a staunch Alliance and later Populist leader, which was called the People's Party;[9] and though it was not successful at the polls in that year, it maintained its identity until its sponsors became People's Party leaders and its members Populists. In 1890 the movement spread further, local independent tickets with Alliance support appearing in that year in counties as widely separated as Jasper,[10] in the southeastern part of the State, and Jack,[11] in the north-central.

From the brief examination of local politics here made it is apparent that the independent movement entrenched itself in all parts of the State during the years 1886–1890. Almost universally it was understood that the rank and file of the independent voters were farmers and further that the majority of them were Alliance men.[12] The agricultural classes were stirring uneasily, then, at the end of the decade, and already they had, by their espousal of

---

[7]*The Southern Mercury*, Aug. 21, 1888 (in the Library of The University of Texas, Austin, Texas).

[8]*Ibid.*, July 30, 1896 (in the State Library, Austin, Texas).

[9]This information comes from the private papers of Dr. Pat B. Clark in possession of his son, Mr. S. E. Clark, of Austin, Texas. If the testimony of those who knew Dr. Clark personally be accepted at its face value, it may be inferred that he saw more clearly the importance of his actions than did most of the local leaders. Presumably he saw the need for a new party to bring together the dissident elements in the North and South and set about deliberately to organize such a party. Further, he called it from the first the "People's Party." Thus his party appears to have been more closely allied with the People's Party as it finally evolved than were the other local movements mentioned.

[10]*The Southern Mercury*, Aug. 7, 1890.

[11]*Jacksboro Gazette*, Sept. 18, Oct. 23, 30, Nov. 6, 1890 (in the office of the *Gazette*, Jacksboro, Texas).

[12]Occasionally, for one reason or another, the local independent candidates did not become identified with the Alliance. Thus in Gonzales County the Alliance was never pledged definitely to support the independent ticket, though more than one effort was made to connect the two. *The Gonzales Inquirer*, July 17, Aug. 21, Sept. 4, Oct. 30, Nov. 13, 1890 (in the office of the *Inquirer*, Gonzales, Texas).

the reform movement locally, given evidence of a deep-seated feeling of dissatisfaction and a willingness to coöperate, even to the extent of quitting the Democratic Party, in an effort to correct the evils which permitted them to be held in bondage.

Further evidence of a deep-rooted discontent was offered by the efforts, halting and ineffectual at first, to organize for action on a state-wide basis. The first such effort came in 1886, when representatives from several counties met and held an "anti-monopoly" convention. The convention was of no intrinsic importance. Again, in 1888, there convened a nameless gathering of Alliance and Knights of Labor men who desired to discuss what steps should be taken in the coming campaign.[13] Those assembled declared themselves independent politically, thus by inference inviting the formation of a new political party, and drew up a list of the demands on which they proposed to act in politics.[14] This meeting was followed by a convention, held in Fort Worth on July 3, which accepted the spirit of its action and nominated candidates for state offices on a non-partisan ticket.[15] Further, on July 5, a convention of the Union Labor Party, meeting also in Fort Worth, approved the action of the non-partisan convention, pledging to its ticket the support of the Labor Party.[16] The presence and activities in these conventions of prominent Alliance men gave rise to the charge that the Alliance had gone into politics,[17] and credibility was lent to the report by the fact that the non-partisans had nominated the President of the State Alliance, Evan Jones, for Governor.

---

[13]*The Southern Mercury*, April 19, 1888. The meeting convened at Waco on May 15.

[14]Ernest William Winkler, *Platforms of Political Parties in Texas* (Austin, 1916), pp. 256–257. Mr. Winkler in this volume has performed the laborious task of gathering and editing the platforms of political parties in Texas. His work is of very great value to the student of the political history of the State. See also the *Dallas Morning News*, May 18, 1888 (in the Library of The University of Texas).

[15]*Ibid.*, July 3 and 4, 1888; *The Southern Mercury*, July 12, 1888.

[16]Winkler, *op. cit.*, pp. 262–263.

[17]Officials of the Alliance were quick to deny the charge, both in the daily press of the State and in the official organ of the order, the *Mercury*. Repercussions of the discussion may be seen in *The Southern Mercury*, as for example in the issue of April 19, 1888.

President Jones, however, struck a lusty blow for his order by refusing to accept the nomination, principally on the ground that, while he had a perfect right to stand for election as a citizen of the State, his candidacy would imperil the Alliance and lay it open to false charges by its enemies.[18]

The strategy of the independents then in nominating the Alliance leader went for naught, and they turned secondly to ex-Lieutenant Governor Marion Martin, who had been nominated for Governor some months before by the Prohibitionists. Governor Martin had a reputation throughout the State which would guarantee him a good following, and in addition he was acceptable to the independents in that he was a staunch Alliance man and a political dissenter. He was therefore nominated, or rather endorsed, by a convention of the "Amalgamated Party," as the non-partisans chose on this occasion to call themselves, which met at Dallas on August 25.[19] He made his campaign as a fusion candidate, receiving the support of the independents, the Prohibitionists, and presumably the Republicans since that party had declined to nominate a state ticket. When the votes were counted, it was found that while he had not even threatened to outstrip the Democratic candidate he had run a strong race.[20] His campaign served to reveal something of the strength of the independent vote and to indicate what its spokesmen might hope for in the future, particularly if they should be able to enlist the support of the Republican Party.

From 1888 to 1890 talk of a new party was constantly in the air, and men found it more and more necessary to take sides on the question of the desirability of a new deal in politics. Among the leaders of the Alliance some, as Dr. C. W. Macune, thought that organization ought to maintain its non-partisan character, on the ground either that participation in politics would invite the destruction of the order or that the Democratic Party remained competent to deal with all problems. Others, as Thomas Gaines and W. R. Lamb, two of the Alliance leaders most active in propagating the new faith, insisted that no hope of relief from the Democratic

---

[18]*Ibid.*, Aug. 7, 1888. He did see his way clear later, however, to announce his candidacy for a place in Congress. *Ibid.*, Oct. 16, 1888.

[19]*Ibid.*, Aug. 28, 1888; *Dallas Morning News*, Aug. 25, 1888.

[20]His vote totaled 98,477, as against 250,338 for his Democratic opponent.

Party could be entertained and maintained that the farmers and laborers as a class must combine into a new party for the pursuit of their common welfare. Under these circumstances the Alliance divided locally, many members criticizing the existing régime and demanding independent action, many others defending the Democratic Party and deploring the new heresy. As the time for making nominations for the elections of 1890 drew near, speculation was rife as to the course which the Alliance would elect to pursue. As we have seen, the Democrats safeguarded their party in that year by nominating Hogg for Governor and accepting many demands of the Alliance program. Thus, temporarily as it proved, virile criticism of the old party died down: the proponents of the old régime prevailed, and the Alliance appeared to be united in support of the chastened Democracy. Not for long, however, was even the appearance of good feelings to be maintained.

It was no more than natural, in view of the circumstances attending the elections of 1890, that the Alliance should expect large favors and concessions from the new administration. Indeed, it was confident that such favors would be forthcoming, and it named a committee to serve as its representative before the Governor and the law-making body in Austin. In another place we have seen briefly how the Governor and the Alliance came to the parting of the ways,[21] so that the order felt it necessary to renounce its fealty to the new administration and take a position as its critic. It now appeared that the Legislature was no more anxious to serve the Alliance than the Governor had been. In fact, a very definite schism developed between some of the Alliance legislators who supported the Governor and the legislative committee of the order, and this rift reached a climax when one of the leading Alliance lawmakers and Harry Tracy, a member of the legislative committee, came to blows on the floor of the House of Representatives.[22] This was the last straw: the relations between the two factions within the Alliance, that is, between those who supported the Governor and those who opposed him, already strained, broke completely. The break came to the surface with the issuance, on March 4, 1891, of what came to be called the *Austin Manifesto*, a document drafted

---

[21]*Supra*, Chap. I.

[22]*Dallas Morning News*, April 23, 1893.

and made public by the Alliance friends of the Governor in the Legislature. The statement contained a severe denunciation of the legislative committee and its activities, which it was alleged were designed to plunge the Alliance into politics and ally it with the incipient third party.[23] Tracy answered in kind, criticizing his wayward brothers in unsparing terms,[24] and the division was confirmed. The Alliance split then on the rock personified by Governor Hogg. Thenceforward neither wing took a backward step; neither proposed a compromise; but both proceeded full tilt toward the point where a legal divorce could be obtained.

In developing the division between the two wings of the Alliance, it was the Hogg branch which forced the fighting, though it found willing adversaries in the camp of Tracy; and the issue which came to the fore was the subtreasury proposal.[25] It was not the subtreasury over which the quarrel originated but the policy of the new administration, and there is no apparent reason why the subtreasury should have been injected into the conflict at this particular time. On the contrary, a campaign had just closed, and ordinarily the question would have been allowed to lie for some eighteen months. The most plausible explanation of the reason for the issue's being raised during this off-season is that it was brought forward at the behest or at least with the consent and approval of the Governor. It is quite possible that he and his advisors were desirous of having the question, which conceivably might be an embarrassing one, brought to a head during an off-year and discussed definitively outside the Democratic Party. It is likewise possible that the Governor read the omens and concluded that the Alliance might prove to be a thorn in his flesh in the campaign of 1892 and that it were better therefore that it be encouraged to suicide.

Whatever the explanation therefor, the Manifesto men called a meeting of anti-subtreasury Alliance adherents to convene on July 10 at Fort Worth. In the call for the meeting its authors announced that the "Tracy type of bossism" must go and that the

---

[23]*Ibid.*, May 31, 1891.

[24]See, for example, his communications in *The Dublin Progress*, March 28, April 11, 1891.

[25]For a brief discussion of the subtreasury plan, see *infra*.

convention would turn its attention to the matter of eliminating it.[26]
The convention met at the time and place designated and proceeded
to come out flatly against the subtreasury and against political
action for the Alliance. A few proponents of the subtreasury, led
by W. R. Lamb, attempted to establish their right to seats in the
convention; but on being informed that the call for the meeting by
clear implication excluded them, they withdrew and held a convention of their own.[27]   The anti-subtreasuryites later perfected the
organization of a second alliance, giving to it the name "The Grand
State Farmers' Alliance" and pledging it to oppose the subtreasury;[28]   and still later this wing of the original Alliance merged
with the Grange, thus losing its identity.[29]   Its history then lends
some credibility to the belief that Governor Hogg sponsored its
organization for the express purpose of effecting a division of the
Alliance and thus bringing about its downfall.[30]

The Tracy faction sprang to arms with equal energy. The "rump
convention" at Fort Worth announced unequivocally in favor of the
subtreasury plan, and in its regular convention for 1891 the Alliance placed itself definitely on record as regards that issue. The
antis there (for a few were in attendance) were refused a hearing;
a reporter from an anti-subtreasury newspaper was ejected from
the hall; the Ocala Demands were endorsed without dissent;[31] and
the subtreasury plan was approved unanimously by specific reference.[32]   Thus did the Alliance answer the administration and the

---

[26]*Dallas Morning News*, May 30, 1891.

[27]*Ibid.*, July 11 and 12, 1891.

[28]*Ibid.*, Nov. 28, 1891. It is interesting to note that one of the leaders of
the anti-subtreasury wing of the Alliance was a young man, determined and
aggressive, named W. H. Murray, known during these later days as "Alfalfa
Bill" Murray.

[29]*Texas Farmer*, April 29, 1893 (in the State Library, Austin, Texas); *The
Galveston Daily News*, May 21, 29, 1893 (in the Library of The University of
Texas, Austin, Texas).

[30]*The Dallas Morning News* took cognizance of a feeling among Alliance
men to this effect in its issue of Aug. 21, 1891.

[31]The Ocala Demands, drafted by the national convention of the Farmers'
Alliance which met at Ocala, Florida, in December, 1890, included the leading principles favored by that organization. They may be read in Hicks,
op. cit., pp. 430–431.

[32]The proceedings of the convention will be found reported in full in the
Dallas Morning News, Aug. 19–23, 1891.

anti-subtreasury men: it accepted the offer of battle, and on the terms named by its antagonist.

The Democrats, who were not of a mind to beat back from their position, advanced further and further, and by a series of declarations defined the term *Democrat* in such a way as virtually to exclude from their party orthodox Alliance men. The first drastic step was taken in October, 1891, when the Dallas County Democratic Executive Committee requested the resignation of one of its members, an Alliance man, who had announced his allegiance to the subtreasury principle. When friends of the Alliance the length and breadth of Texas rose to protest, a Democratic member of the committee felt constrained to explain that body's action in some such terms as these: A Democrat pledges himself to support the platform and the candidates of his party when he becomes a member thereof; the Alliance member is pledged by the action of his order to support no party which does not accept in full the Ocala Demands, which declare in favor of the subtreasury plan. How can a man conscientiously pledge himself to two courses of action which may be diametrically opposed? It is not possible, and for that reason a subtreasury man cannot be a good Democrat and has no right to claim membership in the Democratic Party.[33]

If the action of the Dallas County Executive Committee caused a stir in Alliance circles, a second step in the process which it inaugurated constituted a veritable bombshell. This step came when, some three weeks after the Cole incident, N. W. Finley, Chairman of the State Democratic Executive Committee, issued an open letter " To the Democracy of Texas" wherein he defined the status of the Alliance subtreasury men. The Democratic Party, he argued, had declared against the subtreasury plan in its platform of 1890, if not by specific reference then at least by plain implication,[34] whereas the members of the Alliance were pledged to support of that scheme.

---

[33]The "Cole incident" (the victim of the committee's action was one W. R. Cole) will be found discussed in full in *ibid.*, Oct. 6, 11, 25, 1891.

[34]The plank of the Democratic platform, which Finley interpreted as covering the subtreasury scheme, read in part to this effect: "We oppose the collection and distribution, by the Federal government, of any money . . . . in any way of advancement, or loan to any citizens or class, upon any sort of security, whether government or commercial bonds, farm or other products." Winkler, *op. cit.*, p. 288.

They were pledged, to speak plainly, not to accept the decision of the Democratic Party but to attempt to capture the party and graft upon it a principle which not only was not desired but against which a definite pronouncement had been made by that party. The Alliance had, by adopting the subtreasury plan in the terms which it had used, become a political party, and as such *its members should not be allowed to participate in Democratic primaries.*[35] In short, members of the Alliance were given the alternative of resigning from that order or leaving the Democratic Party, or, as they chose to regard it, of sacrificing their liberty or their party.[36]

While the Democrats were engaged in the business of alienating the Alliance men and driving them from the party, the leaders of the non-partisan groups were preparing to receive them with open arms. Some half-dozen of those leaders, who incidentally also were prominent in the councils of the Alliance, busied themselves throughout the spring and summer of 1891 in spreading the doctrine of independent action in politics. They attended Alliance encampments and labor meetings in all sections of the State, raising everywhere the cry of Democratic perfidy and party bourbonism. Foremost among these early agitators was W. R. Lamb, Union Labor partisan, leader in the State Federation of Labor, and member of the Alliance, who had long been a proponent of independent political action. Lamb attended the Cincinnati convention of reformers of May, 1891, where he was appointed a member of the National Executive Committee of the new Third Party. When he returned to Texas, therefore, he occupied a position which enabled him to speak with some authority concerning the Third Party. On July 4 and 5 he attended a meeting of the State Federation of Labor and in an address delivered there announced that the *grandest People's Party rally* ever held would convene in Dallas on August 17.[37] Thus was called the first People's Party convention ever to meet in Texas.

The convention met according to call, and whatever it lacked in numbers it more than made up in enthusiasm and aggressiveness.

---

[35]*Dallas Morning News,* Oct. 25, 1891.

[36]The Finley ukase, it is interesting to note, was not received with anything approaching unanimous approval in Democratic circles. For Democratic protests, see *ibid.,* Nov. 1, 7, 1891.

[37]*Ibid.,* July 5, 1891.

The fifty delegates were largely Alliance men; indeed the most significant thing about the convention perhaps is the fact that the annual State Alliance convention was in session in Dallas at the time. Most of the People's Party delegates were also delegates to the Alliance meeting, and it need hardly be said that they worked early and late to convert their Alliance colleagues to the cause of Populism. Their success may be gauged from press comments, which complimented them highly on their adroitness and skill at maneuvering and insisted that the Alliance convention had become almost wholly a convention of Third Party men, the protestations of the Alliance president notwithstanding.

In convention assembled, the delegates organized the People's Party of Texas by appointing a state executive committee of seventeen members, two of whom were colored, providing for a hierarchy of committees to coöperate with the state committee and drafting a platform stating their grievances and listing their demands.[38] The meeting then adjourned until February, 1892, when it proposed to meet in Fort Worth to transact additional business in the name of the party.[39] The second convention met as scheduled and endorsed the action of the first, and in June a third gathering nominated candidates for state offices. By the time of the third meeting something of the growth and strength of the People's Party movement could be seen: from a convention attended by no more than fifty delegates in August, 1891, the party's state meeting had grown to more than 1,000 representatives by June of the following year.[40] Further, by the date of the nominating convention there had been organized throughout the State more than 2,000 Populist clubs,[41] and organizers were even then going "out into the hills and down into the valleys preaching their new gospel of political salvation."[42] The leaders of the party, in short, had busied themselves for the year past in building up a state-wide organization, and they had succeeded to an extent which boded ill for their adversaries.

---

[38]The convention is discussed in *ibid.*, Aug. 17 and 18, 1891.

[39]*Ibid.*

[40]Winkler, *op. cit.*, pp. 293, 297, 314.

[41]*Dallas Morning News*, June 7, 1892.

[42]*Ibid.*, April 19, 1892.

Meanwhile those staunch Democrats—and their numbers were legion—affected by the Finley ruling were sorely perplexed. They had all professed undying allegiance to the dominant party, yet they were at the same time confirmed Alliance men and so unswerving subtreasury advocates. They knew not where to turn nor how to proceed, and the result was they floundered about like a rudderless ship for more than six months. In November, some three weeks after the Finley ukase, their leaders met in Dallas as "subtreasury Democrats" to discuss ways and means. The attitude of the Alliance men as a whole may be seen from the statement of an old veteran, General Henry E. McCulloch, a Democrat of unquestioned loyalty and a trusted Alliance man, who remarked petulantly that he had voted the Democratic ticket before Finley was born, that he had always been a Democrat, and that he proposed to remain one notwithstanding the fulminations of the Democratic state chairman![43] His views were shared by virtually every Alliance leader of consequence,[44] excepting the few like Lamb and Gaines who had become affiliated already with the People's Party, and by literally thousands of the rank and file of the order throughout the State.

By the first of the year 1892 the subtreasury Democrats had evolved into the "Jeffersonian Democrats." They met in convention in February of that year and approved a platform which differed only in nomenclature from that of the People's Party adopted previously. One plank of the platform recommended the continued organization of Democratic clubs for the purpose of carrying into effect the principles announced,[45] and to such effect was the work

---

[43]*Ibid.*, Nov. 15, 1891.

[44]Some two weeks after the date of this statement by General McCulloch there appeared in the daily papers a protest against the Finley ruling signed by a large number of the most prominent Alliance men in the State. The protest, which may be read in *ibid.*, Nov. 25, 1891, accused the Democratic leaders of attempted bossism and affirmed the right of all men to petition and make known their desires.

[45]An interesting discussion arose in connection with this plank when a delegate moved to strike out the word *Democratic*. Debate on the proposition became acrimonious, and the motion was lost only after an appeal to the "bloody shirt" by an old soldier had side-tracked the main issue. Apparently its sponsor meant for the amended resolution to be an initial step which would assist in bridging the gap between Jeffersonians and Populists.

For a report of the convention, see *ibid.*, Feb. 11, 1892.

of organization pursued during the next several months that by April the number of local units approached 1,000, with an estimated membership of 70,000.[46] Meetings of "skunk Democrats" were held on every hand, and every such meeting announced the adherence of new converts.[47] From the tenor of the discussions in these meetings, from the pronouncements of the men most active in promoting them, from the criticisms hurled against the movement by its enemies, and from the daily press reports, one is forced to the conclusion that the Jeffersonian Democrats comprised chiefly those members of the Alliance who had not yet seen their way clear to espouse openly the cause of the People's Party. It was apparent that the situation would not long endure, for except for the shibboleth of party name there was no difference between the two and no reason why they should not consolidate. The problem was solved when, early in April, 1892, the Jeffersonian leaders cast the die for the Third Party and Populism. They had accepted already the teachings of that party, based as they were on the Ocala Demands of the Alliance; they now accepted also the name, and the two movements became one.[48]

The authors of the policy of the Democratic Party doubtless had expected some criticism, but certainly they had not anticipated an outright rebellion. They were therefore ill prepared for the full fury of the storm which broke over their heads, and they sought its abatement without delay by both formal and informal offers of

[46]On April 18, there were 700 clubs, with a total membership near the figure named. *Ibid.*, April 19, 1892.

[47]Such a meeting was held by the discontented Democrats of Dallas County about April 1. Chairman Finley had referred to the subtreasury members of his party as "skunk Democrats," and the Jeffersonians delighted so to characterize themselves. *Ibid.*, April 1, 1892.

[48]The merger was effected at a joint meeting of the majorities of the executive committees of the People's Party and the Jeffersonian Democrats which was held at the Alliance building in Dallas. *The Galveston Daily News*, April 12, 1891.

The *Dallas News* reported the coalescence of the two forces in these words: ". . . The Alliance walked over into the camp of the third party and the fortunes of the two bodies were made one." *Dallas Morning News*, April 19, 1892. Note that, according to the interpretation given by the *News*, it was the *Alliance* and not the Jeffersonian Democracy which thus cast its fortunes with the People's Party. The confused terminology indicates merely the identity of the two bodies.

peace. Informally, it was reported, the administration sent emis-
saries to the spokesmen of the Alliance to effect a reconciliation,
offering to modify the Finley manifesto so as to make it acceptable
or, if necessary, to withdraw it altogether. The subtreasury men
listened with patience to the peace offer but informed its bearers
that the time for concession and conciliation had passed.[49] Formally,
the old party ordered a retreat from the too-advanced position into
which it had been thrust by its chairman. The process began when,
toward the end of January, 1892, the Democratic executive committee of Dallas County passed a resolution inviting all persons
to participate in the deliberations of that party who would pledge
their support to its nominees. The *Dallas News* featured this action
under the headline, "BARS LET DOWN," and professed to see
therein a confession by the administration of the error of Finley.[50]
Whatever the effect of the resolution, its intent was plain enough,
though it failed to reconcile that element of the party at which it
was directed. So also did a similar offer by the Democratic chieftains in the call for their party's state convention for 1892.[51] It
was, to speak plainly, too late for compromise.

From the analysis of the inception of the People's Party it is
apparent that Populism sprang from the soil. It came into being
in many sections of the State within the space of a brief period
almost as if by prearrangement, yet there was no relation between
the various local phases of the movement aside from that provided
by the common conditions from which all grew. It was, then, in
its incipient stages a spontaneous, almost explosive force, and its
very spontaneity guaranteed it against artificiality. As it developed
into a force to be reckoned with in the State, leaders came to the
front and presumed to speak for it; and among these leaders, two
stood out. W. R. Lamb insisted from the beginning on the formation of an independent party; he counselled political action on the

---

[49]*Ibid.*, Nov. 28, 1892.

[50]*Ibid.*, Jan. 31, 1892.

[51]*Ibid.*, May 14, 1892. The salient portion of the call (Article 3) read as
follows: "No man should be excluded from the primaries for the reason that
he believes in the subtreasury or any other single principle or measure opposed by the Democratic Party, provided he is willing to support the organized action of the party, and vote for its nominees regardless of their
views upon such principle or measure."

part of Alliance men even before the day when Populism first made its appearance; and he cast his lot with that party in its infancy, nursing it through its minor youthful ills and adversities until it had grown to be a strong young giant. Harry Tracy likewise was deeply interested in affairs political, but despite that fact he remained with the Alliance straight through, leading the subtreasury men through the intermediate stages of subtreasury Democracy and Jeffersonian Democracy to Populism. The People's Party, then, was one of spontaneous and manifold origins; but as it approached the point where consolidation could be effected, aggressive and resourceful leaders appeared, the one to hew a straight line in the direction of open and confirmed independent political action, the other, with the aid of able lieutenants, to follow a more devious route eventuating in the same result. Thus developed the People's Party, which combined a favorable situation with a popular platform to draw into its ranks a vast army of men who sympathized with the program of the Farmers' Alliance.

II

The party whose origin we have examined grew by leaps and bounds. Dissident elements of numerous varieties flocked to its standards, from motives which, it may be assumed, differed as widely as their origins. By far the greater part of the adherents to Populism, however, doubtless affiliated with that party from principle. They were at the same time repelled by the practices of the Democratic Party and attracted by the platform and the program of the Populists. The shortcomings of the Democracy have been analyzed. It becomes necessary now to investigate the other side of the movement and to see what Populism had to offer its converts by way both of theoretical and of practical inducements.

In the beginning, it may be noted that the leaders of the People's Party, to whom one would look for intellectual guidance among its members, were concerned chiefly with practical problems which demanded immediate solutions, rather than theoretical justifications for their position. Their writings, therefore, whether personal works or party platforms, contain relatively little reference to the philosophical content of Populism. Nevertheless one may discern from time to time a thread of reason running through all of these writings; for although Populist authors had little time for logical explanations of their attitudes, they followed certain lines of thought which indicated common acceptance of a basis on which the movement ultimately rested.

The fundamental ideological concept behind the People's Party is to be found in the old American doctrine of the equality of man. With this idea as a starting point, it was a simple and logical step to its corollary which concluded that any variation from exact equality contravened natural and God-given laws and therefore was not to be tolerated. Not only were men created equal; they had certain equal and inalienable rights, of which justice demanded that they be not deprived. The old Alliance doctrine was summarized in the words "Equal rights to all, special privileges to none," and People's Party publicists were not able to improve upon that idea.

The second great hypothesis of Populism, which rested directly on the doctrine of equality and equal rights, may be stated in these terms: Despite the essential and natural equality of man there exist certain economic inequalities which weigh heavily on all workingmen but more especially on the agricultural classes. These inequalities must be eliminated if justice is to be done, and this can be accomplished effectively only through government assistance. Therefore the farmer desired government regulation; then, it that should prove unavailing, government control; and finally, as a last resort, public ownership, not of all industries but only of those affected with the public interest. It was in connection with their suggestions for the elimination of these supposed rank injustices that the People's Party writers, speakers, and platform-makers put forward their first positive proposals for reform.[52]

---

[52]Part of the Populist program, a discussion of which follows, could have been carried into effect through the medium of action by the State Government, while another and very important part could have been consummated only with the aid of the National Government. The leaders of the Third Party in this State, however, discussed state and national issues in a way which revealed their utter lack of ability to distinguish between the two. In their minds the workingman suffered from certain ills which should be remedied, and it was to them a matter of little consequence who had the power to deal with this or that evil. The author has accepted their view on the subject, attempting herein to develop the Populist program in a logical way without

The first great inequality complained of by the Populists had to do with the land. Men "come upon the earth not by any law of government, but by nature's laws, the laws of God, and have a perfect right to the use of the earth, free and unencumbered."[53] Every man, in the theory of the Populists, has a natural right to as much land as is required to enable him to make a decent living, and it should be the concern of the Government to see that he has the opportunity to acquire at a reasonable price such land as he needs. Further, the land problem assumed additional importance in the eye of the People's Party man because he considered land the source of all wealth; and indeed one of the primary grounds on which he based his complaint was that the farmer, who, in his opinion, created all wealth, had so little voice in its ultimate distribution. Notwithstanding the importance of the land problem, particularly in so far as provision for an equitable system of land holding was concerned, Populist spokesmen observed that much land was held in large blocks by railroads, by other corporations, and by alien title holders. They concluded that the Government of Texas had pursued a prodigal policy with regard to its public lands, and they demanded that the policy be reversed in the interest of the citizens of the State. Specifically, they demanded (1) that all public lands of Texas remaining and all that could be recovered be reserved as homesteads for actual settlers; (2) that all grantees who had not complied with the terms of the grant under which they held lands of the State be required to forfeit their lands to the grantor for homestead purposes; (3) that no corporation be allowed to own more land than it actually needed in the prosecution of its business; and (4) that alien ownership of land be not allowed in Texas.[54]

---

regard to the question whether a particular plank demanded state or national action.

[53]Jas. H. (Cyclone) Davis, *A Political Revelation* (Dallas, 1894), p. 102. In the pages following this reference Davis analyzes the land problem from the viewpoint of the Populist, and in other sections of his book he considers other of the chief demands of the People's Party. His book constitutes an excellent contemporary comment on the ideology of the Populist movement.

[54]Summarized from the first platform of the People's Party in Texas, drafted Aug. 17–18, 1891; printed in Winkler, *op. cit.*, pp. 293–297.

A suggestion of the situation against which the People's Party complained is seen in the facts that the State legislative body at various times had granted

It was not sufficient, however, that the Government undertake merely to guarantee a just system of landholding; the farmer must have in addition a means of distributing his produce, for without adequate transportation facilities he must be largely self-sufficient and must therefore be cut off from the "money crops." Concretely, the agriculturist was convinced that the railroads had conspired against him, and he was unrelenting in his demands that drastic measures be taken against them. In the beginning of the revolt, regulation by the Government through the Railroad Commission was acceptable as a means of dealing with the problem. The farmers were not satisfied, however, with the results obtained by the Commission. The People's Party platform of August, 1891, suggested the probable future necessity of public ownership, and that of February, 1892, demanded the construction, ownership, and operation by the State of a railroad from "the deepest water on the Gulf to the most eligible point on the Red River . . . ."[55] Subsequent statements of Populist principles reiterated and amplified these demands, and in 1894 telephone and telegraph lines were added to the railroads as enterprises which should be owned and controlled by the Government.[56] Thus transportation and communication, the second large field in which the Populists found gross inequalities, were to be dealt with by government intervention and control, and the control

---

to railway companies more than 32,000,000 acres of the public domain of Texas, to internal improvement companies more than 4,000,000 acres, and to the Capitol Syndicate (in payment for construction of the State Capitol) 3,000,000 acres. See the *Report of the Commissioner of the General Land Office, 1928–1930* (Austin, 1930), pp. 4–5, for tables showing the distribution of the public domain of the State and the holdings of the railway companies.

[55]Winkler, *op. cit.*, p. 299. This railroad subsequently was much publicized as the "relief" or the "cornbread and bacon" road. It was to be built by convict labor and financed by loans from the State's public school fund. It was to recognize and do business with the tramp steamers which put into Texas ports, which, it was alleged, were boycotted by the railroads at that time. The chief proponent of the Populist "relief railroad" came to be Barnett Gibbs, People's Party candidate for Governor in 1898, who believed that the road could be used to hammer down the rates of the other lines until they had been brought to a point considered fair to the people of the State. See the *Dallas Morning News*, Feb. 24, March 24, April 14, Dec. 22, 1898.

[56]Winkler, *op. cit.*, p. 333.

to be exercised was allowed to assume, early in the history of the party, the proportions of government ownership and operation.

Even if the land and the distribution problems were solved to the liking of the farmer, however; questions of the most serious import would remain to be dealt with in the field of finance. In that realm the greatest single problem had to do with money. Everybody, it seemed to him, always had money except the farmer, who found prices lowest when his goods came to market, who regularly sold his produce for just enough to keep himself going until the next year, and who as a result never had more than enough money for the barest necessities of life. Thus it appeared to the Populist that there was not enough money in circulation, since too little of it fell into his hands. It appeared further that the Government had abdicated its powers in a dangerous direction by having set up national banks with the power to issue money and by having allowed those banks to wax fat in times past by virtue of the privileged position they enjoyed.

The People's Party, convinced of the injustice of these conditions, brought forward sundry proposals pertaining to the medium of exchange. Its spokesmen began with the hypothesis that the currency system was too inflexible and its basis too restricted, and they proceeded, logically enough it seemed to their followers, to suggest means of getting into circulation a more plentiful money which would have some degree of flexibility. First, they followed the lead of the Ocala Demands of the Farmers' Alliance in demanding the abolition of the national banks, insisting that the Government assume full responsibility for the country's financial system. Secondly, their program called for the free and unlimited coinage of silver, as had the Ocala Demands; and every platform drafted by the party until the Democrats took over that issue repeated the demand. Thirdly, the Populists demanded the issuance of legal tender treasury notes "in sufficient volume to transact the business of the country on a cash basis."[57] They computed the amount of money in circulation during the most prosperous period since the War and, finding that amount to have been about fifty dollars per capita, demanded that enough paper money be issued immediately to bring the sum in circulation back to that standard. Nor were they concerned about the basis on which

---

[57]*Ibid.* (quoting from the first People's Party platform drafted in Texas).

their paper money would be issued. The worth of money is governed not by the intrinsic value of the material from which it is made but by the strength of the government by which it is issued; and paper money issued by a sound government therefore is as good money as either silver or gold. Such were the arguments with which Populist partisans defended their demand for a legal tender paper money.

Two problems pertaining to the money system proper remained to be dealt with. The first of these arose from the question, how might money in the amount contemplated by the People's Party program be placed in circulation without causing too great inconvenience and discomfort? The second was that of making the system flexible, which was a matter of the greatest importance in the eyes of the Populist spokesmen. They attacked these problems with characteristic vigor and confidence and found that the two were but phases of the same large problem. Money may be placed in circulation, they postulated, through the medium of appropriations and expenditures, in the form of gifts, and through loans to the citizen on the basis of satisfactory collateral as security.[58] The first is impracticable and the second inequitable, hence there remains the medium of loans as a means for placing large sums of money in circulation in a way at once expeditious and just.

Definite suggestions were not lacking for a plan by which loans might be made easily and safely. The Alliance some years before the inception of Populism had conceived the scheme called the subtreasury plan, and the People's Party inherited it from its progenitor and wrote a demand for the plan "or something better" into their platform. The subtreasury was nothing more nor less than a device by means of which the Government might lend money to the farmer. The plan rested on the idea that the agriculturist has two kinds of property which will serve as satisfactory security for a loan, land and non-perishable farm produce, and on the further hypothesis that he should be allowed to borrow money on his property, within reasonable limits, whenever he may find it advantageous. With these ideas as their basic assumptions, the

---

[58]Harry Tracy, *The Sub-Treasury Plan* (printed as a supplement to Davis' volume above cited), p. 302. This supplement is an able explanation of and argument for the subtreasury plan.

proponents of the subtreasury plan proposed a dual system for making loans to the farmers. First they devised the land loan scheme, whereby money would be loaned by the Government direct to the people who would put up their homes as security. The loans would be made in amounts not exceeding, in any particular case, $3,000 in the aggregate nor 80 per cent of the cash value of the property offered as security; they would run for fifty years and would draw interest at not more than 2 per cent; and they would be granted on application until 50 dollars per capita of loan money had been placed in circulation. As may be seen, this phase of the scheme was designed to increase the permanent volume of money and to provide a means for placing the money demanded in circulation.

The element of flexibility came from what may be called the subtreasury plan proper, which demanded the establishment of numerous subtreasuries throughout the country and the maintenance in connection therewith of government warehouses in which would be stored non-perishable agricultural products given in security for loans of legal tender paper made to the farmers by the Government. The loans were to equal in amount not more than 80 per cent of the value of the produce offered as security, and the interest rate was to be nominal. In this way the farmer would receive substantially the price of his non-perishable crop, thus avoiding the period of stringency which he had always experienced when he had endeavored to market his produce; and the Government would sell his produce at a fair price at any time during the year when a demand for it arose, obviating in this way the glutted market and the consequent low prices which theretofore had always prevailed at certain seasons of the year. The scheme, then, was designed to facilitate the equitable distribution of money and to adjust its volume constantly to the needs and demands of business. Together with the land loan system it constituted the proposal referred to universally as the subtreasury plan, which served the People's Party as one of the chief bulwarks of its program.[59]

---

[59]The author has attempted only the barest outline of the plan. Its details were on the tongue of every Populist four decades ago, and they may be found explained in almost every newspaper of the period. Numerous books and pamphlets also discuss the subtreasury plan, and of these, none is more succinct than the exposition by Tracy above referred to.

Among other problems of a financial nature which constituted a sore spot for the farmers was the system of taxation. It required no savant to see that the general property tax weighed more heavily on the agriculturist, by comparison, than on other classes, and a demand for reform of the taxing system was embodied in the early platforms of the People's Party. The platform of February 2, 1892, for example, insisted that land ought to be taxed on the basis of its actual value without reference to the improvements added by labor.[60] A second demand, incorporated into the first platform of the party in Texas, called for the imposition of a graduated tax on incomes,[61] and Populists continued to advocate the principle of an income tax to the end of the century, becoming bitter critics of the Supreme Court when that body failed to uphold the income tax law passed by Congress.

Yet another important problem of finance involved the matter of governmental expenditures. The Third Party was one of public retrenchment and economy, and its leaders preached reform along those lines from the beginning of Populism to its end. The first platform announced merely in favor of economical and honest public administration,[62] but the second favored a 50 per cent reduction in the salaries of all national and state officers;[63] and the third and subsequent platforms carried the fight for economy to the level of the county, naming maximum salaries for its officers and demanding the abolition of the fee system of payment.[64] Now and again the platform criticised general and specific abuses of the appropriation power, and Populist speakers constantly quoted figures and called names in their charges of official corruption or indiscretion.

The People's Party, then, paid primary attention in the economic world to the trinity of land, transportation, and money, and for the evils suffered in each field it had specific remedies. Along with the principal problems, however, were various ancillary issues of considerable significance, among them the matter of monopolies.

---

[60]Winkler, *op. cit.*, p. 299. The party subsequently beat back somewhat from this bold position.

[61]*Ibid.*, p. 296.

[62]*Ibid.*

[63]*Ibid.*, p. 298.

[64]*Ibid.*, p. 315.

The People's Party was not content merely to denounce the greatest of monopolies, the railroads; its leaders waged active warfare from the beginning on trusts and combinations in general, and soon the party came out with the point blank statement that "We declare the People's Party to be an antimonopoly party . . ."[65] Similarly, and naturally, the party espoused the cause of labor, demanding in its platform the passage of laws providing for an eight hour day for laboring men; the protection, by means of a lien, of artisans, laborers, mechanics, and material men; the establishment of a state bureau of labor and a state board of arbitration; the removal of convict labor from competition with free labor; and the exemption from prosecution as vagrants of laboring men in a condition of enforced idleness. The portion of the Populist program which demanded substantive reform therefore covered a wide range. The party rested its demands on egalitarian assumptions, entering the lists wherever it found a marked deviation from the principles of equality and justice evolved by its leaders.

Acceptance of the fundamental hypothesis of Populism, namely, that all men are equal, leads inevitably to acceptance of what is perhaps its chief corollary, the theory of democracy. And so it came about that the People's Party, intent though it was on obtaining for its adherents a degree of economic betterment, found time to insist on extension of the principles of equality in the field of politics. Populist spokesmen were imbued with a crusading spirit in behalf of the common man who, they were convinced, was a person of fundamental good sense and sound views and who therefore should have a larger voice in the conduct of public affairs.

The democratic theories of the Populists and the practical proposals consequent upon them may be seen first and most clearly from the national platform of the People's Party. That platform, it may be recalled, pronounced in favor of an extension of popular control through the direct election of the President, the Vice-President, United States Senators, and Federal judges.[66] The

---

[65]*Ibid.*, p. 332 (quoting from the platform of 1894).

[66]The evolution of these ideas, which did not appear simultaneously in the national program of the People's Party, may be traced by reference to the platforms themselves which are printed in Kirk H. Porter's *National Party Platforms* (New York, 1924). Something of the ideas and the theories and

People's Party of Texas, by endorsing the national platform, repeatedly approved this pronouncement, and its speakers and writers extended the principle of popular election to all public officials. Further, they insisted that no officer should be allowed to serve for a long term, that repeated reëlection made for monopoly in office, and that the number of terms should be limited to not more than two.[67] Again, they proposed to reduce the stature of public officials by limiting their salaries to a definite maximum figure and by abolishing altogether such additional perquisites as official fees.[68] Yet again, they struck a blow in behalf of minorities with a demand for proportional representation.[69] Finally, they followed the lead of the national party and wrote into the state platform of 1898 a plank favoring direct legislation and the recall, after playing with the idea in a different form in previous platforms. In these various ways did Populism seek to further the control of the common man in public affairs. The proposals had the net effect of serving two ends: First, a democratic system of government, wherein every man had an equal voice with every other man, was instituted; and second, the Government was strengthened and rendered fit to perform the great services demanded of it by the Populist program.

There are critics of Populism who maintain that the platform of the party was so nearly completely economic in nature that its

principles behind them may be seen in Wharton Barker's *The Great Issues* (Philadelphia, 1902).

[67]The spirit in which this principle was accepted appears from the following resolution, which was adopted by a local Populist club of Erath County without a dissenting vote:

"*Whereas*, believing as we do, that, continuance in office is monopoly pure and simple, therefore be it

"*Resolved*, that we will support no able bodied man for a lucrative office for more than two terms." *The Dublin Progress*, May 11, 1894.

To such effect did the People's Party preach this doctrine in Erath County that the two-term rule obtains there to the present day, though in accordance with the spirit of the resolution quoted above, an occasional official is elected for a third or even a fourth term. Several other counties also accept the two-term rule.

[68]*Supra.*.

[69]Winkler, *op. cit.*, p. 334 (platform of 1894).

political demands were of little or no consequence.[70] Many factors
would seem to justify this conclusion with reference to the movement in general, and it is clear that in this State the farmers were
prompted to protest in the hope of obtaining alleviation, by means
of political action, of certain economic ills. It is equally clear, however, that they were convinced that there was no hope for assistance
under the existing political régime. Indeed, it will be recalled, it
was seemingly unwarranted action on the part of "Bourbon Democrats" which provided the occasion for the organization of the
People's Party in this State. Thus it appears that the farmers,
seeking substantive reforms of an economic nature, were forced at
the same time to consider the problem of procedural reforms of a
political character; and as their platform evolved, the two phases
of the reform movement emerged side by side and came to occupy
each a position of first magnitude.

Contemplation of the Populist ideology evokes speculation along
the line raised by the question, to what extent did the Third Party
leaders "trim" the party's platform in their efforts to make it more
attractive and so acceptable to greater numbers of voters? From
the beginning, the new party found itself besieged by woman suf-
fragists, prohibitionists and anti-prohibitionists, and other single
issue proponents in addition to the numerous varieties of reformers
who placed the welfare of workingmen foremost; and more than
a few of its counsellors advised the adoption of one or more of
these side issues. The Apocalyptic city, they recalled, had twelve
gates, three on every side, which indicated that "the citizens thereof
entered in through very different reasons."[71] Similarly the architects
of the People's Party should devise a number of gateways by way
of admitting to its ranks the greatest possible number and variety
of adherents. Early in the life of the Reform party, however, its
prime mover published an open letter to Reformers warning them
against the support of minor issues, even though they might appear
to be worthy.[72] Despite this counsel, subsidiary issues continued to

---

[70]See, for example, Frank L. McVey's work, *The Populist Movement* (American Economic Studies, Vol. I, No. 3), pp. 139, 187.

[71]*The Southern Mercury*, Oct. 1, 1896. The allusion is to the Biblical description of that city, found in Revelation, XXI, 12, 13.

[72]*Dallas Morning News*, Feb. 1, 1892.

come up in such a way as to demand attention, and the party's platform-makers were forced now and again to trim their demands. For example, they were forced to recognize the plain fact that their party must have the support of at least some of the negroes if it was to hope for success and that the vote of the German element was important, and the platform adopted revealed the influence of this knowledge.[73] In various other directions the platform at times demanded this or that concession which apparently was not in every case directly related to the welfare of the farmer. In short, it strayed somewhat afield from the foundation stones of the party— land, transportation, and finance—recognizing apparently that if "the politician must have cattle on a thousand hills," it is not less advantageous for the political party to embrace a variety of interests.

It must not be supposed for a moment that the leaders of the party were oblivious to the effects of these provisions of its platform on the interests affected. On the contrary, questions with regard to which it was thought politic to hedge were threshed out thoroughly on the floor of the convention, and the discussions there revealed a very clear understanding of the probable effects of the various possible courses of action.[74] The party must not be judged too harshly on this score, however, for if now and again an issue was treated softly or mayhap harshly for the sake of effect, if occasionally an overture was made to a portion of the voting population, no principle of importance was sacrificed thereby. On the primary issues of the day, and more particularly on the issues on which it based its existence, the People's Party struck hard and true, announcing its stand in unequivocal language and carrying its program squarely before the electorate for a decision.

A second interesting speculation arises from consideration of the element of continuity in the local People's Party platform. The problem may be seen from the question, to what extent was the

---

[73]*Infra*, Chap. IV.

[74]The daily press was not slow to call attention to the tactics of the Third Party. The leading dailies usually paid high tribute to the skill and dexterity of the party managers in drafting a catch-all statement of principles, while at the same time condemning them for their lack of steadfastness in the cause of the doctrines of Populism. See the *Dallas Morning News*, June 24, 25, 1892, June 21, 22, 24, 1894, July 28, 1898; and *The Galveston Daily News*, June 21, 22, 23, 1894.

program of Populism original with that movement, to what extent inherited from former movements? An examination of the demands of the party reveals that it drew on the programs of the Grange, the Greenback Party, various labor groups and parties, and the Alliance for its inspiration. The result is, there is little of a novel nature in the People's Party program; it served chiefly as editor rather than author, though it did of course introduce such variations as conditions seemed to demand. For example, toward the end of the century when issues had almost failed it, there appeared a demand for a maritime college to be operated by the State of Texas and another for Brazos and Trinity river improvement. The introduction of these issues reveals the flexible nature of the Populist platform, but it betrays at the same time the deterioration of the Reform movement. Populism was not manufactured stuff, nor was its program of such a nature as to require bolstering up. The movement grew up as the champion of the common man; when his cause had been fought, it had served its purpose. The original issues, live and burning in their origin, ran their course and disappeared, some appropriated by rival parties and others forgotten; and the People's Party, finding itself without motive power, followed them shortly into oblivion.

CHAPTER III

THE ROOTS AND SOURCES OF POPULIST STRENGTH

E ARLY in the life of the reform movement it became apparent
what was to be the nature of the Third Party. The Populist
program was designed to elicit the support of the discontented of
every type and class; and the proponents of Populism, far from
becoming apologetic for the resultant influx of diverse and frequently inharmonious elements, congratulated the party on its
manifold origins. They recalled the Biblical Cave Adullam, where
David gathered together the debtors, the distressed, and the discontented,[1] concluding that like the cave of old the People's Party
offered a haven to all who had been buffeted and treated unkindly
in the game of life, or better said, in the game of politics.

Whatever one's attitude toward the all-inclusive character of the
People's Party, the fact was indisputable, for men with every con-
ceivable background sought refuge in the party which promised
them redress of all past wrongs and fair consideration of their
future needs. Some adhered to the Reform Party out of consideration for social and economic factors, and indeed it may be conceded
at once that the primary motive in the minds of most People's Party
men was economic in nature. It will not suffice, however, to study
the party merely as a manifestation of economic discontent, for
other factors were of equal interest, if not quite of equal importance.
Thus it will be necessary to bear in mind that the movement found
its mouthpiece in a political party and to investigate its political
origins and content. And finally, it is a matter of the greatest
significance that the element of religion and religious fervor played
an extraordinary part in the reform movement called Populism.
The People's Party was therefore at the same time a social and
economic, a political, and a religious movement.

I

It may be stated in the beginning that the People's Party was a
"hard times" party. It found its greatest strength among the classes
which felt the reaction most keenly and most directly in the days

---

[1] I Sam., XXII, 1 and 2. See *The Southern Mercury*, Jan. 28, 1897.

of economic adversities. Those classes included the workingman
in general; and since Texas in the nineties was predominantly an
agricultural state, they comprised here largely the farming element.
It is not without significance that the movement had its origin in
this State in the farming counties of what was then West Texas in
the drouth year of 1886; and it is of the greatest significance that
as the conditions of the laboring man, and more especially of the
farmer, grew worse, the party increased in strength until in the
elections of 1894 and '96 which followed hard upon the panic and
the resulting economic depression it threatened to engulf the Democratic Party in the maelstrom of discontent. It is interesting to note
further that as the pall of depression began to lift, the Third Party
found itself facing certain death through a process of gradual
disintegration and decay which was consummated with the return
of normal times.

From these considerations it is possible to proceed at once to a
number of conclusions regarding the nature of the Populist movement. The first of these is that the People's Party was not strong
in the cities of the State, though now and again, of course, extraordinary circumstances arose to change the complexion of a Democratic municipal stronghold.[2] The rural character of the party may
be tested by reference to the accompanying map. It will be noted
at once that the Populist movement in East Texas centered in the
counties of Nacogdoches, San Augustine, and Sabine, while on
either side of this stronghold lay counties almost wholly unaffected
by the movement. The whole of the phenomenon cannot be explained
in such simple terms, of course, but its explanation may be found
in part in the presence or absence of several towns of considerable
size. San Augustine County, for example, had only one town of
consequence, the county seat, while Shelby County, its immediate
neighbor to the north, which kept almost wholly free from the
influence of Populism, had at least four fairly populous towns.
Or turn to the central portion of the State, where Comanche County

---

[2]As for example in 1896, when Jerome Kearby, the Populist candidate for
Governor, polled a large vote in the City of Dallas. Kearby was an able and
popular member of the Dallas bar, and the consideration which the People's
Party received at the hands of the voters of Dallas was due largely to his efforts.

and those surrounding it provided the Populist stronghold. A comparison of, for example, Lampasas County with Brown County, the one as staunchly Populist as any and the other as staunchly Democratic, will reveal the fact that in the former there was but one small town, while in the latter the town of Brownwood dominated by both its size and its influence the elections of the county, which aside from the county seat was almost wholly rural.

Nor are these conclusions regarding the importance of urban centers based upon mere speculation, for the figures of election returns vouchsafe their validity. In 1892, to illustrate, Thomas L. Nugent, the Populist candidate for Governor, ran behind the Democratic candidate in the town of Lampasas by the vote of 199 to 196 but carried Lampasas County by 582 to 316.[3] Again, in the election of 1894, the Populist candidate for Governor lost Brown County to his Democratic opponent by 1126 votes to 926; but if the vote cast in the town of Brownwood be ignored, he won by 806 to 752.[4] The evidence therefore clearly warrants the conclusion that the Democratic-Populist quarrel in an important sense assumed the aspect of a town-country imbroglio, with the consequent result that frequently there developed strained relations between townsmen and their rural neighbors. These animosities may be seen in the disdain entertained by the townsmen for all ideas of Populist origin and in the universal distrust in which People's Party men held the "town ring."

But if the People's Party was essentially a rural movement, it was not a movement entered into by all rural peoples. There were in Texas, forty years ago as now, several varieties of rural dwellers. There was on the one hand the prosperous farmer who cultivated a fertile and sometimes large tract of land. On the other hand there was the farmer whose cultivable holdings were smaller and were situated in a less favored part of the State. Far from being prosperous, such a one rarely made more than a bare living; he was a marginal farmer of the type who knew no surcease from toil at best and who became, when conditions were unfavorable, what the Democratic weekly press called a "calamity howler."

---

[3]*Record of Election Returns, Lampasas County*, No. 1.
[4]*Election Record, Brown County*, No. 1.

The prosperous farmer was reasonably well satisfied under existing conditions or, if not satisfied, was at least hopeful of a change for the better. His attitude, which caused him to continue to vote Democratic, is reflected in the vote cast by the People's Party and, by implication, that cast by the Democratic Party as recorded on the foregoing map (Map I). By reference thereto it will be seen that the heart of the agricultural section of the State remained Democratic throughout the period of the Populist movement. An occasional aberration may be noted, as for example in the case of Navarro County, but special conditions explain this apparent negation of the general conclusion. Among these are the facts first, that the People's Party was very highly organized and ably led in that county and, second, that a Navarro County man was on the Populist ticket for Lieutenant-Governor in both of those years. Other exceptions to the rule are seen in the counties lying to the southwest of Leon in which the People's Party was able to poll a considerable vote. It must be noted, however, that those counties lie in a continuation of the East Texas timbered area called the post oak strip and that, while they have some good farming lands, they are not as fertile or as productive as those counties to the north in the black prairie region or those to the south in the coast prairie country.[5] There is the further important factor of local leadership, and the strength of the People's Party vote in this district may be explained in part in terms of that factor. This is true likewise of those counties lying to the southeast of its southern extremity, where astute leadership and a strong organization enabled the Populists to forge to the front in a country which ordinarily would have been Democratic. An examination of the premise thus reveals its soundness: prosperous farmers fundamentally were Democrats; and though here and there they went into the People's Party in considerable numbers, the heart of the agricultural section remained the bulwark of the Democratic Party in its contests with Populism.

It was the poor, small farmer then who constituted, together with thousands of his fellows, the rank and file of the People's Party,

---

[5]The information concerning the location and relative value of Texas farm lands came from the pamphlet, *Type of Farming Areas in Texas* (Bulletin No. 427, Texas Agricultural Experiment Station, May, 1931).

and reference again to the foregoing map will substantiate this state-ment. As may be seen, the party centered in what is now considered to be Central Texas, though it polled a large vote in the piney woods section of East Texas. The significance of this fact becomes apparent with the further statement that both of the Populist strongholds were found in sections which were not favorable to farming. Those counties of Central Texas lying between Lampasas and Palo Pinto, wherein the People's Party polled its chief vote as compared with that of the Democratic Party, lie to the west of the rich black lands of Texas, whose rainfall has decreased appreciably by the time it reaches these counties; and they are in good part broken by innumer-able sharp hills and ravines, with an occasional stream and its attendant valleys as an alleviating factor. Their people in the nineties were principally farmers, but then as now the farms were comparatively both poor and small. Nor were the Populist counties of East Texas more favorable to large scale or prosperous small scale farming; for while they were blessed with an abundance of rainfall, the heavily timbered nature of their terrain made for small farms, and the comparative poverty of their soil precluded the possibility of any real prosperity.[6] The country then compared with that which lay to the west of the prairies, and neither section approached in productiveness or in wealth the intervening counties of the fertile black lands.

From the accompanying table (Table I), it will be apparent at once that the Democratic counties enjoyed every advantage over the Populist in the field of agriculture. The percentage of improved acreage was larger; the size of the average farm was greater, as was the value of the land and its permanent improvements; the implements and machinery used were better; and the value per acre of farm products was considerably higher.[7] The figures pro-

---

[6]Compare the average farm of the two sections in size (see Table I). Land in the western counties was both cheaper and more readily available than in the eastern.

[7]Delta County, it will be observed, does not conform to type, for notwith-standing the fact that it lies in the black prairie region and therefore should have remained in the ranks of the Democracy, it was a staunchly Populist stronghold. The phenomenon may be explained in terms of the "naturally" independent character of its people (the county polled a large Socialist vote after the People's Party disappeared), its large negro population, and the

duced here offer tangible and incontrovertible evidence of the type of farmer who went into the People's Party, and they reveal at the same time the character of those who elected to remain true to Democratic traditions.

TABLE I

TYPICAL POPULIST AND DEMOCRATIC COUNTIES BY AGRICULTURAL WEALTH AND INCOME, U. S. CENSUS, 1890*

County	Percentage of total farm acreage improved	Average number of improved acres per farm	Valuation per total acre of land, fences, and buildings	Valuation per total acre of implements and machinery	Estimated value per total acre of farm products
(Populist)					
Blanco	13.99	65.8	$ 4.07	$ .10	$ .92
Comanche	39.43	79.0	6.60	.26	2.71
Delta	61.88	56.1	15.43	.59	3.44
Nacogdoches	28.85	39.4	4.46	.22	2.50
Walker	28.94	46.0	5.03	.27	2.61
(Democratic)					
Collin	81.02	67.4	23.03	.82	6.64
Fayette	62.44	67.7	36.45	.56	5.08
Hill	76.34	99.5	16.14	.67	5.63
Robertson	66.95	64.9	11.37	.57	6.82
Williamson	68.43	108.2	15.91	.55	2.71

*Adapted from the *Eleventh Census of the United States*, Vol. I, Table 6.

Further facts of interest in the same connection come to light when the study is pursued within the limits of the county. Reference to Map II, with its accompanying table, will indicate the results which may be expected when one goes down to the level of the voting precinct for data. The county selected for analysis has considerable rough and broken terrain, together with timbered strips called locally the "cross timbers," and this country is very poor for the purposes of agriculture. The inhabitants of the cross timbers, who settled there originally because of the availability of wood and water, were small farmers without exception who were almost total strangers to prosperity. They fell naturally into the People's Party, as the table (Table II) indicates. But if the county has some very bad farm lands, it also has some excellent lands in the dark, rolling prairies which lie between the two strips of timber. There the farms were larger, the soil much more productive, and the farmers more prosperous than their neighbors of the

strength of local Populist leadership. The county was not a typical Populist habitat and is included here merely as a matter of making the record complete.

MAP II

LOCATION OF VOTING BOXES IN COOKE COUNTY WITH
REFERENCE TO TYPE OF FARM LANDS*

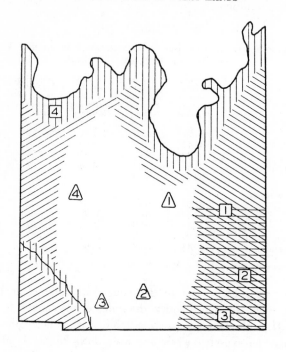

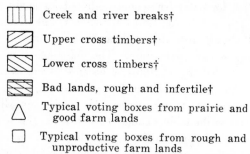

	Creek and river breaks†
	Upper cross timbers†
	Lower cross timbers†
	Bad lands, rough and infertile†
△	Typical voting boxes from prairie and good farm lands
☐	Typical voting boxes from rough and unproductive farm lands

*Located from map in office of County Judge of Cooke County.

†Information obtained by personal interviews with men familiar with Cooke County.

TABLE II

VOTE CAST FOR GOVERNOR IN CERTAIN TYPICAL GOOD FARMING AND CERTAIN TYPICAL BAD FARMING AREAS OF COOKE COUNTY, 1892–1900*

	Boxes located in good farming areas†				Boxes located in bad farming areas†			
	1	2	3	4	1	2	3	4
1892								
Democratic	858	97	148	66	82	40	50	56
Populist	264	47	9	6	71	92	95	93
1894								
Democratic	999	144	150	138	56	35	40	35
Populist	438	69	47	2	90	84	90	127
1896								
Democratic	1223	166	200	201	89	62	61	65
Populist	817	94	32	12	93	94	108	106
1898								
Democratic	737	144	122	123	50	55	44	18
Populist	75	30	14	----	11	72	36	32
1900								
Democratic	1140	178	143	200	99	73	48	59
Populist	----	----	----	----	----	----	----	6

*Record of Election Returns, Cooke County, Vol. 2.
†These boxes identified as such by numerous Cooke County citizens in personal interviews.

cross timbers; and there the Democratic Party held undisputed sway. It was forced to bow to the inevitable and accept the dominion of Populism over the cross timbers, but it yielded not an inch out on the prairie.[8] And what the party in power conceded in Cooke County it granted of necessity throughout the State, namely, that the People's Party had an irresistible appeal for the impoverished farmers of the State.

One who pauses for a moment to seek an explanation of the strength of the People's Party among the agricultural classes will call to mind at once, among other less significant factors, the espousal of Populism by the Farmers' Alliance.[9] The physical relationship between the Alliance and the Third Party may be understood when it is called to mind that the former originated in Lampasas and Parker counties, which became the focal points for

---

[8]The acceptance by the Democrats of the situation described may be seen in a statement made by Lieutenant-Governor M. M. Crane in a speech delivered in Cooke County. Mr. Crane said, "I am proud that most Democrats live on the prairie and are well-to-do people. The cross timbers are full of Populists." *The Gainesville Signal*, Oct. 31, 1894 (in the office of the *Signal*, Gainesville, Texas).

[9]*Supra*, Chap. II.

its expansion,[10] and that the People's Party later achieved its greatest strength in the same section of the State (see Map I). Moreover, it is demonstrable that virtually every county in which Populism met with a friendly reception boasted a strong Alliance.[11] It is not meant to suggest that a vigorous Alliance organization was sufficient in itself to guarantee success locally to the Third Party, but it is indisputable that such an organization was a most helpful adjunct to the cause of Reform.[12]

It is clear, therefore, that the People's Party depended for its strength very largely on the agriculturists. Other elements of some importance entered into its composition, however, and among these were the sheep ranchmen of West Central and West Texas. The frontier of the cattle kingdom in the nineties was constantly receding, the old cattlemen giving way steadily to sheep ranchers. Emphasis thus was shifting from beef and hides to wool, and the new industry depended, or believed that it depended, on the protection offered it by a high tariff duty. Sheep ranchmen therefore inclined toward the Republican Party, though the tradition under which they had been trained led many, perhaps most, of them to vote in 1892 for the Democratic Party and Cleveland. The state of mind of the sheepmen perhaps can be imagined when that party permitted the tariff duties on wool to be abolished. Wool which had sold for 18 cents per pound dropped in price to 6 and 8 cents, and "hard times" struck the wool grower. He considered that he had been betrayed by the Democrats; and while the Third Party might have

---

[10]*The People's Journal*, Jan. 6, 1893 (in the Library of The University of Texas, Austin, Texas).

[11]The State Secretary of the Alliance, writing after the close of the campaign of 1894, made the statement that a comparison of the election returns with the records of the Alliance revealed that the People's Party candidate for Governor carried those counties where the Alliance was active and strong and concluded that this was due to the Alliance educational campaign there. See *The Southern Mercury*, Jan. 10, 1895.

[12]It is worthy of note that if the People's Party had a most worthy ally in the Alliance and its official organ, the *Mercury*, it had an implacable foe in another state farmers' organization, the Grange, and its organ, the *Texas Farmer*. The Alliance, however, without question was much stronger than the Grange in the early nineties.

been much more definite in its tariff policy, he concluded nevertheless to cast his lot with the Populists in the hope of securing an
adjustment.[13]

The third element of importance which entered into the composition of the People's Party, unlike the farmers and stockmen,
was not dependent upon the soil for its livelihood, for it comprised
the laboring men of the State. The sympathy with which the laboring classes might be expected to regard Populism was revealed early
in the history of the Reform movement when half a dozen of the
most trusted champions of labor became leaders in the organization
of the People's Party.[14] As the movement developed, labor organizations here and there pronounced for a third party;[15] prominent
Alliance and Populist orators addressed audiences of laboring
men; the People's Party platforms took cognizance of the needs
of labor;[16] mass meetings of workingmen came together now and

---

[13]See *The Southern Mercury*, March 26, 1896, for the plaint of a sheep man
who wrote a letter explaining his position.

Reference to Map I reveals that Kimble County voted Populist in two elections, a fact difficult to explain except in terms of the low price received for
wool. That county is essentially a ranching country; there is little arable
land within its limits.

It was during the days of worthless wool that People's Party men told the
following story. A Populist (the story goes) was riding along the road when
he came upon a man shearing sheep. The usual mode of shearing was to
begin at the head and shear toward the rear, and the Populist observer was
somewhat surprised to see that the man had reversed the process, beginning
at the tail and shearing toward the head. "My friend," he inquired, "you are
shearing your sheep backward. What is the reason for this strange perform-
ance?" "Well, stranger, I'll tell you," the sheep man drawled, "I voted for
Cleveland in 1892, and since then I just ain't had the nerve to look a sheep
in the face!"

[14]Among them were W. R. Lamb, W. E. (Bill) Farmer, J. J. (Jake) Rhodes,
and L. L. (Lee) Rhodes. All of these were active from the beginning in
advocating the cause of the Third Party, and Lamb was more prominent than
any other in effecting its organization.

[15]See, for example, the resolutions of the "Federated Union of Labor,"
which met at Dallas on Jan. 5, 1891. *The Galveston Daily News*, Jan. 6, 1891.

[16]In the convention of June, 1892, for example, a plank was written into the
platform calling for the establishment of a state department of labor. The
party also demanded a shorter working day for the laboring man. See the
Dallas Morning News, June 25, 1892; *The Galveston Daily News*, June 21, 1894.

again to endorse Populist candidates;[17] the *Southern Mercury* received the laboring men with open arms—in short, every indication pointed to the almost universal conversion of labor to Populism.[18] It is true that the People's Party was not strong as a usual thing in the urban precincts, which may be supposed to have been the stronghold of labor, but that fact was to be attributed rather to the relatively small number of organized laboring men than to their lack of faith in Populism. The editor of the *Texas Farmer* went so far, indeed, as to insist, with reference to the elections of 1892, that the Populist candidate for Governor polled his chief vote among the wage-workers of the towns and cities who, he charged, rushed pell-mell into the party without having given its platform sufficient consideration.[19] Such a position cannot of course be maintained, for even a superficial examination of the election returns reveals its falseness. And indeed, one might have pointed out to the editor that large numbers of laboring men pursued their way almost wholly unaffected by Populism.[20] The statement, nevertheless, reveals an attitude based on a fact of indisputable validity, namely, that most of the wage earners supported the cause of Populism and voted for the candidates nominated by the People's Party.

When the Populist party left the farming and laboring classes and sought strength elsewhere, it found that while Populism might be received with tolerance and civility on the part of other classes of society, it could not hope to find there the enthusiasm which

---

[17]*Dallas Morning News*, Aug. 24, 31, 1894.

[18]A local editor, whose comments were typical of those of the country press, identified the People's Party with the "Union Labor-Greenback Party" of 1886, concluding, with regard to the fulminations of the Populists, that "Their howlings are identical with the howlings that went up in that year." The *Palo Pinto County Star*, Aug. 6, 1892 (in the office of the *Star*, Palo Pinto, Texas).

[19]See the issue of the *Farmer* of Nov. 12, 1892.

[20]There were, for example, the sawmill laborers of East Texas who voted as they were directed to vote by their employers and who consequently cast few ballots for the People's Party. Map I reveals the fact that Montgomery and Angelina counties, each adjoining a hotbed of Populism in the piney woods district of East Texas, remained free from domination by the People's Party. The explanation of this phenomenon is found in the fact that both were lumbering counties, with several hundred laborers employed in their sawmills, and that the sawmill vote was a controlled vote.

characterized its reception among workingmen. There were, for example, the merchants. The Farmers' Alliance, convinced that its members were being robbed by the non-producers, among whom were the storekeepers, had fostered coöperative stores in those counties where its membership justified that course; and the "Alliance store" had become an institution through which supplies were furnished to the farmer at cut-rate prices. Naturally enough, it was looked upon as an interloper by the merchants of the locality who attached to the Alliance, and so perforce to the People's Party, the odium deriving from the operation of its store. There was the further fact that the merchant was a member, though mayhap an humble one, of the capitalist class and as such was not one to question the existing order or demand a radical change. Hence the People's Party included in its ranks very few merchants, who refused to be converted to its teachings.

There were also the professional classes, and among them, the lawyers. The People's Party listed among its leaders three or four of the State's foremost lawyers, and here and there locally an attorney took up the fight. The latter were frequently men young in the legal profession who were desirous of furthering their careers and who saw in the People's Party an opportunity to place themselves, perhaps in a favorable light, before the public. Notwithstanding the names of some lawyers, a few of them of marked ability, on the rolls of the Third Party, it may be surmised that not more than one attorney in one hundred forsook the old parties and became a Populist. And what was true of the lawyers was true also of the schoolteachers, for while there appear to have been more schoolmasters in the People's Party than attorneys, there were not enough to raise the level of literacy among its members by an appreciable degree. Nor did the doctors embrace Populism in any considerable numbers. It is true of this as of other professions that there were some physicians who were Populists, and a few of these filled positions of trust in the party; but the presence of these few served merely to emphasize the absence of doctors as a class. Members of the professional classes, therefore, did not go into the People's Party with anything like the enthusiasm with which that party was accepted among the laboring classes.

The social and economic composition of the People's Party thus is seen to have hinged on the acceptance of the doctrines of Populism by the farming classes and more particularly, among those classes, by the marginal farmer. The farmer whose lands were comparatively poor, whose implements were cheap and undeveloped, and whose produce sold for barely enough to enable him to keep operating was usually a confirmed Populist.[21] Exceptions to this rule of course were many, but its general applicability cannot be controverted. Aiding and abetting the impoverished farmer were the sheep rancher who indirectly also found his sustenance in the soil, and the laboring man who looked to the People's Party for relief and aid in the directions promised him by its board of managers. Other classes of society heard the plaints of the Populists, sometimes with good grace and sometimes with bad, but they were not visibly affected by the arguments advanced. They kept to their several courses and left the Third Party to those in whose behalf it had been launched in the beginning.

II

Politically, many professed to believe that Populism had sprung from a single source and that it drew its strength from one group or party. Some supposed the Third Party to be a latter day manifestation of Greenbackism; others insisted that it was merely a left wing branch of the Democratic Party; still others believed that its chief strength came from the Republican Party; and some zealots identified it with Socialism. There was an element of truth in each of these explanations, but the fact of the matter is that the People's Party commanded a considerable vote from each of the parties in question and from the Prohibition Party as well. The Reform movement therefore assumed a cosmopolitan political character, for it depended for its support not upon one party but upon all.

To those who were so inclined, it was not difficult to associate the People's Party with the Greenback-Independent movement of the eighties. The platforms of the two parties, while not identical, were so similar as to require a second reading to distinguish them.

---

[21]As one staunch old Democrat put it to the author, "Where you found the hogs running loose, there were lots of Populists; where you found them penned up, the Democrats were in the majority." If one follows the significance of this statement, it must be conceded that there is an element of truth in it.

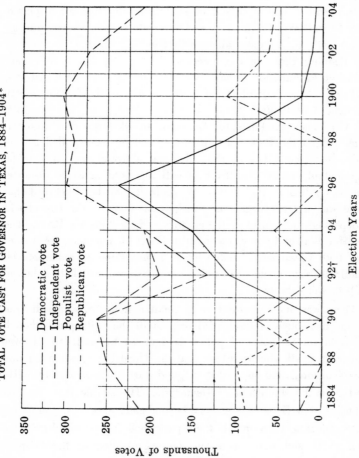

CHART I

TOTAL VOTE CAST FOR GOVERNOR IN TEXAS, 1884–1904*

— Democratic vote
---- Independent vote
— Populist vote
-- Republican vote

Thousands of Votes

Election Years

*Election Register of State and County Officers, 1884, 1888, 1890, 1892, 1894, 1896, 1898, 1900, 1902, 1904.
†Two Democratic candidates ran in 1892.

The leaders of the new Third Party previously had been the leaders of the old, and the rank and file of the Populists had voted for the Greenback candidates in 1884 and for the Independents in '88. Populism was of course a broader and stronger movement than its progenitor, and it cannot be said truthfully that all Populists were Greenbackers. The reverse of that statement, however, approximates truth, for virtually all true Greenbackers became members of the People's Party in the nineties. Strong Populist counties are found on examination to have been also strong Greenback districts, and this is true particularly of those counties of the People's Party stronghold of Central Texas. In Comanche County, for example, the Greenback candidate for Governor in 1884 ran only fourteen votes behind the Democratic nominee, and the vote polled by the Independent candidate in 1888 also was a strong one. It is to be expected of course that the rule will not hold in every instance, but as applied to the State as a whole it may be concluded that there was a large degree of overlapping between the Greenback-Independent movement of the eighties and the People's Party. The vote for Walker County, recorded in Chart II, indicating as it does that both Greenback ("Independent") and Populist gubernatorial candidates ran strong races there, reveals something of the relationship between the two.

There was another aspect of the matter, however, which did not escape the notice of thoughtful men or of the daily press, though it might for purposes of policy be ignored by partisans. It was apparent to all who would see that the Third Party, odious or not, was sponsored and supported in good part by men who formerly had been the staunchest of Democrats. The simple fact was that many old line Democrats, goaded beyond endurance by the supposed autocrats into whose hands their party had fallen, withdrew from that party and participated in the organization of the People's Party.[22] And if in the ranks of the new party they found themselves side by side with the old Greenback men and the more recent Independent advocates, they consoled themselves that these too had been good Democrats in their day and had only taken offense and withdrawn from the dominant party at an earlier date than they.

---

[22]*Supra*, Chap. II.

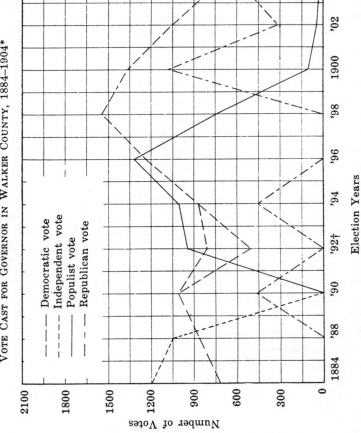

CHART II

VOTE CAST FOR GOVERNOR IN WALKER COUNTY, 1884–1904*

— — — Democratic vote
— – – — Independent vote
———— Populist vote
— — Republican vote

Number of Votes

2100 1800 1500 1200 900 600 300 0

1884 '88 '90 '92† '94 '96 '98 1900 '02 '04

Election Years

*Election Register of State and County Officers, 1884, 1888, 1890, 1892, 1894, 1896, 1898, 1900, 1902, 1904.
†Two Democratic candidates ran in 1892.

Thus all were Democrats, they argued, and they were never convinced of their alleged treason. It was the Democratic Party, so-called, which had broken loose from its moorings and renounced time-honored Democratic principles, and those stigmatized as renegades were in reality the bone and sinew of the party who had undertaken to turn it back to the traditions it had foresworn. One might differ from the conclusions reached by men of the type who led the insurrection, but there was little room for question of their major premise or its leading corollaries.[23]

The validity of the hypothesis which traced the major portion of the Populist legions to Democratic origins may be tested by reference to the election returns for the elections of the nineties. If one turns to a study of the figures for the election of 1890 as compared with that of 1894,[24] he is at once struck by the fact that although the total vote for the State increased by 31 per cent during those four years, that of the Democratic Party decreased by more than 21 per cent (Chart I). A further startling fact arises from contemplation of the vote polled by the People's Party candidate, which grew from nothing at all in 1890 to more than 150,000 in 1894. The conclusion seems compelling that Populism drew its chief strength during these years from the Democratic Party. Some votes doubtless came from the Republican camp; but they could not have been many, for that party polled almost as many votes in 1894 as was its custom at that time. Some also doubtless came from other non-Democratic sources, as for example from the Prohibition Party, which commanded a scattering vote over the State. If the Republican and the Prohibition parties be credited with their greatest vote since the War and that vote be subtracted from that of the non-Democratic groups, however, there remain more than 100,000 votes to be accounted for; and these votes could have come only from the Democratic Party, or from classes over the State reckoned ordinarily as being Democratic in their affiliations.

The argument acquires additional weight when it is observed that the People's Party, as compared with the Democratic, was strongest

---

[23]See an editorial on the nature of the People's Party in *The Galveston Daily News* of Dec. 1, 1892.

[24]The year 1892 is omitted intentionally, inasmuch as the campaign and election of that year were in no wise typical.

in a section of the State, the central portion, where there were naught but Democrats. The point may be illustrated by recourse to figures in this fashion: In those eight counties of Central Texas in which the People's Party ran first in three or more elections (see Map I), the Democratic Party polled a total of 11,604 votes in 1890 as against a Republican total of 427. In 1894, however, the same counties polled a total of 7,828 votes for the People's Party and only 6,533 for the Democratic. It is therefore quite apparent that in this part of the State the Third Party originated in a rift in the ranks of the Democracy. The relation between the Democratic vote and that of the People's Party in a typical county of the section may be seen from Chart III which substantiates the conclusion reached on the basis of a study of Chart I, namely, that the People's Party depended in good part on the support of disaffected Democrats for its voting strength.

But if Populism might hope by dividing the dominant party to get within striking distance of success, it could hardly hope to reach its ultimate goal without the support of the Republicans, who would hold the balance of power in the event the Democratic Party should divide about evenly. The Populist strategists, therefore, sought to convert to Populism those elements popularly supposed to vote Republican. The Republican managers, on their part, recognized in the People's Party a young giant which might best their ancient rivals, and they saw fit on two occasions to throw their strength into the balance in favor of the Populist candidates. The result of their decision may be seen from Chart I which records a very definite relation between the large Populist vote of 1896 and the failure of the Republicans to put a candidate in the field in that year. The sharp decline in the People's Party vote from 1898 to 1900 also is of interest, especially in light of the fact that in the latter year the Republicans chose to enter the field again with straight party nominees leading their ticket. The resultant shift of the vote warrants the conclusion that the People's Party vote of 1898 was not only partly but largely Republican in its complexion.[25]

---

[25]The conclusion seems further warranted by the fact that the Democrats in 1896 nominated Bryan for the Presidency on a free silver platform, thus paving the way for the return of Populists to the Democratic Party.

CHART III

VOTE CAST FOR GOVERNOR IN COMANCHE COUNTY, 1890–1906*

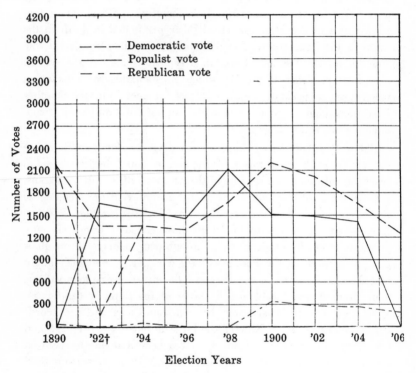

Election Register of State and County Officers, 1890, 1892, 1894, 1896, 1898, 1900, 1902, 1904.

†Two Democratic candidates ran in 1892.

Consideration of the situation in various counties of the State leads in the direction of the same conclusions regarding the relationship between the Populist and the Republican vote. Charts II, III, and IV which record the votes of counties widely separated reveal alike a Populist vote which rises with a declining Republican vote and falls with the nomination of Republican candidates. Chart IV is of special significance, for it appears to offer something tangible on which to base definite conclusions regarding the composition of the People's Party in one county in 1898. For the years 1898 and 1900 in that county the total vote cast was substantially the same. From the first election to the second, the People's Party lost about 1,900 votes, while the Democrats gained 405 and the Republicans increased from nothing to 1,425. Thus the Democratic and the Republican parties gained about as many votes as the People's Party lost, the total vote remaining the same. Computations based on these figures reveal that about 78 per cent of the Populist vote was lost to the Republican Party and about 22 per cent to the Democratic. Thus, ignoring the negligible vote polled by the Populist candidate in 1900,[26] we may conclude that in 1898 the People's Party in Bastrop County was about 78 per cent Republican in its composition.

One is not, of course, to conclude forthwith that the People's Party of Texas was three-fourths Republican in its composition in the heyday of Populism. In 1892 and '94 it was much nearer 75 per cent Democratic, for in those years the Republicans had candidates whom they preferred to those of the Third Party. Further, some of the staunchest Republican counties in the State escaped almost wholly the influence of Populism. The fusion election of 1896 brought into the party a large element of Republican strength, however, and by 1898 the erstwhile Democrats had withdrawn from its ranks in such numbers that the Republicans remaining constituted a majority of its membership. Hence it was a matter of no surprise when, with the nomination of a straight Republican ticket once more in 1900, the party fell into a position of moribundity from which it never recovered.

Those who stigmatized the People's Party as a party of Republicans thus had something to argue in behalf of their point of view.

---

[26]The party polled only 121 votes in the county in 1900.

CHART IV

VOTE CAST FOR GOVERNOR IN BASTROP COUNTY, 1890–1906*

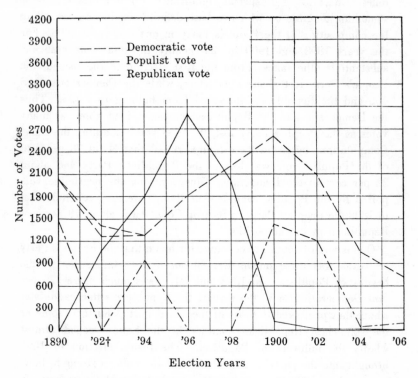

------- Democratic vote
———— Populist vote
— — Republican vote

Number of Votes

Election Years

*Election Register of State and County Officers, 1890, 1892, 1894, 1896, 1898, 1900, 1902, 1904.
†Two Democratic candidates ran in 1892.

There were those, however, who insisted that the party was controlled by Socialists, and these were able to summon much evidence in support of their contention. To begin with, many of the men foremost in the propagation of Populist principles previously had been active in directions which had gained for them such opprobrious reputations as were implicit in references to "the anarchist Bill Farmer," "the union labor agitator W. R. Lamb," and others of like nature. These men reputedly were Socialists, and a degree of odium attached, in the minds of partisans, to any movement with which they became affiliated. Again, the Third Party adopted a platform calculated to confirm suspicions already existent and to create new ones, calling as it did for public ownership and control of numerous industries and government regulation of practically all others. Yet again, while the spokesmen of Populism vigorously defended their party against charges of socialism so long as the movement was on the upgrade, their attitude changed markedly toward the end of the century. Such terms as "the class struggle" and "the army of the proletariat" came to be employed; Eugene V. Debs himself was mentioned by leading Populists as their choice for presidential candidate; and the *Mercury* changed its tone completely concerning Socialism.[27] Finally, when the People's Party had demonstrated beyond peradventure its inability to overcome the Democracy, scores of Populist leaders veered from their course and espoused the cause of Socialism.[28] Their several defections and subsequent careers revealed that the newly organized Socialist Party in Texas was headed by men who until 1900 were Populists, and this served as the final link in the argument of those who would identify Socialism and Populism as the two were practiced in Texas.

Concrete proof that the relationship was not illusory may be had from a brief comparison of the votes of the two parties by

---

[27]The changing attitude of the *Mercury* may be seen in its issues of the latter half of 1899 and the whole of the year 1900.

[28]Among them were the ubiquitous Bill Farmer; the Rhodes brothers (one of whom had served in the Legislature as a Populist), who ran each in turn as the Socialist candidate for Governor; Reddin Andrews, a former candidate for Congress on the People's Party ticket, who ran for Governor twice as a Socialist; and E. O. Meitzen, once candidate for State Comptroller as a Populist, whose son was the Socialist candidate for Governor in 1914.

counties. In the elections of 1912, a typical year, the Socialist candidate for Governor polled a vote in each of fifteen counties equal to 25 per cent of that polled by the Democratic candidate in those counties. Of the fifteen counties in question, four were of little consequence politically in the days of Populism; they were western counties casting a very small vote, and for the purpose of the comparison here they may be ignored.[29] Of the eleven remaining, all cast a very heavy Populist vote. Four were among the strongest Populist counties in the State, and in the remaining seven the People's Party ticket regularly polled a large vote, winning now and losing then but always keeping the standard of the party well toward the front.[30] The implication of this analysis becomes even more definite with a comparison between the Socialist vote polled in certain representative Socialist precincts and the Populist vote polled there. The figures of Table III reveal a distinct correlation between the two votes and indicate beyond question the affinity between the former People's Party and the latter day Socialist Party.

Experience reveals that a third party ordinarily will be called upon to consider and accept or reject innumerable reform principles in which the public has betrayed some interest.[31] The People's Party, confessedly a party of reform, perhaps had to cope with more than its share of these *isms,* and among the side issues thrust upon it none was more vexatious than that of Prohibition. In the very beginning of Populism, Third Party leaders were forced by

---

[29]These counties were Cottle, Haskell, Menard, and Zavala. Even here, it is interesting to note, the People's Party usually received a good vote.

[30]The eleven counties in question were Angelina, Bowie, Comanche, Eastland, Henderson, Jasper, Leon, Palo Pinto, Rains, Somervell, and Van Zandt. Comanche, Palo Pinto, Rains, and Somervell counties were as strong for Populism as any in the State. See Map I.

[31]Robert Michels in his *Political Parties* (New York, 1915) has put a similar idea in these words (p. 95):

> Every vigorous political party which is subversive in its aims is predestined to become for a time an exercise ground for all sorts of innovators and quack-salvers, for persons who wish to cure the ills of travailing humanity by the use of their chosen specifics, employed exclusively in smaller or larger doses—the substitution of friction with oil for washing with soap and water, the wearing of all-wool underclothing, vegetarianism, Christian science, neo-Malthusianism, and other fantasies.

one of their own number to take action on the question, which they did by voting down overwhelmingly a resolution denouncing the liquor traffic.[32] Thereafter the party pilots attempted consciously to steer their craft clear of the liquor issue: they were careful not to brand the Third Party as an organization favoring the liquor interests, but they were equally careful not to permit it to become known officially as the Prohibition Party.

TABLE III

THE RELATION BETWEEN SOCIALIST AND POPULIST VOTE IN THE INDIVIDUAL VOTING PRECINCTS OF CERTAIN TYPICAL COUNTIES, AS SEEN IN THE VOTE FOR GOVERNOR, 1894, 1896, 1898, 1912, 1914

	Charleston (Delta County)*	Moccasin Rock (Erath County)†	Muldoon (Fayette County)‡	Bazette (Navarro County)§	Wayland (Stephens County)‖	Rocky Hill (Angelina County)¶	Farmer's Chapel (Comanche County)**
1894							
Democratic	27	49	61	24	43	24	16
Populist	157	136	85	97	95	27	61
1896							
Democratic	43	69	89	45	57	28	37
Populist	173	175	103	90	108	41	46
1898							
Democratic	76	63	65	27	36	32	7
Populist	197	126	108	63	112	18	48
1912							
Democratic	90	9	31	31	40	11	3
Socialist	94	28	30	24	30	23	29
1914							
Democratic	88	5	28	27	23	19	4
Socialist	97	18	23	27	27	17	30

*Record of Election Returns, Delta County, Vol. I.
†Record of Election Returns, Erath County, Books I, II, and III.
‡Record of Election Returns, Fayette County, Vols. I, II, and III.
§Record of Election Returns, Navarro County, Vols. I and II.
‖Record of Election Returns, Stephens County, Nos. I and II.
¶Record of Election Returns, Angelina County, No. II.
**Record of Election Returns, Comanche County, Vol. I.

In light of these facts, it seems strange that the reputation of the People's Party should have spread as the champion of Prohibition. The phenomenon may be explained in rather simple terms after all, however, for the plain fact was that the People's Party enveloped the Prohibition movement, and the leaders of the old anti-liquor party became trusted advisors of the new Third Party.

---

[32]*Dallas Morning News*, June 24, 1892.

Further, while that party announced formally its support of the principle of local self-government in the convention of 1894, at the same time it betrayed its connection with the old Prohibition forces by nominating among its candidates for state offices two of the leaders of the anti-liquor movement in the State.[33] Yet again, while the state organization maintained its formal independence, the People's Party locally was summoned frequently to the aid of Prohibition. In Navarro County, for example, it was allied definitely with the local Prohibition forces through the agency of its leaders there, and in Cooke County the Populists were considered to be the Drys.[34] In practice, therefore, it was inevitable that the People's Party should become identified closely with the cause of Prohibition.

From a consideration of all the factors involved in the political origins and makeup of the People's Party, one is led to the conclusion that that party depended upon divers sources for its strength. The old Greenback-Independent contingent came into its ranks bodily; the Democratic Party contributed liberally to its membership; the Republicans in more than one election conspired by their support to increase its vote markedly; the Socialists found themselves perfectly at home among Third Party men and contributed whatever of strength they could muster to the cause of Populism; and the party of Prohibition found in the People's Party a haven of refuge afforded its members nowhere else. Populism thus became a true reform movement: it embraced the discontented from every group and faction and united them into a party which enabled them to speak as one in announcing their own candidates for office and giving voice to the principles on the basis of which they demanded reform.

III

It remains now to examine the religious content of the Third Party by way of determining to what extent and in what directions that party was able to identify its own interests with those of the

---

[33]Addison Clark, long a devout Prohibitionist, was nominated for State Superintendent of Public Instruction, and E. L. Dohoney, an equally stuanch Dry, was named candidate for the Court of Criminal Appeals.

[34]*The Gainesville Signal*, Oct. 31, 1894.

From *The Young Populist*, Sept. 27, 1894.

The attitude implicit in this cartoon reveals unmistakably why the People's Party became known as the champion of Prohibition despite the liberal pronouncements of its spokesmen.

members of the religious groups existent in the State in 1890. Those groups numbered among their members and communicants 677,151 persons, out of a total population of 2,235,523. Of that number 99,691 were Roman Catholics, while 577,460 were divided among the various Protestant sects.[35] It was generally known that virtually all Mexicans were Catholics and that the strength of that church centered in the southern (Mexican) counties of the State.[36] The Protestant sects on the other hand found members in good numbers in all parts of the State except the southernmost counties, with apparently little concentration of strength worthy of the name. It is evident then that any political party which sought success in Texas in the nineties must be primarily Protestant in its religious makeup, though it could not with impunity ignore the Catholic vote in the Mexican counties of South Texas.

Of the parties active in the State during the days of the agrarian revolt, none was able to appeal to the religious prejudices of the people more strongly than the Third Party. The spokesmen of Populism depended heavily on the bulwark offered by their religious beliefs and those of their followers, using scriptural teachings and quotations to buttress their conclusions. And indeed, under the habits of thought which not only permitted but endorsed this appeal to authority the necessity for teachers largely disappeared. Any man could read the Bible and learn there what was right and what wrong, what might be done and what might not. Every man thus became his own tutor, arriving at certain principles of justice whose uniformity among countless readers need occasion no surprise in view of their common origin. Further, the principles so arrived at were regarded as having special sanctity; they were of divine origin, and all believers rallied to their defense with a zeal

---

[35]*Eleventh Census*, III, 38–42. Of the total number of church members and communicants, 36.7 per cent were Baptists; 32.3 per cent were Methodists; 6 per cent were Disciples of Christ; 5.6 per cent were Presbyterians; and 4.7 per cent were affiliated with various other non-Catholic sects.

[36]In Texas in 1890, eleven counties had populations which were Mexican to the extent of 50 per cent or more. These eleven counties had a total of 40,689 church members and communicants, of whom 33,398 were affiliated with the Catholic Church. Note that more than 82 per cent of the religious elements in those counties were Catholic and that those elements included some 33 per cent of all the Catholics in the State. See *ibid.*, pp. 81–83 and 245–246.

not commonly found in so material a realm as politics. The People's Party thus became a tabernacle under which gathered all those bent on the defense of the divine laws of justice against those who put worldly affairs first and sought to ignore them. It became, in short, a semi-religious order, its members zealots for the cause of justice.[37]

The old partisans in the beginning did not sense the full import of the factor of religious zeal, but they were brought ere long to a realization of the fact that they had in the People's Party a foe of a wholly new type. Here were no blustering, swaggering, drinking soldiers of fortune such as one might associate with an insurrectionary movement. Here rather were men, of mature years, most of them, whose life-long training had taught them well the lessons of patience, sobriety, and self-restraint. Here were men who could sit, or stand, for the whole of a four-hour debate on the issues of the day in the broiling Texas sun of a midsummer afternoon; men to whom all luxuries were strangers and who therefore were not keenly aware of their bodily discomforts; men who, convinced of the justness of their cause, were prepared to give freely of their time and energy with little hope of recompense—here were men, in short, without training in politics and new at the business, who might nevertheless wield a powerful influence on the course of affairs. The State's leading daily newspaper, after following the proceedings of a Third Party state convention, made this significant observation regarding the delegates in attendance there: "Their earnestness, bordering on religious fanaticism, has a touch of the kind of metal that made Cromwell's round heads so terrible a force in the revolution that ended with bringing the head of Charles I to the block. It would be supreme folly to despise and belittle a movement that is leavened with such moral stuff as this."[38]

The general effect of seriousness was further heightened by the comparatively large number of ministers and former ministers in the ranks of the party. It was a standing pleasantry that the Third

---

[37]This attitude is revealed in the following statement taken from *The Southern Mercury* of Nov. 1, 1900: "Populism is a practical religion. To vote according to our best convictions of right is a duty we owe to the Creator, as well as to our fellow men. For a Populist to fail to vote is to be derelict to a sacred duty."

[38]*Dallas Morning News*, June 25, 1892.

Party was composed of "one-gallus" farmers and Campbellite preachers, and the statement contained an element of truth. It at least reveals the popular impression that the People's Party had more than its share of Gentlemen of the Cloth. Concerning the upper reaches of the party less of circumspection is demanded, for among its leaders one found a considerable concourse of ministers and former ministers, chief among whom was the redoubtable Stump Ashby.[39]

There appears, therefore, to be little room for question of the main hypothesis, namely, that Populism rested on a fundamentally religious basis. Nor is it difficult to show definitely by reference to figures the general religious composition of the party. It is a significant fact that in the Census report on churches the counties of Palo Pinto, Comanche, Mills, Hamilton, Somervell, and Sabine, all Populist strongholds in Central or East Texas (see Map I), were not listed in the tables showing the distribution of Catholics and further that in the strong Populist counties of Blanco, Erath, Lampasas, Nacogdoches, and San Augustine (Map I) Catholics numbered only 4 per cent of all church members and communicants.[40] On the other hand in the eleven strong Mexican counties above mentioned (p. 84n), where 82 per cent of the church members and communicants were Catholics, People's Party candidates ordinarily polled a negligible vote: in 1894, for example, the Democratic candidate for Governor received a vote in those counties larger by six times than that of the Populist nominee.[41] These facts warrant the conclusion that the Third Party was preponderantly if not wholly Protestant in composition.

Accepting as it did the support of active ministers, boasting of, or at the least acknowledging, its distinctly religious complex, and employing the terminology and the appeal to authority characteristic of religious orders,[42] the People's Party found itself on

---

[39]See *The Galveston Daily News*, Sept. 28, 1894, for sketches of some fifteen of these "preacher Populists." Of the number sketched, the *News* characterized nine as Methodists, two as Baptists, two as Campbellites, one as Presbyterian, and one as Cumberland Presbyterian.

[40]*Eleventh Census*, III, 81–83, 245–246.

[41]See *infra*, Chap. IV, Table VIII.

[42]See *infra,* Chap. VII.

more than one occasion forced to answer the charge that it was a church party. Specifically, it was alleged that the Third Party was allied with the American Protective Association (A. P. A.), an organization with a pro-American, anti-Catholic program. Such an alliance would have stamped the party as the descendant of the old Knownothing faction, and the effect would have been injurious to its cause, if not disastrous. Hence the Populist managers were quick to deny the charge,[43] and they continued to deny it, with undoubted sincerity, until the A. P. A. cloud had passed away. The Populists were confessedly a deeply religious people, but their quarrel was only with those who seemed to forget the scriptures or refused to be bound by their teachings. They ignored church lines and were innocent of factional strife. If they favored one church above another, it was the great church of Populism, whose principles they considered to be those of Christianity and whose subjects were found among laboring men.

The People's Party then rested on divers social and economic bases: operating as it did under a program designed primarily for the benefit of that class of society called the producers, it drew its chief strength from the ranks of the farmer and the laboring man, although it welcomed and to some extent received the support of other classes. So too, it welcomed men of all political creeds and beliefs, providing only they would accept the new faith of Populism; and though as was but natural the new party drew most heavily from the membership of the dominant party of the State, it received also the support of such dissident groups as the Socialists and the Prohibitionists and occasionally that of the Republicans as well. Further, Populism took on a distinctly religious cast, to the extent almost of becoming a new religion; and the zeal of its adherents proved to be a source at once of strength and of embarrassment. In fine, the People's Party was a reform party, and as such it profited from the support of every group that was dis-contented under the existing order.

But if Populism found its ranks swelled by the adherence of dissentient groups of all types whatsoever, it found itself at the same time the depository of all the cares and woes of its component

---

[43]*The Southern Mercury*, June 6, 1895.

parts. It found further that the support of this group or that was not always an unmixed blessing, for quite frequently a faction brought with it greater liabilities in the nature of odium attaching to it or of ill-concealed skeletons from the past than assets in the form of votes. It was no more than was to be expected that the established party would seize upon every weakness of this nature and magnify it a thousandfold. The People's Party thus became the "all isms" party, the receptacle for political driftwood from every malcontent faction, and the proponent of every vagrant scheme that seemed designed to catch the popular fancy. Democratic commentators of course greatly overstated the divers character of Populism, for they had a case to make, but fundamentally their observations were based upon facts. At worst, the People's Party had the appearance of being "an asylum for all the cranks in the universe."[44] At best, the cranks played a minor if active role; the great body of the party was composed of men of various origins and allegiances who were united for the time honestly and seriously in the pursuit of reform. And this latter, whatever may have been the indications to the contrary on occasion, was the true character of Populism.

---

[44] A Populist brother once so characterized his party in a moment of exasperation. *Ibid.*, Feb. 11, 1897.

CHAPTER IV

THE RACIAL COMPLEXION OF THE PARTY

IN 1890 Texas had a total population of 2,235,523, of which a majority was of white, native American origin. There were, however, considerable colored and foreign elements in her population which added greatly to the complexity of politics during the time of the People's Party. Of the total population of about two and one-quarter millions, 488,171, or approximately 22 per cent, were colored, and an additional 15 per cent were either foreign-born or native-born of foreign-born parents.[1] This means, to shift the emphasis, that no more than 63 per cent of the State's population was native-born of native white parents.

The significance of these figures becomes apparent when it is recalled that in the nineties the colored man quite frequently exercised the franchise right, as the so-called foreign elements and their descendants do until the present day. Thus the political party which aspired to success in the State must find a large following among the colored and foreign voters, who unless divided would cast the determining vote in the event that the native American vote should be divided, or it must depend upon the native vote for its strength.[2] The latter alternative presented a forlorn hope, for the party which rested solely upon the native American vote must poll a minimum of 80 per cent of that vote in order to win; and it was of course next to impossible for a third party to draw into its ranks so overwhelming a majority from any class or group. It becomes, therefore, an interesting question, to what extent was the People's Party successful in combining under its standard the

---

[1]Henceforward the term "foreign" will be applied to that portion of the State's population which was foreign-born or native-born of foreign-born parents. The term is not thus used in a strictly accurate sense, though for our purposes it may be employed with a reasonable degree of satisfaction to distinguish such persons from the colored portions of the population and from that portion native-born of native white parents.

[2]The words "native" and "native American" are employed synonymously in this discussion to refer to that portion of the population which was native-born of native white parents.

various racial elements of the State? Here were racial groups which may be classified in order as native American, Negro, Mexican, and German, with several minor groups, including Czech, Swedish, and Polish, worthy of mention. A study of the political affiliation of each group for the decade of the nineties will go far toward explaining the successes and failures of the People's Party.[3]

I

We have seen how the People's Party originated essentially with the division of the Democratic Party into subtreasury (Alliance) and anti-subtreasury factions, the former espousing the cause of Populism, the latter remaining true to the traditions of the old party.[4] Now, both the Alliance and the Democratic Party found large numbers of their adherents among the colored and non-American groups. Suballiances were organized among German constituents, and among the Bohemians, and among the negroes, so that the farmers' organization came to rest upon a broad racial basis.[5] Similarly, the dominant party drew its support from all: in certain negro and German counties, it found a worthy foe in the Republican Party, but in most sections of the State it experienced no great difficulty in repulsing the assaults of its adversary. Thus both the Farmers' Alliance and the Democratic Party, the two sources from which sprang the People's Party, drew strength from every racial group, though from the nature of things each was dominated by native white membership.

Notwithstanding the divers character of its parent organizations, Populism was from the beginning essentially a movement among the native American farmers. Newspapers recognized the true nature of the party;[6] and while occasionally, usually for the purpose of pointing out alleged questionable tactics on the part of its leaders, the Democrats attempted to identify the movement with a foreign or colored racial group, even its chief adversaries were

---

[3]The figures used here, and those on which were based the percentage computations as well, were taken from the *Compendium of the Eleventh Census of the United States*, 1890, Tables 2, 13, and 19.

[4]*Supra*, Chap. II.

[5]If suballiances were organized among the Mexicans, that fact was not recorded in the columns of the contemporary press.

[6]See the *Dallas Morning News*, Aug. 6, 1896.

forced to agree that it depended primarily for its support upon the solid, pioneer, native white farming classes. And the tradition spread throughout the length and breadth of the State until the typical Populist came to be looked upon as being a "long-haired, post-oak," staunchly American citizen whose politics might be questioned but whose origins were as ancient and as honorable as any.

The validity of this conclusion in general may be tested by casual reference to Maps III, IV, and V below, which portray the distribution of the various racial groups in Texas, in comparison with Map I, which reveals the distribution of the People's Party vote in the State. The party attained its greatest strength, as may be seen, in that section where there were neither negroes nor foreigners, that is, in those counties of Central Texas from Lampasas to Palo Pinto. Further pursuit of the subject by means of contrast leads in the same direction, for it appears at once that the People's Party achieved little success in those portions of the State where the colored and foreign population was greatest as compared with the native white. But if these casual comparisons and contrasts be considered merely indicative and not definitive, the validity of the conclusion becomes apparent when the investigation is carried into the county. There it may be tested finally by reference to representative native white voting boxes situated in colored and foreign counties, where such boxes may be studied as exceptions to the general rule which determined the vote of the non-white or non-native boxes surrounding them. In this connection, the figures presented in Table IV are of the greatest significance. Robertson and Gillespie counties remained entirely free from People's Party influences, so far at least as Map I reveals, and Goliad County was by no means a Populist stronghold; yet in each of the three there was a voting precinct preponderantly native American in its population, and in every case that precinct was a hotbed of Populism. Of even greater interest was the situation found in Fayette County, where 74 per cent of the population was either colored (20.5%) or foreign (53.5%). The county contained but four native white boxes, whose political complexion is portrayed in Table IV. Each of the four was surrounded by German, Czech, and negro boxes, yet each was a stronghold of the People's Party, and the four combined to give the candidate of that party some 30 per cent of the total bonafide Populist vote polled by him in the county, notwithstanding there were thirty-four voting boxes in the county. Contemplation of these facts substantiates beyond question the conclusion that the People's Party in Texas depended primarily upon the allegiance of the native white citizen and that its success was greatest where it found a population free from the complications induced by varied racial groups.

TABLE IV

POPULIST NATURE OF THE VOTE IN TYPICAL NATIVE AMERICAN BOXES* IN CERTAIN COLORED OR FOREIGN COUNTIES, WITH SPECIAL REFERENCE TO FAYETTE COUNTY, AS SEEN IN THE VOTE FOR GOVERNOR, 1892–1900

	Bald Prairie† (Robertson County)	Harper‡ (Gillespie County)	Sarco§ (Goliad County)	Colony‖ (Fayette County)	Ledbetter‖ (Fayette County)	Muldoon‖ (Fayette County)	West Point‖ (Fayette County)	Total vote, Native American boxes‖ (Fayette County)	Total vote, all boxes¶ (Fayette County)
1892									
Democratic	29	2	**	40	14	83	126	263	1670
Independent Democratic	----	6	**	10	13	27	54	104	3415
Populist	86	42	**	101	33	19	61	214	556
1894									
Democratic	35	6	4	21	22	61	63	167	2867
Republican	----	19	----	32	----	33	57	122	2016
Populist	93	46	56	115	50	85	112	362	1144
1896									
Democratic	58	30	19	26	46	89	113	274	4236
Populist	84	45	42	138	35	103	104	380	2454
1898									
Democratic	63	30	22	31	32	65	123	251	4731
Populist	56	37	44	123	36	108	78	345	1258
1900									
Democratic	59	36	48	42	46	106	133	327	3792
Republican	9	53	8	37	28	75	72	202	2103
Populist	----	----	14	60	3	39	5	107	188

*Identified as native American by many citizens of the respective counties in personal interviews.

†*Record of Election Returns*, Robertson County, No. 2. Population of county largely colored.

‡*Record of Election Returns*, Gillespie County. Population of county largely German.

§*Record of Election Returns*, Goliad County, Vol. I. Population of county partly Negro, German, and Mexican.

‖*Record of Election Returns*, Fayette County, Vols. I and II. Population of county largely Czech, German, and Negro.

¶*Record of Election Returns*, Fayette County, Vols. I and II.

**Returns not available.

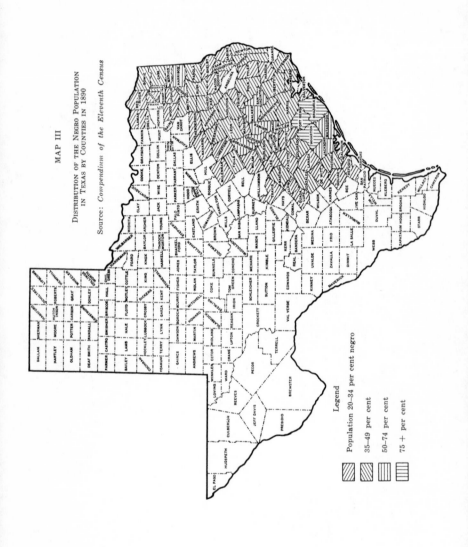

MAP III

DISTRIBUTION OF THE NEGRO POPULATION
IN TEXAS BY COUNTIES IN 1890

Source: *Compendium of the Eleventh Census*

Legend

Population 20–34 per cent negro

35–49 per cent

50–74 per cent

75 + per cent

Notwithstanding the great faith placed in the native white citizen by the People's Party, it was generally recognized by the Populist strategists that support from that group alone would not avail to bring to the party unqualified success. The simple fact was: The State in 1890 had a negro population equal to almost 22 per cent of her total, descendant largely from the old slave negroes, of which prior to the War Texas had a large number.[7] The centers of slave-holding in the State had been in the counties along the lower Brazos River and its tributaries, whose fertile valleys offered excellent lands for the culture of cotton and sugar cane, and in those of East Texas lying about the old river port of Jefferson, in Marion County, which served as one of the principal inland gateways to the State in the early days. From these two centers the old slave negroes and their descendants had filtered inland along the rivers to such effect that by 1890 no less than seventy counties of East Texas counted each in its population negroes in the number of 20 per cent or more of its total, and of this number sixteen had populations which were colored to the extent of 50 per cent or more (see Map III). Sheer numbers did not of course make of the black man an important personage in affairs political, but the significance of his presence in such numbers becomes apparent with the observation that in 1890 he exercised the right to vote, and thus was important as an elector.[8] In sixteen counties he controlled by sheer force of numbers, while in as many as fifty more he cast the determining vote when the whites divided among themselves.

---

[7]Texas is not usually thought of as having been a great slave-holding state. Lying as it does far to the west of the older states of the Old South, it is classed ordinarily as a western rather than a southern state. Nevertheless the Census of 1860 reveals the fact that of a total population for the State of 604,215, 30 per cent (182,566) were slaves. See the *Preliminary Report on the Eighth Census, 1860*, Table 1.

[8]As a matter of satisfying his curiosity on this point the author indulged in a bit of arithmetic to measure negro participation in politics in Texas during the nineties. Making use of the population figures of the United States Census Reports and the election returns for 1894, he calculated that in that year in Grimes County 85.4 per cent of the negroes voted; in Marion County, 75 per cent; in San Jacinto, 96.7; in Waller, 90; and in Camp and Jackson, 120 per cent and 116 per cent, respectively!

Thus the negro was an object of solicitude on the part of politicians and party managers, for he must be reckoned with on election day.

Since the emancipation of the slaves, the Republican Party had been looked upon as the guardian of the negro, who under the guidance of its leaders had established himself as a factor of considerable importance in politics during the days of Reconstruction. The Democrats had been able to wrest the Government of the State from the hybrid party in the early seventies, though a few colored members were elected to the Legislature as late as the nineties; but it was a matter of much greater seriousness to stamp out Republican rule in the counties where the negro controlled by sheer force of numbers. In those districts, there were in effect but two practical options offered to the Democrats: they could circumvent negro rule by use of force or by expert counting of the ballots cast,[9] or they could "play ball" with the blacks. The truth of the matter was that by 1890 the negro had become fair prey in the game of politics. Still traditionally Republican in his allegiance,[10] he was found nevertheless to be open to conviction when approached by the Democratic managers. Hence there originated the game of organizing and voting the negroes; and while it was a game fraught with dangers, it was also one offering the high stakes of public office.

That the People's Party leaders were not slow to see the necessity for pacifying the negro and the opportunity to do a remunerative work in attempting his conversion to Populism is attested by their early interest in the colored voter. The first convention of the party recognized him by appointing as members of its State Executive Committee two negroes for the State at large,[11] and subsequent conventions likewise flattered the black in ways designed to win his support.[12] Again, the official Reform press repeatedly urged

---

[9]Such legal devices as the direct primary and the poll tax were invented only toward the close of the century.

[10]See the accompanying table (Table V).

[11]*Dallas Morning News*, Aug. 18, 1891.

[12]For example, the convention of 1894 included in its platform a plank designed especially, the press believed, to catch the negro vote, in the resolution pertaining to the public free schools of the State. *Ibid.*, June 22, 1894. The resolution read: "We favor an effective system of public free schools for six months in the year for all children between the ages of six and eighteen years, and that each race shall have its own trustees and control its own schools." Winkler, *op. cit.*, p. 333.

the negro to consider his plight and come into the People's Party where relief awaited him.[13] In the field, organizers went out to effect the organization of negro Populist clubs; negro orators made hundreds of speeches to colored and mixed audiences in the black districts, the colored leader J. B. Rayner, of Calvert, Texas, being especially active in this work;[14] colored picnics and barbecues were

TABLE V

REPUBLICAN NATURE OF THE VOTE IN CERTAIN TYPICAL NEGRO BOXES,*
AS SEEN IN THE VOTE FOR GOVERNOR, 1892–1900

	Cotton Gin (Freestone County)†	Fannin (Goliad County)‡	Hawkins Plantation (Matagorda County)§	Mumford (Robertson County)‖	Wharton (Wharton County)¶
1892					
Democratic	141	††	89	160	190
Independent Democratic**	161	††	23	112	484
Populist	95	††	----	----	2
1894					
Democratic	106	34	14	78	172
Republican	193	118	85	185	519
Populist	112	48	10	----	2
1896					
Democratic	172	37	59	235	696
Populist	258	133	76	109	53
1898					
Democratic	113	82	121	147	††
Populist	135	57	----	----	††
1900					
Democratic	109	42	26	46	169
Republican	213	101	60	83	230
Populist	13	13	----	----	----

*Identified as negro boxes by numerous citizens of the respective counties in personal interviews.
†*Record of Election Returns*, Freestone County, Vol. II.
‡*Record of Election Returns*, Goliad County, Vol. I.
§*Registration of Election Returns*, Matagorda County, Vol. A.
‖*Record of Election Returns*, Robertson County, No. II.
¶*Record of Election Returns*, Wharton County, Vol. I.
**The independent Democratic candidate received the support of the Republicans.
††Returns not available.

arranged, with the dinner preceded and followed by Populist orations; colored days were designated for white Populist camp-meetings; and the negro was given official recognition at the hands

---

[13]See, for example, the *Texas Advance*, June 30, 1894 (in the Library of The University of Texas, Austin, Texas).

[14]See *infra*, Chap. V.

of Populist officers which he had not theretofore received—for example, he was summoned for jury service.[15] In short, the People's Party went out to the limit of its means after the colored vote; it recognized the importance of that vote; and it worked long and diligently in its effort to convert it to Populism.

Its labors, however, met with only a modicum of success. In the first place, in those counties where the negroes constituted a large majority of the population, there was no room for Populism. The white people of those counties were too much concerned with a thing which was more vital to them than Populism, or Democracy, or Republicanism: they were concerned with the issue of white *versus* black rule, and factional bickerings were subordinated before this one great issue. All white men turned in a common direction in a final, titanic effort to oust the so-called Republican leader and his black henchmen from control. In such a situation the People's Party knocked in vain for admittance.

In the second place, the simple truth was that the negro vote was purchaseable. Hence, while in a great many counties with a large negro population the People's Party managed to convert one-half or more of the native white vote, it had still to compete with the Democratic Party for the control of the negroes. In county after county the identical story was told: the white vote divided about equally between the Democratic and the Populist parties and the negroes held the balance of power. In such a situation the strategists of the two parties went out on the open market to deal with the negro voter, and circumstances combined to throw so great an advantage on the side of the Democrats that they were able ordinarily to return with the larger vote to show for their efforts.[16] In these simple terms may be explained the failure of the People's Party to make a better showing among the negro counties of the State.

The validity of the leading conclusion, that is, that the People's Party ordinarily failed to win the support of the negro voter, may be tested by reference to the accompanying table (Table VI). There it will be seen that in those counties whose populations were preponderantly colored the People's Party candidate for Governor in

[15]In Nacogdoches County. *The Galveston Daily News*, Oct. 19, 1894.
[16]See *infra*, Chap. VII.

1894 ran not only second, but third, both in the number of counties carried and in total vote polled. The Democratic candidate polled a large plurality which, extended to all of the negro counties of East Texas, enabled him to go into the white portions of the State with a safe lead over his Populist rival. To be sure, one is inclined to doubt the correctness of the returns from certain counties. It is not for us at this time, however, to question the returns or the methods by which the vote recorded was obtained. The figures here given were legal; they were those on the basis of which candidates were declared elected or defeated; and they reveal an impressive advantage in favor of the Democratic Party and its candidate for Governor.[17]

TABLE VI

VOTE CAST FOR GOVERNOR IN 1894 IN THOSE COUNTIES WHOSE POPULATIONS
WERE COLORED TO THE EXTENT OF 50 PER CENT OR MORE*

	Culberson (Democrat)†	Makemson (Republican)†	Nugent (Populist)†
Brazoria‡	§	§	§
Brazos	1,304	1,412	702
Camp	640	441	335
Fort Bend‡	§	§	§
Gregg	593	236	637
Grimes	1,978	520	1,669
Harrison	4,362	109	169
Jackson	276	247	203
Marion	852	612	509
Matagorda	134	274	44
Robertson	1,931	2,390	968
San Jacinto	452	147	793
Walker	864	454	1,004
Waller	610	917	737
Washington	2,356	1,939	834
Wharton ‡	369	951	89
Total	16,721	10,649	8,693

*Population classified as more than 50 per cent colored by figures from *Compendium of the Eleventh Census, 1890, Part I,* Table 13.
†*Election Register of State and County Officers, 1894.*
‡The populations of these counties were colored to the extent of 75 per cent or more.
§No returns were made in 1894.

From this it is not to be inferred that the Democratic Party was uniformly successful in its efforts to marshal the negro in support

[17]An interesting commentary on Democratic control over the negro vote in East Texas is seen in the fact that in Marion County, where the negroes had always been used to bolster up the Democratic ticket, an arrangement was perfected in 1898 whereby a white man's party was organized and the negro barred from politics. The county immediately and for the first time returned a Populist majority for Governor.

of its candidates. Table VI indicates that both the Republican and the People's parties were able occasionally to persuade the black man to vote their tickets.[18] Indeed, there were as many as half a dozen counties in the negro section of the State on which the Populists could depend with some degree of certainty. Among them,

TABLE VII

Populist Influence on the Vote in Typical Negro Boxes* in Certain Strong Populist Counties, as Seen in the Vote for Governor, 1892–1900

	Cedar Creek (Bastrop County)†	Plantersville (Grimes County)‡	West Nacogdoches (Nacogdoches County)§	Ironosa (San Augustine County)‖
1892				
Democratic	116	44	155	28
Independent Democratic	93	164	92	7
Populist	37	5	238	108
1894				
Democratic	56	107	289	53
Republican	128	62	41	1
Populist	67	90	293	117
1896				
Democratic	71	119	309	61
Populist	235	160	332	108
1898				
Democratic	89	205	325	70
Populist	178	257	339	90
1900				
Democratic	94	¶	327	66
Republican	151	¶	198	72
Populist	13	¶	238	36

*Identified as negro boxes by personal interviews with numerous citizens of the respective counties.
†*Record of Election Returns*, Bastrop County, Vol. I.
‡*Record of Election Returns*, Grimes County, Vol. I.
§*Election Returns*, Nacogdoches County, Book I.
‖*Election Returns*, San Augustine County.
¶Returns not available.

Grimes and San Augustine may be considered as being representative. Both had large negro populations; and with regard to both the rule that in such counties the support of the negroes was prerequisite to success held true, for in both the People's Party polled a majority of the negro vote. In both also the same explanation of this phenomenon may be offered: a fearless local leader turned Populist, announced his candidacy for sheriff, paraded his guns

---

[18]See also Tables V and VII.

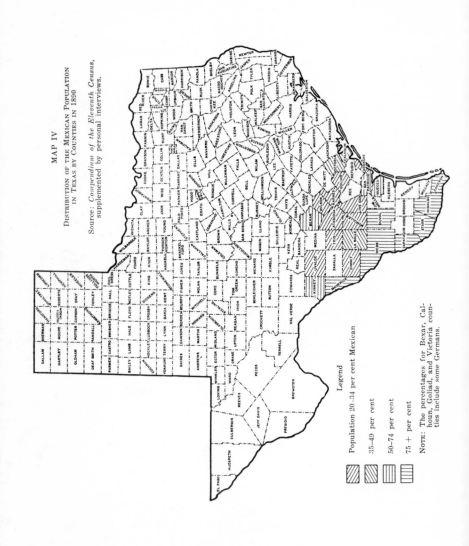

MAP IV

DISTRIBUTION OF THE MEXICAN POPULATION
IN TEXAS BY COUNTIES IN 1890

Source: *Compendium of the Eleventh Census*,
supplemented by personal interviews.

Legend

Population 20–34 per cent Mexican

35–49 per cent

50–74 per cent

75 + per cent

NOTE: The percentages for Bexar, Calhoun, Goliad, and Victoria counties include some Germans.

before the eyes of his simple watchers, unloosed a generous supply of liquor among them, and marched them into the polls in squads on election day.[19] The formula worked perfectly. True, it led in both of these cases to feuds and numerous violent deaths, but it was uniformly effective as a temporary expedient. Unfortunately for the People's Party, there were relatively few men in its ranks who could manage such a situation. The party, therefore, was not strong as a general thing in the negro sections; and where exceptions to the rule are found, they may be attributed universally to some force other than the logic of Populist argument—and that force usually was to be found in a dynamic character who was at the same time an able advocate and a practitioner of direct action.[20]

III

If the negroes constituted the most important racial group in the State aside from the native white Americans, the Mexicans or persons of immediate Mexican descent easily took second place.[21] The forbears of these people long had inhabited the country from Bexar County south; and as one progressed southward from San Antonio in 1890, one found a Mexican population which increased in strength as one approached the Rio Grande until, in the counties bordering that river on the north, a preponderant majority of the total population was Mexican or of direct Mexican origin (Map IV). That section of the State, therefore, was dominated by the Mexican vote. To succeed in politics locally, a party or candidate must draw heavily from the ranks of the Spanish-speaking portion of the population. In state politics the Mexican vote, while not controlling,

---

[19]See *infra,* Chap. V.

[20]Another county very similar to those mentioned was Nacogdoches. There the Populist manager (who was also the county sheriff) was accused openly by a local newspaper of voting the negroes in herds for his ticket. The editor estimated that the whites of the city of Nacogdoches voted Democratic by a majority of three to one, while the negroes voted Populist by ten to one. *The Daily Sentinel,* Nov. 7, 1900 (in the office of the *Sentinel,* Nacogdoches, Texas).

[21]It is, of course, not accurate to refer to the Mexican population of the State as comprising a "foreign" element, for in truth those people were the natives and the Anglo-Saxon invaders the foreigners. By 1890, however, the latter had come to predominate in the State at large; and the Mexican population, constituting as it did a distinct minority racial group, may therefore be classed for the purpose of this examination as a foreign element.

was by no means a negligible factor, and it were well for the party which hoped for state-wide success to attempt at least to divide that vote if not to control it.[22]

In view of the acknowledged importance of the Mexican vote, it is strange that the People's Party did not turn its attention in the direction of building up a following among that group. That it did not, however, may be inferred from the facts first, that no spokesman of the Mexican voters ever came before the state convention and, second, that that body paid no attention to the matter of making the party's platform acceptable to the Mexican element. Locally, the leaders of the Populists now and again made conscious efforts to carry their cause to the Mexican voter. For example, a Spanish newspaper was established in San Antonio under the guidance of a Mexican editor, but it failed to attain to any considerable success, and was suspended after a brief period. Again, a few Populist clubs were established here and there among the Mexicans, and an occasional address was delivered in Spanish to Mexican audiences. Yet again, even the state leaders gave evidence now and then that they were not wholly oblivious to the importance of the Mexican vote by defending the party against charges calculated to injure it in the Mexican sections of the State. Such notice was, however, wholly incidental, for those leaders considered that there were other fields more important than that relating to the conversion of the Mexican voter. Hence they denied, or ignored, the pleas of local leaders for assistance in the southern counties of the State, with the result that almost no attention was given to what should have been an important field of action.[23]

In light of these facts, it is a matter for no surprise that the People's Party drew almost no support from the Mexicans. In a few counties, it is true, local strategists of the party were able temporarily to convert to Populism a Mexican following of some

[22]See *The Southern Mercury*, May 14, 1894, for a letter in which a Populist leader from South Texas called attention to the importance of the Mexican vote. That he did not overemphasize its significance may be seen readily by reference to the election returns from the larger Mexican counties for any year.

[23]*The Southern Mercury*, May 14, 1896. The writer noted the need for propaganda work among the Mexicans and made a plea for such financial assistance as would enable him to wage an active campaign in the Mexican counties.

consequence. Thus in Wilson County, where the Mexican voters held the balance of power, the Populists nominated one Vicente F. Carvajal for a county office, succeeding thereby in dividing the Mexican vote to such an extent that they were able to control the county for four years. This was recognized, however, to be an unusual occurrence. The Third Party considered ordinarily that its candidates labored under an unfavorable handicap measured by the strength of the Mexican vote; that they were correct in their appraisal of that vote is evidenced by the election returns tabulated in Table VIII. The figures entered there reveal the weakness of the People's Party among the Mexican voters, indicating also by clear implication an important cause for the failure of that party to achieve a large degree of success in the State.

TABLE VIII

Vote Cast for Governor in 1894 in Those Counties Whose Populations Were Mexican to the Extent of 50 Per Cent or More*

County	Culberson (Democrat)†	Makemson (Republican)†	Nugent (Populist)†
Bexar	4,813	2,005	1,586
Cameron‡	2,763	491	-------
Duval‡	307	493	1
Hidalgo‡	835	12	1
Kinney	186	46	1
Maverick‡	333	181	274
Nueces	1,297	318	163
San Patricio	491	28	147
Starr‡	1,247	567	-------
Webb‡	1,452	920	134
Zapata‡	324	14	-------
Total	14,048	5,075	2,307

*Population classified as non-native American in *Compendium of the Eleventh Census, 1890, Part I,* Table 19, as Mexican by many citizens throughout the State in personal interviews.
†*Election Register of State and County Officers, 1894.*
‡The populations of these counties were Mexican to the extent of 75 per cent or more.

If an explanation be sought for the comparative weakness of Populism in the Mexican counties, it may be found in several factors which combined to retard the cause of Reform there. In the first place, wholly aside from the fact that there were certain natural factors which conspired against the party in those sections, its leaders did not work for the conversion of the Mexicans with any degree of enthusiasm. In the second place, the Farmers' Alliance, the foundation stone of the People's Party, was less strong in the southern portion of the State than in any other, and the

Populists thus had a poor base on which to build. In the third place, its non-alien makeup and its alleged anti-alien program cast about the Third Party a cloud of Knownothingism so that reasoning Mexicans regarded Populism with doubt, while the unthinking masses took fright and stampeded outright when the party was mentioned. In the fourth place, the Mexican vote forty years ago was a controlled vote. Political bosses in the counties of South Texas voted the Mexicans as they pleased; and if there were not enough votes on the Texas side of the river, there were more where those came from.[24] Since these local princelings were almost universally Democrats, the vote of their followers was overwhelmingly Democratic. Table VIII indicates something of the situation, though the figures explain nothing of the spirit behind the vote cast.[25] From the table, it is patent that the Democratic Party was so firmly entrenched in the Mexican counties as to be almost invulnerable; and this fact, together with the positive handicaps under which the People's Party labored among the Mexicans, serves to explain the fatal weakness of Populism in the important section of the State south of San Antonio.

IV

Another racial group found in Texas in considerable numbers in 1890 comprised the German inhabitants and citizens of German extraction. These people had immigrated to Texas in the days of

---

[24]Those who undertook to control by use of questionable methods among the Mexicans were aided and abetted by the liberal provisions of the law which extended the right to vote to any male alien who complied with the usual requirements and who had, *at any time prior to the election* in which he sought to vote, declared his intention to become a citizen of the United States. *Revised Civil Statutes of the State of Texas, 1895*, Article 1731. Under this law the local Democratic chieftain could summon as many votes as he might need and aliens were imported in droves from Mexico, it was said, and marched to the polling places with their trousers still damp from having waded the river. Tales of the "wet" and the "muddy" vote of the Rio Grande valley became legendary, and there is ample evidence that they rested on a foundation of truth.

[25]A better index to this latter may be found in the vote for the election of 1898, when several of the counties listed in Table VIII returned votes ranging up to 3,000 for the Democratic candidate and *none at all* for the Populist.

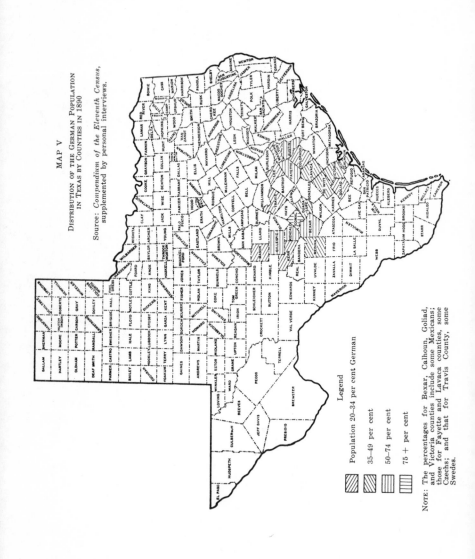

MAP V

DISTRIBUTION OF THE GERMAN POPULATION
IN TEXAS BY COUNTIES IN 1890

Source: *Compendium of the Eleventh Census,*
supplemented by personal interviews.

Legend

Population 20–34 per cent German

35–49 per cent

50–74 per cent

75 + per cent

NOTE: The percentages for Bexar, Calhoun, Goliad,
and Victoria counties include some Mexicans;
those for Fayette and Lavaca counties, some
Czechs; and that for Travis County, some
Swedes.

the Republic and the early days of the State, settling in the districts lying about Austin and Comal counties.[26] By 1890 they constituted the majority of the population in four or five counties, while in as many as a dozen more they were found to the extent of 25 per cent or more of the total population (Map V). Numerically then they were an important element in the population of the State, and their significance in public affairs was accentuated by their interest and participation in politics.[27] Moreover, the German was a voter of very high type: there was little or no boss control in the German communities, for the citizens there were jealous of the franchise right and demanded to be free in its exercise.

In politics, the German voter was looked upon generally as being a Republican. The popular characterization was not wholly accurate, however, for among German citizens there were many Democrats. Indeed, the inclination of the German immigrant originally was to vote Democratic, which he did by large majorities until the time of the War. With the rise of the slavery issue, he found himself caught between two fires. On the one hand, it appeared to him that the impending war bade fair to be a contest in behalf of an institution he did not favor for an end (disunion) he did not desire. But on the other hand he was a Democrat: he had landed in a country of Democrats and had been cordially received there, and he resided even then in a community surrounded on every hand by men of the Democratic faith. In such a predicament, discretion called for a quiet and tranquil policy on his part.

Among the Germans, however, there were those who were staunch Abolitionists, and their voice came to be identified with that of the German people of the State. Democratic spokesmen, and especially the Democratic newspapers, adopted a bitterly denunciatory tone regarding the objectionable political activities of the Abolitionists.[28] The conflict so engendered, beginning innocently enough in a discussion of the slavery problem, waxed ever warmer in the years immediately preceding the War until by 1861 the Germans had been

[26]Rudolph Leopold Biesele, *The History of the German Settlements in Texas, 1831–1861* (Austin, 1930).

[27]The reader interested in studying the foreigner as a voter may learn some significant facts concerning German participation in politics by comparing the Census population figures with the election returns for the German counties.

[28]See Biesele, *op. cit.*, Chap. X, for the pre-War struggle here alluded to.

branded definitely as Unionists. The intolerance of the secessionists precluded the possibility of a pacific settlement of the quarrel, which reached a climax when the authorities chose to regard certain actions on the part of the Union sympathizers in the western German counties as rebellion against the Confederacy and to send Confederate soldiery into those counties to quell the alleged disturbances. Before the Confederate troops the Unionists, having no desire to test the issue by resort to arms, were driven either to bushwhacking or to flight, and either alternative was as dangerous as it was distasteful. The bushwhackers were ferreted out one by one and dealt with summarily. Several bodies of fugitives made their way into Mexico, where they found a haven; but many were less fortunate, falling before their pursuers ere they had reached the Rio Grande.[29]

TABLE IX

VOTE CAST FOR GOVERNOR IN 1894 IN THOSE COUNTIES WHOSE POPULATIONS WERE GERMAN TO THE EXTENT OF 50 PER CENT OR MORE*

County	Culberson (Democrat)†	Makemson (Republican)†	Nugent (Populist)†
Austin	1,653	1,152	517
Comal‡	759	176	84
Fayette	2,867	2,016	1,144
Gillespie	260	653	473
Kendall	155	213	198
Total	5,694	4,210	2,416

*Population classified as non-native American in *Compendium of the Eleventh Census, 1890,* Part I, Table 19, as German by many citizens of the respective counties in personal interviews.
†*Election Register of State and County Officers,* 1894.
‡The population of this county was German to the extent of 75 per cent or more.

In fine, differences arising over the slavery controversy, together with the events of the War, sealed the decision for separation. The Germans, formerly good Democrats, remained Democratic in part,

---

[29]The most flagrant case of this nature, from the point of view of the Germans, was the massacre called the "Battle of Nueces River," which took place on Aug. 10, 1862. A band of sixty-five men, nearly all Germans or of German extraction, attempting to make their way into Mexico, was set upon on the Nueces River, in Kinney County, by a force of 100 men under a Confederate officer. The Germans, poorly armed and taken completely by surprise, offered but slight resistance, and half of their number were slain by the Confederate force. See John W. Sansom's *Battle of Nueces River* (San Antonio, 1905).

but a large portion of them affiliated with the Republican Party, and this was true especially of those who resided in the westernmost of the German counties where the military rule of the Democrats had been most stringent. Tables IX and X reveal in general the

TABLE X

REPUBLICAN NATURE OF THE VOTE IN CERTAIN TYPICAL GERMAN BOXES,*
AS SEEN IN THE VOTE FOR GOVERNOR, 1892–1900

	Biegel (Fayette County)†	Comfort (Kendall County)‡	Fredericksburg (Gillespie County)§	Germantown (Goliad County)‖	San Geronimo (Medina County)¶
1892					
Democratic	23	27	9	††	17
Independent Democratic**	141	91	361	††	39
Populist	3	57	38	††	7
1894					
Democratic	65	44	143	21	19
Republican	91	86	236	65	25
Populist	11	57	37	32	6
1896					
Democratic	70	93	268	16	13
Populist	115	42	163	117	36
1898					
Democratic	158	156	346	89	53
Populist	4	8	63	32	5
1900					
Democratic	73	63	151	56	30
Republican	76	99	325	75	29
Populist		2	4	2	

*Identified as such by many citizens of the respective counties in personal interviews.
†*Record of Election Returns*, Fayette County, Vols. I and II.
‡*Record of Election Returns*, Kendall County, No. 2.
§*Record of Election Returns*, Gillespie County.
‖*Record of Election Returns*, Goliad County, Vol. I.
¶*Record of Election Returns*, Medina County, No. II.
**The Independent Democratic candidate received the support of the Republicans.
††Returns not available.

nature of the German vote in the nineties. From the figures presented in Table IX it appears that the strongest German counties in the State had comparatively large Republican votes, though the Democratic Party still predominated in the most populous of those counties.[30]

---

[30]It is not without significance that Gillespie and Kendall counties, the scene of operation of the Confederate disciplinary troops, were the strongest Republican counties of the five noted.

The People's Party from the beginning recognized the importance of the German vote. In the Populist state convention of 1892, a candidate of German parentage was nominated for State Superintendent;[31] and again in 1894 concessions were made to the German voters in the nomination for Comptroller of E. O. Meitzen and in the adoption of a resolution in behalf of local self-government which, translated into practical terminology, meant Sunday beer for the Germans.[32] Nor were the German electors neglected by the Populist field men. Lecturers and speakers addressed them in their own tongue; a German Populist newspaper was established;[33] and organizers went among them attempting to transform the sub-alliances (of which there were many among the German communities) into People's Party clubs. In short, no effort was spared to convert the German voters to Populism.

The results of these efforts were disappointing in the extreme. Of the five counties whose populations were German to the extent of 50 per cent or more, only one ever returned a vote favorable to the People's Party candidate for Governor, and that county, Kendall, voted Populist only in 1896 when the Republican Party endorsed the Third Party candidate. Indeed, only two strong German counties ever returned majorities or pluralities for the Populist candidate aside from the year 1896. One of these, Medina, went Populist in 1892, and the other, Lavaca, only in 1894. It was in the former county only, among the German sections of the State, that the People's Party may be said to have achieved any appreciable success. There three or four prominent German citizens became converted to Populism, and they were able, largely by their personal influence, successfully to bridge the gap between a strong local Alliance and a moderately strong Populist organization.

There were sundry reasons why the People's Party was treated with such scant courtesy by the Germans. In the first place, it appeared from the beginning that that party was so wholly American in its complex as to be almost unavoidably anti-alien. Indeed,

[31]*Dallas Morning News*, June 25, 1892.

[32]*Ibid.*, June 22, 1894. This was a direct bid for German support, and it was denounced as such by a member of the platform committee which recommended the plank. He was frowned down, however, and the resolution passed by an overwhelming vote.

[33]*The Southern Mercury*, July 2, 1896.

Populist spokesmen were at no pains to conceal their attitude: slighting references to the alien, and to the German in particular (by implication) as a "base element of our country" were made naturally and perhaps unconsciously, and they inevitably found their way into the press.[34] The opinion to which this attitude gave rise hardened into conviction with the coming of the Knownothing movement called the American Protective Association, with which the People's Party was at once identified in the mind of the German voter. He conceived the party as favoring the restriction of immigration, the more rigid definition of citizenship and the process of naturalization, the safeguarding of native labor at the expense of the alien—in short, the People's Party became, in his eyes, the reincarnation of the old Knownothing movement, anti-alien, anti-Catholic, and anti-liberal, and he refused to affiliate with it.

In the second place, the German voter looked upon the Third Party as the party of righteousness. By a custom as old as his race he gathered on Sunday with his fellow men and passed the day at cards and beer drinking which, in his mind, were innocent pastimes concerning none but those participating in them. Naturally then he feared lest the Government fall into the hands of an illiberal faction which would deprive him of his hard-earned pleasures, and he distrusted especially any movement which smacked of Prohibitionism. The People's Party, it appeared to him, was both anti-liberal and Prohibitionist. True, it had refused to espouse the cause of Prohibition actively, but the German could not forget what was the composition of the party. He remembered that it was filled to overflowing with preachers and that the old Prohibitionist, E. L. Dohoney, was prominent in its councils. Moreover, he insisted that "The implications of the platform outweigh(ed) the explicit provisions a thousandfold."[35] Populism thus came to symbolize

---

[34]See, for example, the quarrel which reached a head in the *Mercury* of May 29, 1890.

[35]*The Texas Vorwaerts*, March 23, 1894 (in the Library of The University of Texas, Austin, Texas). This paper characterized the local self-government plank as "bait to catch mice," and opined that no thinking German would be gulled by it. See the issue of Aug. 17, 1894. Outbursts against Populist preachers may be read in *ibid.*, May 29, 1896, and June 26, 1896.

to the German voter all that was distasteful of the idealist movements of the day; it became a "blue Sunday," Prohibition party, and as such he did not consider it worthy of his support.

Aside from these objectionable features of Populism, there was much in the Populist program which appealed to the German voter. For example, the demands for an income tax, the extension of the principle of popular election, and public ownership of the railways were in no wise unacceptable to the progressive citizenry of the German communities.[36] Other aspects of the platform, however, either expressly stated or implied, dictated the course of the German voter. The *Texas Vorwaerts*, a liberal paper of the progressive wing of the Democrats, lampooned the Populists as "boys from the piney woods *(Fichtenknaben)* of East Texas;[37] it regarded Meitzen as a "German worm dangling from the political fishhook of the Populists to attract German bites;"[38] and, in short, it made the whole movement the object of such satire and sarcasm and ridicule as one rarely finds in the columns of a newspaper. The editor of the *Vorwaerts* carried his opposition to greater lengths than most of his contemporaries, though few left room for doubt as to their attitudes concerning the People's Party. That party found little sympathy among the German people of the State, as is evidenced by the vote which its candidates polled in the sections where those people resided in large numbers.

V

Among the minor racial groups in Texas in 1890, the Czech, the Polish, and the Swedish elements are worthy of brief note. The strongest of these groups, the Czech, was found largely in Fayette and Lavaca counties, where a considerable percentage of the total population was Bohemian or of immediate Bohemian descent. The Poles constituted a large portion of the population of no county: there was a Polish settlement in Robertson County and another in Wilson, and outside of these two centers (and neither was very

[36]*Ibid.*, Sept. 15, 1893. Indeed, a convention of Germans pronounced in favor of the first two of these principles forty years before the People's Party. See Biesele, *op. cit.*, p. 198.

[37]*The Texas Vorwaerts*, July 28, 1892.

[38]*Ibid.*, Aug. 28, 1896. In another connection Meitzen was referred to as the "long-eared gentleman" *(Eselskopf)* from Lavaca. Dec. 25, 1896.

populous) that element was of little or no consequence. The Swedes resided in considerable numbers in and around the city of Austin, in Travis County, and in the south central part of Williamson, though they did not constitute a majority of the population in either county.

Notwithstanding the fact that each of the three groups was recognized as being of some importance in the politics of the counties wherein its members resided, the state organization of the People's Party ignored all. The campaign methods and propaganda techniques employed by the party leaders to effect the conversion of the negroes and the Germans were wholly lacking with reference to the minor groups, except in the case of the Czechs. A few Populist clubs were organized among the Bohemians, and an occasional speaker addressed them in their native tongue;[39] but these were feeble efforts which succeeded in engendering no great amount of enthusiasm.

The results of the attitude of the Populist strategists on the vote cast might have been foretold with complete accuracy months before any particular election. The Czechs as a usual thing were by inclination Democrats: they had become accustomed to consider themselves members of that party early in their career in this country, and nothing had happened to turn them to another. Further, the older men among them, remembering the difficulties they had experienced with paper money in the old country (Austria) back in the fifties, counselled their countrymen against the fiat money schemes of the Populists.[40] Again, the Czechs took exception to the unguarded and ill-considered references made by People's Party sympathizers to non-American peoples.[41] Finally, they were more subject to control than certain other racial elements—than

---

[39]*The Southern Mercury*, July 2, 1896, announced a number of addresses to be delivered before Czech audiences in Texas by T. K. Ringsmuth, editor of the newspaper *Svit*, of Cedar Rapids, Iowa.

[40]See a letter published in the La Grange (Fayette County) *Svoboda*, Sept. 15, 1895 (in the Library of The University of Texas, Austin, Texas).

[41]For example, back in 1888 a letter appeared which classed the Bohemians along with the Chinese as undesirable aliens, and representatives from seven Bohemian suballiances met and denounced the letter and protested against the policy of the *Mercury*, which had neglected or refused to print their reply to it. See *The Southern Mercury*, Dec. 6, 1888.

for example, the Germans—and among the members of any group where this was the case the old party from the nature of things had a large advantage.[42] It is not a matter for surprise, therefore, that while some few Czechs voted for Populist candidates, a large majority remained with the Democratic Party.[43]   Moreover, what was true of the Czechs was true also, in general, of the Poles. They voted Democratic, and the most the Populists could hope for in the Polish settlements was a division of the vote which would prevent the Democratic ticket from rolling up too great a majority.

Among the Swedes, as among Czechs and Poles, the People's Party found little welcome.   The Swedish voter who immigrated direct from Sweden was by preference a Democrat; his brother who came to Texas from the northern states in this country was by training a Republican.   Whether Democrat or Republican, however, the Swede took great pride in the right to vote, demanding to be left free in the exercise of that right.   Hence he was never organized along with other of his countrymen into a race-conscious group, or for that matter into a close organization of any description.   He voted Democratic or Republican largely from preference and continued so to vote despite the promises held out by Populism.

The several minor racial groups of the State therefore remained in good part Democratic during the days of the Third Party campaigns.   But little effort was made to cause them to change their political allegiances; and while small numbers from each element voted for the Populist candidates every two years, the election returns reveal unmistakably the lack of campaign and propaganda work among them.   The general character of the Czech, the Polish, and the Swedish vote may be seen from Table XI, which reveals that the typical community of each group always returned a Democratic majority, with the Populist candidate a poor second and sometimes even a third choice.

---

[42]The writer of the above mentioned letter in *Svoboda* alluded to herd voting by his countrymen and concluded that evidently they did not know what they were doing, inasmuch as they voted Populist on this occasion.

[43]*Svoboda*, Nov. 22, 1894.

TABLE XI

DEMOCRATIC NATURE OF THE VOTE IN CERTAIN BOXES TYPICAL EACH OF A
MINOR RACIAL GROUP,* AS SEEN IN THE VOTE FOR GOVERNOR, 1892–1900

	Bremond (Polish) (Robertson County)†	Hutto (Swedish) (Williamson County)‡	Praha (Czech) (Fayette County)§
1892			
Democratic	283	182	10
Independent Democratic	273	70	94
Populist	57	46	6
1894			
Democratic	326	184	83
Republican	119	37	1
Populist	51	121	41
1896			
Democratic	275	325	132
Populist	137	92	6
1898			
Democratic	366	208	104
Populist	3	50	4
1900			
Democratic	278	299	96
Republican	31	31	7
Populist	——	10	4

*Identified as to race by many citizens of the respective counties in personal interviews.
†*Record of Election Returns*, Robertson County, No. II.
‡*Record of Election Returns*, Williamson County, Nos. II and III.
§*Record of Election Returns*, Fayette County, Vols. I and II.

The subject developed above reveals beyond question the chief source of strength of the People's Party. That party depended primarily upon the support of the native white American citizen, and in the districts where that type of citizen predominated to the virtual exclusion of all others Populism was strong. There were, however, numerous colored and non-native elements in the population of the State which must be taken into account by the party which hoped to succeed. It was precisely in this direction that the People's Party failed most signally. It made valiant efforts to convert the negro vote to Populism; and though the attempt proved futile in large, it is significant that in the counties of East Texas the party succeeded almost exactly in the proportion that it was able to carry the negro boxes. It made some attempt also to convert the German vote, but in this field its efforts met with even less success than in the black belt section of the State. The Mexican vote it ignored almost entirely, as also that of the minor groups, the Czechs, the Poles, and the Swedes. The party strategists then were guilty of the fatal error of stressing the Anglo-Saxon vote too greatly at the expense of that of other racial groups. The symbols which they summoned and the tocsins which they sounded rallied on the one side a multitude of native whites and some colored men and arrayed on the other many staunchly Democratic natives, many negroes, and a multitude of foreigners —and the latter prevailed over the former by sheer force of num-bers, even as the Democracy prevailed over the cause of Populism.

CHAPTER V

LEADERSHIP

THE importance of the element of leadership to the new political party can hardly be overstated. The third party appears with no well-defined or generally accepted program: instead, in its incipiency, there are innumerable reform movements in the air, and from the issues presented by these movements it must draft a platform which will have the widest possible appeal. Further, in the infancy of the third party the forces of reform are scattered and discrete, yet out of this mass of inharmonious elements must be molded an organization which will present a united, closely-knit front against the charges of the enemy. To these labors is adequate only the undivided attention of the most skillful of leaders who must be tireless in their efforts and astute in their analyses. Ordinary acumen and perseverance will not suffice to secure success to their cause, which demands for its consummation a large measure of perspicacity and ingenuity on the part of those who speak in its name.

The implications of these remarks are of special consequence to one who would understand the People's Party as it operated in Texas. That party, nurtured through an uncertain infancy by men whose watchful care saved it from coming into the world still-born, never ceased to require the solicitous attention demanded by all infants—it never attained that position in the State, long occupied by the Democratic Party, which permitted its adherents to relax for an instant their vigilance. The element of leadership, therefore, of gravest moment to the minor party, was particularly important in the case of the People's Party in this State.

When one turns from a recognition of the significance of leadership to a consideration of the leaders, however, one turns from a field in which there is general agreement to one in which every conclusion reached may be controverted. None will deny the influence of the Reform leaders; but concerning such matters as the motives of each, the character and capacities of each, and the contributions of each to the People's Party, there is nothing even approaching a common opinion. Midway between the position

of the partisan who sees all Populist leaders as patriots and that
of the critic who views all as office seekers, however, is one which
permits the observer on the basis of the information at hand to
make an objective study of these several leaders and reach an
impersonal conclusion as to the part played by each and by all
in the People's Party movement.

An investigation conducted from such a point of view will dis-
close the fact that the Third Party summoned to its support men
of sundry personalities, motives, and abilities.   It will reveal
further that, while the state leaders of the party played much the
more spectacular role, the part of local managers in organizing
People's Party clubs and in getting out the vote was of the greatest
importance to the success of the party.   The state leader and the
local leader indeed were complementary, and both must be considered in any attempt to evaluate the factor of leadership.

I

The men known throughout the length and breadth of Texas
as the leaders of the Third Party submit themselves to satisfactory
classification into more groups than one.[1]   It seems best, however,
to strike at once to the heart of the matter by adopting as the
basis for approaching the subject the contributions to Populism of
the leaders contemplated.   What were the services performed by
each, and what was his role in the development—and the decay
—of the party?   Selecting six leaders each of whom exercised an
undoubted influence on the course of his party, let us examine
each briefly with an eye to his background, his station in life, his
personal characteristics, his techniques, his abilities, and his services to Populism.   When this is done it may be possible to reach
a reasoned conclusion regarding the leaders of the Third Party in
Texas.

A political party is strengthened immeasurably in its popular
appeal if it is able to personify in its leaders the myth of rightness on which it stakes its claim for support.   The People's Party
in Texas found more than one great or good man in the ranks of

---

[1]One suggestive category, for example, contains the names of those leaders
classified according to their political origins and their backgrounds.

its prophets, and foremost among them was Thomas L. Nugent, twice Populist candidate for Governor and acknowledged leader of his party in this State to the very end of his too-brief life. Born in 1841 of a family in moderate circumstances, Nugent as a youth had the advantage of a college education, completing with an excellent record the work necessary for graduation from Centenary College in Louisiana. With the coming of the War he enlisted in the Southern army where he served with distinction to the end of hostilities. Then he followed school teaching until 1870, when he was admitted to the bar and began the practice of law. An omnivorous reader, he was a student of the classics as well, and his learning soon made for him a reputation which called him to the attention of the powers that were. Further, he served commendably as a member of the Texas Constitutional Convention of 1875. Hence when a new judicial district was created in his section of the State in 1879, it was no more than natural that he should receive the appointment to preside over the new court. At the end of the first term, he was elected to succeed himself, and when that term expired, he was re-elected. It was during this third term as district judge that his name was brought up for the Democratic nomination for the court of appeals; and though he was not nominated, he received a substantial vote in the convention. In 1888, when it became apparent that his health demanded a change in climate, he resigned his judgeship and moved to another part of the State where he engaged again in private practice of the law.

As a boy Nugent was a serious-minded, studious youth set apart from those of his own age by his meditative nature and sober mien. Encouraged by the deeply religious atmosphere which pervaded his father's household, he became a close student of the Bible and a confessed Christian before he had reached his majority. As he grew older he delved more deeply into the mysteries of life, turning to various philosophers and eventually to Emanuel Swedenborg, of whom he became and thenceforward remained a staunch disciple. Far from being irreligious or non-religious, as his opponents in politics subsequently frequently charged, he was most pious in his attitude and Christlike in his practices. He was kind, gentle, courteous to the point of being courtly, quiet and self-contained, dignified, and withal a Christian gentleman in the best sense of the term.[2]

Here then is the background which led to the espousal of Populism by Judge Nugent. There were those who traced his defection from Democracy to his failure to secure the judicial nomination he sought back in the eighties,[3] but the beginnings of the break may be seen before that event occurred. Indeed, one need not seek far for an explanation of Judge Nugent's political career. His super-sensitive nature, his inborn sympathy for the unfortunate, and his long residence in a district (Erath County) where the Alliance was strong and where an independent political movement already had wrested control locally from the Democrats—these factors combined to foredoom him to Populism.

If it seemed only natural that Nugent should profess a preference for the People's Party; it was no less to be expected that he would come to the front as a leader of that party. In public address he was not markedly effective: he told no stories nor anecdotes; he used few gestures; and he refused to attack his opponent personally. On the contrary, he relied on a simple, logical, straightforward presentation of facts, and his addresses appealed, therefore, to the intellects and not the emotions of his audience. Nor were his writings (for he addressed frequent communications to the press) inspired by extraordinary literary power, though it is probable that he was as effective in writing as in speech. Hence he was not a strong campaigner; there were others, many others, in the People's Party who surpassed him in the art of making converts.

There was none, however, whose reputation as a gentleman overshadowed that of Nugent. No man had heard him use unseemly language; no man had seen him drink. No man had known him to lose his equilibrium, or to raise his voice even in heat of argument above a well-modulated tone. Nor was his sense of fairness ever impeached: more than one of his political enemies

---

[2]See Mrs. Catharine Nugent, *Life Work of Thomas L. Nugent* (Stephenville, Texas, 1896).

[3]Charles A. Culberson, his opponent for the Governorship in 1894, professed to find the explanation here. *Dallas Morning News,* Oct. 25, 1894.

have confided to the author that they practiced law in his court for years while he was on the district bench and that no word ever fell from his lips which in the least reflected discredit on the judiciary or the magistrate. Such a man was of necessity, it seemed, a stranger to the art of making enemies, while friends were his as a matter of course by the thousands.

It may be supposed by the reader, as it was supposed by some not acquainted with Judge Nugent in the nineties, that he was something more or less than a man and that in any event he must have been of colorless and passive personality. Such was not at all the case; for if Nugent was dignified in his mode of expression, he was at the same time vigorous; and if he was fair, kind, and considerate, he was nevertheless firm in his convictions and positive in his statements of opinions. He was in truth a man of great courage, if mayhap also of poor judgment, as is evidenced by his steadfastness in his unpopular religious and political creeds, to which he clung tenaciously even when some slight compromise would have made his way much easier. If Nugent's sense of honesty and his strong mind and unyielding will had had the support of a powerful body, he would have been a veritable giant among the leaders of Populism, but this was not to be. His health forced him to conserve his strength wherever possible, and thus to circumscribe his activities at times and places when otherwise he might have done valiant service for the Third Party. And by the measure of his physical disability was his usefulness as a Populist leader diminished.

It is not strange that there should grow up about this religio-political idealist a tradition of righteousness and justice which gave him a much stronger popular appeal than he ordinarily would have enjoyed. His character came to symbolize the whole Reform movement, to epitomize all that was best of Populism. Thus he was made to serve as the focal point of the movement, and the "Nugent tradition" became the rallying cry for Reformers the State over. His death in December of 1895, which appears at first blush to have dealt a heavy blow to the Reform movement, in reality served to accentuate the importance of the tradition; for his survivors forthwith canonized the martyred leader, with the result that the name Nugent was almost if not quite as significant in 1896 as it had been in 1894.

When death overtook Judge Nugent the People's Party was put to the necessity of finding another leader about whose standard it might rally the forces of Reform for the campaign of 1896. The name of an acceptable substitute came to mind at once; and if the mantle of the talismanic Nugent hung a little awkwardly from the broad shoulders of Jerome C. Kearby, it might nevertheless be made to fit his figure with some alterations. Kearby was not a pious, kindly shepherd, but he was a man of unquestioned ability; and if he could not be made over into a "good" man, perhaps he might be found to have some of the attributes of greatness. He became, therefore, with little preliminary advertising the great man of Texas Populism.

Jerome Kearby was born in Arkansas in 1848.[4] Service in the armies of the Confederacy precluded the possibility of early formal training, and it was not until the end of the War that he was able to turn his attention to study. After a few years of reading in private law offices, he became a member of the Dallas bar in 1875, where he soon rose to a position of eminence which he never relinquished. Early in his career he concluded to "throw off the Democratic collar," remaining thereafter an independent in politics. Nonconformity was no new thing for him, then, for he had had two decades of experience in dissenting when the People's Party was organized. His background made it only logical, as his superior ability made it inevitable, that he become a leader of that party in the State.

Kearby was one of the best known criminal lawyers in Texas during the days of Populism. His fame spread as the "boy soldier," the youngest man enlisted on the side of the South during the War, and his personality and appearance enabled him to capitalize on the handicap furnished by his reputation and to add many cubits to his stature. He was possessed of a sincere, straightforward manner and a pleasing address which made new friends at sight. Recognized universally as a man of ability, he profited also from a splendid physique which together with his wide knowledge and his

---

[4]See the *Dallas Morning News*, Aug. 7, 1896, for a brief account of the life of Jerome C. Kearby.

prowess as an orator made him one of the strongest campaigners in the State. Nor were his motives open to question: he was a political dissenter of twenty-five years standing, and all who knew him could vouch for his steadfastness in the cause of reform and his courage in defending his creed.

Fortified by these attributes, Kearby slipped easily into the position vacated by his predecessor. There was for him little of the reverence manifested toward Judge Nugent by those who knew him best, but there was a wholesome respect for his ability and a supreme confidence in his integrity. He became therefore the champion without peer of the cause of Reform, and the Populist hordes transferred their regard without violence from Nugent, the priest of Populism, to Kearby, the commander.

The new director of the Third Party suffered nevertheless from two weaknesses. First was his alleged immoderate use of intoxicating liquors. This was understood in his home city of Dallas and allowance made for it; but the People's Party out in the provinces was the party of Prohibition, and it added no strength to Populism for its champion to come there with the charge of intemperance upon him—and this more particularly if the district should happen to be "dry," as it was frequently, under local option. Second, Kearby's religious beliefs were open to question. It was alleged that he was a heretic, a charge demanding instant and conclusive refutation if the accused desired to continue in the good. graces of the rank and file of the party. The refutation was never made to the satisfaction of all, and the subject's reputed failing for liquor was ignored completely. Hence it may be questioned whether Jerome Kearby, perhaps the ablest man in the People's Party, brought to the party more strength by his adherence than his personal habits and attitudes repelled from it.

From the discussion of Nugent and Kearby, it may be concluded that the Third Party in Texas was able to personify its leading myths in a satisfactory manner in the characters, real and legendary, of its leaders. There is much to be done, however, even after the political party has succeeded in canonizing its foremost chieftains, for what does it profit a party to be led by saints and super-men if its light be hid under a bushel? It must, for all the respect enjoyed by its head, carry its message effectively to the people, and for this work it must have orators and organizers. The People's

Party in Texas boasted several leaders whose talents fitted them either to popularize the cause of Reform from the stump or to marshal the voters into one or more of the various organizations sponsored by the party.

Foremost among the orators was James H. (Cyclone) Davis, whose voice was heard by greater multitudes than that of any other state speaker. Davis was born in South Carolina in 1854, though his family came to Texas immediately thereafter.[5] The educational advantages afforded him were limited to the opportunity to attend a country school and to do some special work under a local schoolmaster. Young Davis was of an inquiring turn of mind, however, and improved his spare time by delving into various fields, one of which was the law. As a young man he tried his hand at several professions, among them schoolteaching, politics, and newspaper work, but by 1890 he had gravitated into the practice of law at Sulphur Springs, in Hopkins County, where he continued to serve also as editor of the *Alliance Vindicator*. He was never satisfied, however, with the prosaic life of the practicing attorney but was on the lookout constantly for something of a more exciting nature. His ready vocabulary made for him a reputation throughout his section of the State as a public speaker while he was yet a young man, and he lost no opportunity to appear in public and speak on the issues of the day. He was not eligible to become a member of the Alliance, but his speech-making proclivities resulted in his being made a "political lecturer" of that order, in which capacity he lectured through most of the country, becoming widely acquainted and imbibing thoroughly the doctrines of the Alliance.

By 1890 the fame of Davis had spread through the State. His semi-religious fervor, which had won for him the pseudonym "Methodist Jim," forced him to explain frequently that he was not and had never been a minister of the gospel. It came to be accepted as a matter of course that Methodist Jim Davis would appear on all worth while programs which involved the discussion of questions of public interest, and as time passed it was generally understood that he would be found in the ranks of the minority, whatever the

---

[5]For a sketch of the life of James H. Davis, see *The Galveston Daily News,* April 20, 1894.

question to be debated. He became, in short, a personage: men came from far and near to hear (and to see) him speak.

With the formation of the Third Party, the dissentient Davis lost no time in professing Populism. In his home state, where he came soon to be regarded as one of the mightiest of Populist leaders, he was nominated more than once for high office by his party. His fame spread abroad, however, and he was much in demand as a speaker in other sections of the country. More than willing always to answer any call made of him, he travelled extensively during the nineties, visiting states as widely separated as North Carolina and Oregon, as Idaho and Louisiana. On one trip into Kentucky the newspapers referred to the "cyclones of applause" which his efforts evoked, and thenceforward the name "Cyclone" was applied to the speaker himself. Newspaper headline references to "The Cyclone from Texas," "The Burning Eloquence of Cyclone Davis," "The Inimitable 'Cyclone' Davis," and the like gave evidence of the effectiveness of the campaign which he waged in other states. If he was somewhat less effective where he was better known, it was in part because he neglected local fields of endeavor for missionary work abroad.

The source of Davis' strength lay in his tremendous power as an orator. Possessed of every natural qualification, including a giant frame (which at the age of almost eighty years is still as straight and strong as that of a man of forty) which never tired, a booming voice which could be heard for blocks with no apparent effort on the part of the speaker, a sense of humor which he communicated to his listeners, a vocabulary which never failed him, a knack of carrying his audiences with him through thick and thin, and a flair for stage play, he was one of the most powerful public speakers of his day.[6] In personal appearance he commanded attention at once: he stood near six feet three inches in height, and his full beard and somber dress gave to him a patriarchal aspect which singled him out in any assemblage. When he mounted the platform

---

[6]Davis was also well known as an author, his numerous letters to the press and his *Political Revelation* playing a considerable part in his party's propaganda campaign. See *infra*, Chap. VII. While his literary efforts reveal a forceful mode of expression and a not unpleasing style, his reputation and his effectiveness as a prophet of Populism nevertheless rested very largely on his ability as an orator.

with his ten ponderous tomes of Jefferson's works and such other stage properties as he wished to employ,[7] one knew from the hush which fell over the meeting that the Cyclone had arrived. And from that time forward, for perhaps as long as four hours, he was complete master of the proceedings. He wove a spell about his audience, painting with the skill of an articulate Raphael word pictures which held them entranced for hour on hour. Men sat speechless in his wake after he had finished, seemingly unaware that the séance had ended and that they must return again to the workaday world of reality. His contemporaries remember Davis as being in his prime the equal of William Jennings Bryan, and whatever the value of that comparison, the fact is indisputable that the Democrats were never able to match forces with him by strength alone; he was barred from the political arena, for there was none to do battle with him in debate.[8]

Notwithstanding Cyclone Davis' matchless power over the multitudes, he was not invulnerable, for his very strength made him disregardful of the small things the proper evaluation of which is called political acumen. He was guilty on occasion of the grossest violation of simple rules whose observance in the minds of most politicians would have been dictated by the principles of plain common sense.[9] He was not, therefore, an astute political strategist. A second shortcoming arose from the reputation which he acquired as a soldier of fortune in the game of politics. Even during the days of the Third Party, it was charged frequently that he was not wholly consistent in his public utterances. Further, he confessed toward the end of the decade that his expenses were paid

---

[7]Sometimes he made use of a British flag which he waved with telling effect in the face of his audience.

[8]A leading daily made the following comment: "Cyclone Davis, who spoke here last week, is the most adroit Populist speaker in Texas. He carries the people along, he stimulates their prejudices and excites their hopes, he praises their faults and kicks their enemies, and he exalts their self-esteem and avoids everything that would give offense." *The Galveston Daily News*, Oct. 31, 1893. See also the issue of the same paper of July 31, 1892.

For further press evaluations of his efforts, see the *Dallas Morning News*, June 23, July 3, 1892, and June 22, 1894; *The Comanche Vanguard*, Aug. 2, 1913; etc., etc.

[9]For evidence of this lack of political perspicacity, see the *Dallas Morning News*, the issues of Jan. 24 *et seq.*, 1895.

on one of his speaking tours through Texas by the fusion Populists of Nebraska.[10] Some of his own colleagues thus became convinced that he was a time-server and that he accepted pay for his oratorical efforts. Since 1900 he has spoken in behalf of numerous causes: he campaigned for Prohibition; he became enamored of the Ku Klux Klan and defended that organization staunchly; he has assisted various candidates by taking the stump in their behalf; and he has sought election to office in his own right more than once.[11] Those who survive among his old Populist colleagues view his ceaseless activities with mingled emotions, but among those who have no cause to be generous in their attitude it is generally agreed that he is an opportunist in politics, ever restless and ever eager for battle.

Similar to Cyclone Davis, yet sufficiently different in both character and methods to warrant separate consideration, was that restless soul who never found his place in life, Harrison Sterling Price (Stump) Ashby.[12] Born in Missouri in 1848, Ashby, like most of his colleagues in the People's Party, was forced to forego an early formal training in favor of service in the armies of the Confederacy, and like many he came out of the War with no definite plans for the future. He drifted first into amateur acting, creating a sensation as Joe Morgan in "Ten Nights in a Barroom." His parents would not hear to his becoming a professional actor, however, and he came to Texas where he tried successively the life of a cowboy, schoolteaching, and the ministry. His success in the last-named field was phenomenal, but his alleged use of liquor kept him in the bad graces of his superiors who shifted him about continually in the hope that eventually he would regain his equilibrium. His pastorates became less and less desirable until in the late eighties he found himself located in a small town where there were five preachers to

---

[10]*The Southern Mercury*, Jan. 18, 1900.

[11]His latest venture in politics was his campaign, waged in the July and the August primaries of 1932, for the Democratic nomination for a place as Congressman-at-Large from Texas. He was defeated by Joseph Weldon Bailey, Jr., son of one of the bitterest foes of Populism in the ranks of the Democracy.

[12]There are more stories concerning the life and experiences of Stump Ashby than of any other member of the People's Party. By some he is credited with having been a circus clown in his youth, though apparently that story grew out of his activities as an amateur actor. What appears to be as nearly a correct brief sketch of his life as any may be found in the *Dallas Morning News* for Sept. 16, 1894.

do the work that could have been done by one. He concluded then, as he confided to his friend Cyclone Davis, that God's business there was on the verge of bankruptcy by reason of fratricidal competition, and he resigned his charge and took up farming.[13] As a farmer he came into contact with the Alliance, where his native ability and his experience in public address soon won him an appointment as a lecturer of the order. From that position, concluding that heroic measures would be necessary to right the evils which existed, he drifted naturally into the People's Party.

Throughout the course of his varied career it is not recorded that Stump Ashby once found himself without a multitude of friends. His was a naturally happy disposition; endowed with a rich fund of humor, he knew no moments of fear and anxiety, or knowing them, he concealed them perfectly from his acquaintances. There were no dull intervals in Ashby's presence, private or public, for that worthy fitted himself without effort into any company and took a leading part in any discussion, whatever the subject. Nor did his forwardness descend to arrogance, for of all persons Ashby was most kind and least affected. There were those who questioned his sincerity, particularly in his espousal of Reform, but apparently without basis except for some vague, undefined doubt of his motives. There was none, however, who denied his courage—that had been tested as minister, as Alliance man, and as Populist—or the vigor with which he defended his beliefs. Ashby was not a man who commanded universal respect, but there were many thousands throughout the State who liked him tremendously and who counted among their friends plain Stump Ashby, the most natural of the Populist leaders.

From the time of his adherence to Populism, Ashby was recognized as one of the more able of the People's Party leaders. His colleagues had large faith in his executive ability, but it was on the platform that he performed the greatest service for the Populist cause. As a public speaker he was second only to Cyclone Davis, and indeed if his type of address be borne in mind, it is not too

---

[13]It was charged that Ashby was forced to resign from the ministry, but he always denied that charge with vehemence. He maintained that he resigned of his own free will and accord and insisted that he was eligible to return to that profession if he should so desire.

much to say that he was unsurpassed. Davis controlled his audience through sheer power of oratory; Ashby won his listeners by relating innumerable stories and anecdotes, some of which were not up to the drawing room standard, and by employing biting sarcasm, stinging ridicule, and deadly invective. Thus it was that while Davis was the more impressive of the two in straight public address, in joint debate Ashby was without peer. If it happened that he won the draw and took the floor first, his opponent was beaten from the start, for the audience normally had stampeded before the close of his opening address. He employed all of the histrionic talent which had made of him a successful actor as a young man; by his remarkable control over his facial expressions he ran the gamut of human emotions from darkest gloom to ecstasy. He practiced also the arts of the ministry. Frequently he left the platform and proceeded down an aisle among his listeners, his rich voice the while rising and falling, now softly and tensely, now vigorously and without restraint. Throughout the audience he went, up one aisle and down another, until, near the end of the time allotted him, he returned to the platform and in a final peroration turned the meeting over for the time being to his opponent. That unfortunate, however, as a usual thing could read the signs without difficulty. His efforts were only half-hearted, for Stump Ashby had stolen the show and the main act was over. Indeed, it happened not infrequently that an audience refused to hear the other side of the question; Stump had spoken, and his auditors were satisfied with his efforts.

On the platform, then, Stump Ashby was a tower of strength to the cause of Populism. His one great fault was his alleged intemperate use of intoxicating liquors, though unfortunately that was a grave one. Among his Prohibitionist colleagues were those who regarded it as fatal, and even among those of a more liberal attitude it was conceded that on occasion Stump and his wine brought embarrassment on the party. To illustrate, surviving members of the Texas delegation to the national Populist convention of 1896 tell a story of how several of the famous "Texas 103," Ashby among them, appeared on the floor under the influence of liquor. Tales of such incidents, whether or not they were correctly reported, gained credence; and to the extent to which Ashby reputedly was responsible for them he was a millstone about the neck of his party.

Midway between the orators who appear above and the organizer who follows was the negro leader J. B. Rayner, a centaur-like individual who served the Third Party in the dual capacity of speaker and organizer. Born into slavery in North Carolina in 1850 of a white father who was prominently identified with the public life of that State and a negro mother who was a direct descendant of the kin of a President, he was given the advantage of a college education in the years following the War. After ten years in his native state as teacher in its rural schools, constable, magistrate, and deputy sheriff, he came to Texas, settling in Robertson County.[14] From 1881 forward he followed various pursuits: he taught school for a few years, then preached for a while; he played an important role in politics among his people, though never offering for public office himself; and he worked for several years with various societies for the advancement of his race. He was, in short, what a friend of his called "a public man." He lost no opportunity to appear before his people to urge them on to greater efforts in a campaign for their enlightenment or to present their cause and defend it before those whites who were in positions to be of assistance to him and his race.

When Rayner arrived in Texas in 1881, he was, almost of necessity, a Republican. In the early nineties, however, he became convinced that his people had little to hope for from the party which by tradition was their friend and benefactor, and he seized the opportunity offered by the rise of Populism to renounce Republicanism and to affiliate with the new party of the whole people. During the several campaigns waged by that party, he worked among his people to such effect that he won the repeated recognition of its leaders.

Rayner's chief value to the Third Party lay in his power as an orator, though he was recognized also as an organizer of large ability. He thus played a dual role as a propagator of Populism: during the interval between campaigns, he worked incessantly, speaking to the members of his race assembled at picnics, barbecues, encampments, and ordinary mass meetings, organizing colored Populist clubs himself, and directing the work of organization by

---

[14]*The Galveston Daily News* for Aug. 9, 1896, carried a brief biography of J. B. Rayner.

means of a corps of colored assistants who worked in conjunction with him. When the campaign came on, he took the stump in behalf of the Populist ticket. Up and down the State he roamed, to the uttermost limits of the negro empire, preaching always the doctrine of Populism, with special reference to the hope which it held for the colored man. His favorite setting was a rural one, and his favorite audience was colored, though he took considerable pride in the interest which his appearance always engendered among the white people who delighted to hear his rousing periods in behalf of Populism. Thus it was that he frequently addressed mixed audiences, and on more occasions than one he spoke to white men only, from the same platform as white speakers.

He was, if the truth be told, as able a speaker as one would find ordinarily. A portly man, of good physique, his features revealed his negro blood only to those familiar with his origin. In speech his articulation was clear, his voice good, his vocabulary wide and varied, and his choice of words apt and effective. Further, he was blessed with a sense of humor by which he was able to win the sympathy of his audiences and a sense of proportion which stamped him as southern bred and made him acceptable to the old rebels with whom he worked. He was, in fine, fitted by nature and by training for the role he assumed to play, and by ability for that of a leader among his people. Barring Cyclone Davis and Stump Ashby, he was as effective a speaker on his merits as any man in the party. There is no doubt of the significance of Rayner's conversion to Populism; for no man was better able to present a cause to the negroes of the State than he, nor did any work with greater enthusiasm for the success of the Third Party.[15]

If the orators of Populism assumed a position of primary importance in propagating the principles of the People's Party, they were followed at no great distance by the Populist organizers whose work entitled them to generous credit for the showing of the Reform

---

[15]The value of the services performed by Rayner was universally recognized among the strategists of the People's Party. Their attitude was reflected in a statement made by Stump Ashby, while he was State Chairman of the party, to the effect that he had arranged with Rayner to spend several months in the field among his people in the interest of the Populist Party. The statement concluded with the words, "The work I want Rayner to do no white man can do." *The Southern Mercury*, June 13, 1895.

candidates. And among the organizers of the party, none performed greater services than the ubiquitous Harry Tracy. Tracy's early history resembled that of countless of his Populist contemporaries: born about 1840, he was drawn into the armies of the Confederacy, from which he emerged at the end of the conflict to take up farming in Texas. About 1885, when he had managed by his industry to place himself in easy circumstances, he gave up his farm life, placed his property in the care of his brother Nat, and entered the field as an Alliance lecturer. From that time until the birth of the People's Party he served that order faithfully. He professed allegiance to the tenets of the Democratic Party; and when that party nominated Hogg for its gubernatorial candidate in 1890, he took the stump in his behalf, making over a hundred speeches throughout the State. With the break between Hogg and the Alliance, Tracy became a "Jeffersonian Democrat," confessing freely his disappointment with the Democratic Party but maintaining his fealty to true Democratic principles. He was among those to whom the Finley manifesto proved especially galling; he considered, indeed, that he had been read out of the party of his choice, and he reconciled himself to the organization of a new party which, as he conceived it, would stand for the true principles of Democracy.[16] Until 1891, he was as loyal an Alliance man as Evan Jones; after that date, he was as staunch a People's Party advocate as any man in the State.

Tracy's distinguishing attributes were his complete honesty and openness and his unfailing energy. His fairness was admitted by all, and he was open to conviction on any question until he had arrived at a conclusion. Thereafter, his mind was firmly fixed; he espoused the cause dictated by his opinion with a zeal which made of him a most respected partisan. His was the unswerving faith of a prophet and the courage of a lion; he knew nothing of the art of hedging and little enough of compromise. His reputation spread, then, as a poor politician, though the high quality of his particular abilities was universally recognized. He referred to himself once as a "hunch-backed little clodhopper," but the inaccuracy of the characterization, which implies something of humility and artlessness, was apparent to all who knew him. There were few who

---

[16]*Supra*, Chap. II.

counted themselves friends of Harry Tracy, but there were many who entertained for him a most wholesome respect.

Tracy was essentially an executive, by nature and by training. This is not to say that his value to his party as a propagandist was negligible, for he played a not unimportant part as a preacher of Populism. Thus he contributed frequent articles to the press and wrote a supplement to Cyclone Davis' book which revealed his ability as an author, both in mode of expression and in reasoning power.[17] And on the platform he was an effective if not a polished speaker. His *forte*, however, was the work of organization. During the years 1891 and (more especially) 1892 he went out into the unmarked spaces of the State preaching Populism; up hill and down dale he travelled, into the furtherest fastnesses unreached by the railroads, and everywhere he left behind him a trail of newly-organized Populist clubs. It is not too much to say that the surprising showing made by the Reform candidates in the elections of 1892 was due as much to his work with these clubs as to any other factor.

As in the case of other Populist leaders, the spokesmen of the Democrats were wont to impute to Tracy a selfish purpose in espousing the cause of reform. The evidence which may be summoned in his defense is overpowering, however, and leaves little of the case built against him. In the first place, he refused more than once to permit his name to be mentioned for public office. In the second place, far from profiting either by reputation or financially from his allegiance to the Third Party, he actually sold his properties piece by piece to obtain funds for the pursuit of Alliance and, later, Populist projects.[18] His loyalty to the cause in truth eventually reduced him to the verge of ruin.[19] Tracy then was not accused justly of being a self-seeker, for he followed the People's Party far past the point where his selfish interests demanded that he withdraw and attend to his private business.[20]

---

[17]*Ibid.*

[18]The chief enterprise in which Tracy became interested was the publication of *The Southern Mercury* and the *Texas Advance*. See *infra*, Chap. VIII.

[19]See an open letter written in his defense by his brother, Nat (who remained a staunch Democrat), in *Texas Advance*, Aug. 4, 1894.

[20]Second only to Tracy in his reputation as a Populist organizer and second to none in enthusiasm and energy was one of the younger leaders of the party,

Nugent, Kearby, Davis, Ashby, Rayner, Tracy—the list is not complete, for many of the most renowned of the Populist leaders are passed over by design, but among these names will be found those of the men who contributed most, according to their various talents, to the cause of the People's Party in Texas. Nugent was the good man of Populism and Kearby the great man, and the two symbolized the Populist myths of honor, rightness, and justice to all mankind. Davis, Ashby, and Rayner were the orators of Reform; they performed the important service, whatever their incidental activities, of placing Populism before the people, and none will deny that they did their work well. Tracy was the best of the Populist organizers, though he was ably assisted, in the negro sections of the State, by Rayner. Thus were the interests of the Third Party subserved on three fronts by the leaders whose contributions we have examined.

It remains now to weigh the capacities of these men as leaders, not as judged by their services to the party, but as measured by certain standards which may be set up. Professor Charles E. Merriam has listed the common attributes of the political leader;[21] let us attempt in summary to measure these six Populist leaders in accordance with the standards which his list suggests. The first test is, with what degree of sensitiveness to the "strength and direction of social and industrial tendencies" did these leaders react to the situation in Texas from which evolved the People's Party? An examination of the life history of each reveals that none was sluggish in interpreting the signs of the times from 1885 to 1890. Every man among them was connected either as member or as sympathizer with the Farmers' Alliance, while several, as Ashby and Tracy, were high in the councils of that order; and most of them also bore reputations as political dissenters of some years' standing. These men therefore not only were not slow to sense the movement of economic and social unrest which boiled over as the Populist movement: they played large roles, with only one or two exceptions, in the crystallization of that unrest.

Thomas Gaines. Gaines' ability brought him to the front as a leader in the youth of Populism, and his untimely death in 1894 was a serious blow to the Third Party. See *The Comanche Vanguard*, Aug. 2, 30, 1913. See also *infra*, Chap. VIII.

[21]See his *Four American Party Leaders* (New York, 1926), Introduction.

This brings us to the second criterion: With what acuteness of perception did the leaders in question gauge the "possible courses of community conduct" and take action thereon? Judged by this measure, the directors of Populism qualify again as political leaders of more than ordinary ability. They interpreted the situation as one demanding independent political action; and while they appeared loath to proceed to the organization of a new party with undue haste, yet they nursed the discontented along until it became certain that such a party would receive widespread support. They appear therefore to have been neither too forward nor too slow in taking advantage of the third party agitation but to have seized upon and capitalized it at precisely the right time. Apparently they did not estimate accurately the potential strength of the incipient movement, for it appears that they not only hoped but may have expected to carry the State on at least one occasion. That their calculations went awry in this respect probably was due more to the appropriation of their program by the Democrats than to any other single event.

A third measure of leadership is found in the leaders' "facility in group combination and compromise." First, how well did the Populist leaders coöperate together in pursuit of the common goals of Populism? The answer involves manifold problems of party relationships, but briefly it may be said that the relations between the leaders were not always of a sort to foster mutual trust and confidence. For example, the motives and the tactics of Cyclone Davis were questioned by more than one of his colleagues, and Tracy and Ashby did not have the kindliest of feelings toward each other. And after 1896, the fusion quarrel divided the party, and with it the leaders, into two irreconcilable factions. A second question is this: To what extent were the leaders of the Third Party able to reconcile the divergent groups upon whose support they must depend for success in the State? In the realm of the political in particular were the leaders able to reconcile various conflicting elements, as Democrats, Republicans, Socialists, Prohibitionists, and Greenbackers, under the standard of Populism. Economically and socially, however, the Third Party rested on the poor farmer, to the almost total exclusion of other classes, and racially it depended upon the support of the Anglo-Saxon natives, plus a considerable vote from the Negroes. Thus vital elements were barred from the party, and it became in the final analysis a "single-shot" movement, which proved fatal to the ambitions of its leaders. It may be urged in defense of its managers that they were bound by the limitations of the Populist program, but this is merely to say that they stated the program of their party in such uncompromising terms as to make it impossible for them to engage in the business of give-and-take with a variety of factions. In their enthusiasm for the regulation of alien land ownership they overstated their position and stamped their party as an anti-alien and so naturally as a Knownothing party, and in their anxiety to placate the small farmer beyond peradventure they alienated other important classes. It is true that on certain questions, as Prohibition, they attempted to hedge, but with little success. The conclusion seems inescapable, then, that the leaders of the People's Party were undistinguished as diplomats and that they failed miserably in the consummation of the final combination and compromise which might have brought success to their party.[22]

In the matter of "personal contacts with widely varying types of men" the leaders of the Third Party in Texas enjoyed somewhat more success. Most of them were quite approachable and counted many friends throughout the State, though some, as Nugent and to a less degree Kearby, were known largely only by reputation. Davis, Ashby, and Tracy had multitudinous connections far and wide, and Rayner was as well known as any among his people. After all, however, it must be granted that the personal contacts of the leaders in question were largely one-sided: they were acquainted widely among the farming and laboring classes, but outside the ranks of the workingman they were not well known personally. And this appears to have constituted another weak link in the Populist armor.

With the facility believed to be necessary for "dramatic expression of the sentiment or interest of large groups of voters," the People's Party leaders were well supplied. They were possessed of simple formulae for the cure of recognized ills, and they were able, while appealing to a particular economic and social group, to phrase their remarks in terms which were summarized in a demand for justice for the workingman whose interests thereupon

---

[22]Chapters II, III, and IV, *supra,* deal in detail with the various aspects of the problem raised in this paragraph.

were identified with those of all mankind. Further, they counted among their number men of various talents who were able to present the Populist program to the greatest possible advantage. The Third Party did not want for dramatic championship, for it boasted leaders whose greatest fault was that they were too enthusiastically Populist and therefore too little considerate of the desires and needs of minor groups of voters.

Nor did the party want for men of courage to guide its destinies. It required considerable of physical courage to be a confirmed Populist in some portions of the State, while it was downright dangerous for a Reform speaker to appear there. Rayner, for example, took his life in his hands when he went into certain counties of East Texas, and even the white speakers of the party were molested more than once. But more than mere physical bravery, it required a great deal of moral courage to cast loose from the dominant party and launch out as a leader of a new and untried party, for such a course was regarded as being, if not traitorous, at least suicidal in so far as hope for achievement or political preferment was concerned. The latter would not have been conceded entirely by the Populist leaders, who hoped to make their influence felt directly through the agency of the new party. And it may be their hopes would not have been denied fulfilment if they had profited from the "dash of luck" which might reasonably have been expected. Fortune smiled on them a few times in the incipiency of their party, as for example when the Democratic State Chairman issued his famous manifesto;[23] but thereafter she turned from them, and they were denied the break which might have meant for them the difference between failure and success.

Finally, in our weighing of the leaders of Populism in Texas, it is worth while to ask the question separately, what were their abilities as political inventors? What resourcefulness did they reveal in introducing new formulae or in adapting the old to their ends? The question may be examined from two points of view. First, as to technique, it may be said that the Populists were responsible for little that was novel in the matters of organization and campaign tactics. It is true that they based the organization of their party on the local club, and that the political club was almost

---

[23]*Supra*, Chap. II.

unknown until the Third Party organizers popularized it in the early nineties. That, however, was because the Democrats had not seen the need for such a unit and not because they were unacquainted with it. It is true further that the Populist leaders adapted the campmeeting to the needs of their party and so introduced a distinctly religious tone into their propaganda efforts and that this adaptation constituted a real innovation in campaign methods in this State.[24] Moreover it appears that the Reformers of Texas had as good claim as any to the honor of having originated the campmeeting as a party weapon. With this single important exception, however, the campaigns of the nineties resembled those of any other day in propaganda and campaign technique. Second, as to program, it may be said again that the Populists were able to find little that was new. Their platform rested on those of earlier dissident groups, with little of a novel nature added by their spokesmen. Nor were the Reform leaders able to add new principles that were sufficiently attractive to hold their party together even when it was a matter of life or death to them. A few feeble efforts were made to rejuvenate the party's program after 1896, but nothing came of them.[25] It is clear, therefore, that the leaders of the People's Party in Texas were not men of brilliantly resourceful natures in finding new methods and new issues; they were not what one would call political inventors.

The leaders studied, then, seem to have been very able as measured by four of the seven standards set up on the basis of the suggested common attributes of the political leader. They were sensitive to the social and economic unrest evident in the State in the late eighties, and they perceived with sufficient clarity what course was demanded and took action thereon. The program upon which they agreed was ably launched and dramatically defended, and in the campaigns which followed there were many situations to test their courage, which was found adequate to all needs. In three important particulars, however, they failed to measure up to a high standard: they emphasized phases of their program which alienated certain important groups, thus encountering relative failure in the important field of group combination and compromise; thanks to

---

[24]See *infra*, Chap. VII.
[25]See *supra*, Chap. II, and *infra*, Chap. X.

the background of most of them they failed to develop personal contacts among various types and professions of men, though as a whole they counted hosts of friends among the farming classes; and they failed in the field of political invention. In these respects, therefore, the leaders of the People's Party proved incapable of carrying satisfactorily the burdens placed upon them as the confessed leaders of their party.

II

One feels that the People's party, notwithstanding the shortcomings of its state leaders, would have had an even chance of success if the campaigns could have been limited to tournaments between those leaders and their Democratic adversaries. They were not so limited, however, for if there was one aspect of the campaign which saw the cause of Populism effectively presented, there was another, the local phase, which frequently if not usually proved to be the determining factor. The truth of the matter was, then as now, that although a party were ever so well organized and ever so ably led throughout the State as a whole, it must carry its fight home to the voter if it desired to succeed, and more especially it must have able representatives in the voting precincts on election day to bring out the vote. The People's Party left little undone in so far as its state campaign was concerned, if the limited financial resources at its command be taken into account. Its local campaigns, however, with whose success was bound up inextricably that of the state ticket, were more frequently than not poorly managed, with resultant effects disastrous to the hopes of the party for success in the State.

The reasons for the disparity between state and local campaigns were manifold, and not least among them was the matter of mediocre local leadership, as contrasted with the comparatively able leadership enjoyed by the party in state affairs. Local leaders of the People's Party usually were merely farmers who had concluded to try their hands at politics; they were without experience in the ways of the game so new to them, and they managed their campaigns clumsily and ineffectively. On the Democratic side of the ledger, it may be noted that the old politicians, the office-holders and the local managers, remained almost solidly Democratic, to give the dominant party every advantage in the matters of experience and expertness in political management. The local Populist managers thus found themselves, inexperienced and unskilled as they were, in combat with adversaries whose business for a quarter of a century had been to study and to practice the rules of the game of politics. The results of the unequal contests might have been foretold in most instances without the necessity of casting and counting ballots.

The local leaders of the People's Party in the counties where that party was comparatively successful may be classified into three groups for the purposes of the present analysis. In the first place, there was the apostle of direct action who employed force to gain his ends. Such leaders thrived only where there was a large controllable vote, and inasmuch as that vote was confined largely to the negro and the Mexican counties, they were limited almost entirely to East and South Texas. Furthermore, bossism on the part of the People's Party failed to develop in the Mexican sections of the State, so that the Populist boss was found exclusively in the negro districts. There an occasional manager arose who was able by forcible control of the negro vote to make himself a power in local politics.[26] Such leaders would be called, in these latter days, pragmatists, but during the days of Populism they were known (by the Democrats) as "nigger men." Their tactics were similar, and they were uniformly effective. They involved, in their essentials, herd voting of the negroes who had been prepared for the proper exercise of their sovereign right to vote by a liberal display of firearms— and mayhap a generous distribution of firewater. The ballots voted under the direction of these leaders were straight Populist ballots usually, bearing the names of the People's Party candidates for every office from top to bottom, and here is the significance of the advocates of violence for the People's Party. They wanted primarily to be elected to offices in their several counties, but in order to gain the end desired they espoused the cause of Populism and had their followers vote the Populist ticket. In some part, then,

---

[26]More than one Populist sheriff enjoyed the reputation of having won office through manipulation of the colored vote.

the People's Party became a boss-controlled negro party, notwithstanding the protestations of its leaders to the contrary. The importance of the bosses in the negro counties may be seen from a study of the election returns in the light of local events. Grimes County first revealed a strong Populist vote in 1894, when Garrett Scott began to interest himself in the People's Party; and that party died a violent death there when in 1900 the faithful among the Democrats, in a pitched battle growing out of Scott's activities among the negroes, killed his brother and seriously wounded Scott, forcing him to leave the county. Similarly in San Augustine County the party came to an abrupt end in a feud which cost the lives of half a dozen men, among them the Populist sheriff George Wall. In Nacogdoches the Third Party leader A. J. Spradley escaped a violent death, and his party died of anaemia some years after it had expired of apoplexy in Grimes and San Augustine. In the case of these three counties, then, the relationship between local leadership and the success of the People's Party may be seen clearly.

In the second place, among the local leaders of Populism, there was the popular haranguer who appealed to the voter by public address for his support for Populism. This type of leader frequently was little more than a demagogue, though occasionally there was found one who relied upon reason and argument for his strength. Such leaders were Judge H. C. Maund, of Sabine County, and W. H. (Wick) Blanton, of Wilson. Judge Maund, who had had considerable experience as a Democratic chieftain, was an able speaker of the rough-and-ready type, with little of polish but much of force in his remarks, and he was also an organizer of some ability. Mr. Blanton, an excellent speaker for all his youth, carried his cause directly to the voter by means of an intensive, vigorous, and thorough speaking and hand-shaking campaign. He provided the life spark for the People's Party in his county, as did Judge Maund in Sabine, and without these men that party probably would have experienced little or no success in those districts.

In the third place were such local leaders as C. K. Walter, of Gonzales County, and N. J. Shands, of Erath, who, while having some reputations as public speakers, were known chiefly as still-hunters. Walter is credited by old Democratic leaders with having placed the People's Party in the position of strength which it occupied in Gonzales. He had been a farmer until almost middle life then had taken up the study and shortly thereafter the practice of law. Desirous of forging to the front, and doubtless convinced also of the justice of the Populist cause, he bestirred himself in the organization of People's Party clubs in the very inception of the Reform movement, and to such effect did he work that he had thrown over the county a veritable network of local units before the Democrats were much more than aware of the existence of the Third Party. Further, once its organization was effected, Walter's ability as an organizer and his proclivities for hand-shaking enabled him to keep the party's forces intact for several elections. Similarly, in Erath County, N. J. Shands revealed large abilities as an organizer and a man-to-man campaigner; and while he found conditions there more favorable than those which confronted Walter in Gonzales County, the work done by him is not to be minimized. He kept the members of the party in line, as did his contemporary in Gonzales, past the point where, in the absence of such leadership, they would have remained loyal to Populist principles.

The importance of local leadership may be further tested by brief reference to those counties wherein the People's Party failed to poll a large or a winning vote. In the "sugar bowl" counties of Brazoria, Fort Bend, Matagorda, and Wharton, and indeed in nearly all counties where the negroes constituted 50 per cent or more of the total population, little effort was made to advance the interests of the party, and there were few Populist leaders worthy of the name. In the Mexican counties of the State, little or no effort was made to propagate the Populist faith; local leadership was of no consequence; and the party failed to poll a strong vote. Among the German counties, little was heard of the People's Party as a usual thing, though it is significant that in the one German county (Medina) where several substantial German citizens became converted to Populism that party achieved a considerable degree of success. On the other hand, in these same counties local Democratic leadership usually was very strong. In Robertson County, for example, where there were more negroes than whites, the People's Party had organized well under the leadership of the negro leader, J. B. Rayner, only to have Democratic bosses come among the negroes on election day while they were in the very act of voting and disperse two bands of several hundred each with volleys fired into the air from their revolvers. The People's Party in that county lacked the services of a Garrett Scott to answer fire with fire, and there was nothing for the negro Populists to do but withdraw under the threat of armed intervention by the local Democratic leaders.

The presence of able local leaders, therefore, apparently was prerequisite to any considerable measure of success for the Third Party. The oratorical offerings of the state leaders of the party were of first rate interest and significance, of course; but while they doubtless made many converts to the cause of Reform, they did not bring out the vote on election day. That remained for the local leader; and unless he performed well the task delegated to him, the Third Party developed little local strength.

Into the People's Party as state leaders came men of every type, men of a wide variety of characters, men seeking from the party a variety of benefits, and contributing to its welfare a variety of advantages. Superficially, they seemed to give to it an able and well-rounded corps of leaders, for what one lacked another seemed to supply: where one was too liberal in his views, another balanced the scales with his conservatism; where one imbibed too freely, another was a staunch Dry; where one was an idealist, another was a practical-minded politician; and where one was possessed of talents along a particular line, another came forward with abilities of a wholly different nature. Fundamentally, however, the Populist leaders were too narrow in their interests, their affiliations, and their appeals to give their party a sufficiently broad basis to guarantee its success. As advocates and defenders, therefore, they fulfilled every need, but as diplomats and inventors they left much to be desired; and it was only by virtue of their vigor and energy afield that the cause of Populism was given serious consideration by the voters despite the poor strategy which accompanied its presentation.

Similarly, men came into the party at the level of the county with a variety of purposes and a diversity of talents. The local party organization offered greater opportunities than did that of the State, for it required considerable ability to come to the front among the state leaders of the party, whereas in a county not strongly Populist a person of mediocre talents might take command and assume a position of some importance. The truth is, the local Reform leaders ordinarily were not men of outstanding ability, even as compared with the local Democratic leaders. In those instances where the party was able to convert to the cause of Populism able and astute local men, it managed to poll a good vote, a vote whose strength was in direct ratio to the ability and the vigor of the leaders in question. And here appears a fatal weakness of the People's Party. Its state leaders waged an heroic battle and sent the ticket out to the counties with considerable strength behind it, but the local managers proved inadequate to the occasion. They were not strategically distributed, nor were they sufficiently numerous or strong to perform the yeoman service in the polling precincts demanded by all political parties. Hence the party failed, in part for want of local organizers who could marshal its forces and bring out the vote.

CHAPTER VI

ORGANIZATION

HAND IN HAND with leadership as an element affecting vitally the
success of a political party is the factor of organization, which
is of particular consequence to the young party seeking to become
a permanent force in the politics of the state or of the nation. A
brief period of success may be achieved by strength of leadership
alone or by the espousal of a significant issue, but the party which
wishes to enjoy more than an ephemeral existence must marshal
its members in an organization which will keep constantly before
them the principles and the ideals on the basis of which their support was enlisted. As the party grows older it tends to ripen into
an institution, and traditions and dogmas may be made to serve
in part the purpose of the organization which formerly was its
chief source of strength. Even so, however, the utility of organization is recognized by the party leaders who turn, when crises confront them, to the methods which served them so well in the youth
of their party.

In Texas in 1890 the party machine characteristic of the recurrent
conflict almost may be said to have been non-existent. The old
parties had learned to play the game of politics under the rules
of the one-party state, which minimize the need for party organization. The young and vigorous People's Party was no respecter of
traditional forms of procedure, however, and it set about at once
to establish an organization which would bring success to its cause.
It sent speakers and organizers into the field to carry the message
of Populism to remote places, with the result that in an almost
unbelievably short time it had created a machine which made of it
a foe worthy of the respect of any adversary.

The organization of the People's Party in Texas may be examined
with profit from several points of view. First, it is necessary, if one
is to comprehend the tremendous momentum gained by the party in
the brief space of a few months, to understand something of the
Alliance background of the Populist hierarchy of clubs and conventions. Secondly, the working organization of the People's Party
as such—the clubs, conventions, and committees—must be examined

and evaluated with some thoroughness. Thirdly, it will be of advantage to investigate the workings of certain ancillary bodies which had a very definite value as focal points for the upbuilding of the Populist tradition. Finally, the leaders of the People's Party did not fail to recognize the value of the military appeal, and they provided the party with a militia which must be investigated by one who would comprehend that organization in all its phases.

I

The organization of the Alliance was based upon a unit cell called simply the Farmers' Alliance, or familiarly, the suballiance. A suballiance might be organized with not fewer than five members, male or female, who must be white and over sixteen years of age.[1] Each Alliance was given a charter by the state organization upon its establishment; and it was designated for official purposes by a number given it in the order of the issuance of its charter, though it was allowed to assume whatever name it chose. Thus were found such local Alliances as Black Jack Alliance No.—, Hickory Grove Alliance No.—, etc. To such effect did the officers of the State Alliance carry forward the work of organization that by 1891 the order boasted a total membership of more than 200,000 distributed among some 4,000 suballiances.[2]

Immediately above the local was the county Alliance, which, composed of delegates from the suballiances, met quarterly, accepting invitations in turn from the various local Alliances. Above the county Alliance was the congressional district Alliance, which included delegates from each county body and which met semiannually.[3] At the top of the Alliance hierarchy was the State

[1]*Constitution of the Farmers' State Alliance of Texas* (Dallas, 1890). Art. V, Sec. 1. Farmers, farm laborers, country school teachers, country physicians, ministers of the gospel, stock raisers, mechanics, and mill hands were admitted to the order. Merchants, except those in the service of the Alliance, were excluded from membership by specific provision of the Constitution (Art. V, Sec. 2). Ladies were encouraged to become members and were relieved of the payment of fees.

[2]The Dublin Alliance in June, 1891, was Alliance No. 3945. *The Dublin Progress*, June 27, 1891.

[3]The Constitution of the edition of 1890 made no provision for the congressional district Alliance. That such Alliances were in existence and doing business, however, is evidenced by direct references to them in various parts

Alliance, whose annual meeting comprised one delegate from each county Alliance, chosen by and as a representative of that body. In organization all of the several Alliances were similar. Each elected its own officers, among whom the lecturer occupied a position of first importance. The local and the county lecturers, whose sole important function consisted in expounding Alliance principles, filled prominent places on the programs of their respective bodies. The state lecturer was a full time official, and in addition to the business of explaining and defending the ideals of the Alliance, he supervised the work of organization, aided by a number of assistant lecturers and organizers appointed by the State President. Aside from the individual officers, each Alliance named various committees, whose activities emphasized both the importance of the order in the lives of its members and the hierarchical nature of its machinery.[4]

The importance of the Alliance organization may be seen if one can grasp the spirit in which the activities of the order were carried on. Its members were almost wholly farmers, who from the nature of their business enjoyed few opportunities for social intercourse. Hence when the day came, once a month, for the meeting of the local Alliance, the farmer forgot his fields, loaded his whole family into his wagon or surrey, together with a bountifully filled picnic basket, and made his way to the place where his neighbors for miles around would meet to do business in the name of the Alliance and to spend the day pleasantly in making group social calls. The Alliance work, however, was not subordinated to the social aspects of the meeting. The farmer was always present when the session began; moreover, he remained in his seat when, business done, the lecturer took the platform. That individual usually was the most learned man of his neighborhood and the ablest speaker. It was his duty to deliver an address on some question of public importance, and his farmer friends sat patiently while he made known to them the fruits of his intellectual labors. Nor did the

---

of the State. See, for example, *The Southern Mercury*, Oct. 2, Nov. 20, 1890, and *The Gonzales Inquirer*, May 21, 1891.

[4]The organization of the Alliance is summarized largely from the Constitution of the order cited above. That document is explicit in its provisions concerning the subjects here dealt with and concerning others of interest as well.

discussion always end with the delivery of the lecturer's formal address, for a question from the floor frequently precipitated a general debate. Each question in this manner was threshed out to the satisfaction of the members of the local Alliance, who departed for their homes at the end of the day confident that they had learned something of value and looking forward already to the next meeting one month away.

The meeting of the county Alliance was similar to that of the suballiance, and so also in part was that of the (congressional) district Alliance, though as progress was made from the lower to the higher bodies something of the spontaneity and earthiness of the local meeting was sacrificed for a more businesslike and formal procedure. The Alliance lecturers at these levels were able nevertheless to keep alive in the minds of their listeners the thirst for knowledge which they brought with them from their local meetings.

The annual convention of the State Alliance was of importance chiefly for the service which it performed as the clearing house for ideas coming up from the county Alliances, which in turn served in similar capacities for the thousands of suballiances. The process, generally, by which Alliance principles came into being was this: A local Alliance, after discussing a question of public interest, reached certain conclusions which were communicated to the other suballiances of the vicinity through the medium of the county Alliance. That body considered and adopted the conclusions, tempering them somewhat to make them generally acceptable. The county Alliance then sent a delegate to the State Alliance meeting, which was able thereupon to arrive at a conclusion, with regard to a specific question, acceptable to the membership of the order throughout the State. In this way, Alliance men gradually and imperceptibly absorbed first the information necessary and second a common viewpoint, until with regard to any particular matter the spokesmen of the order were able to announce a definite Alliance policy.

Meanwhile, it may be noted parenthetically, the same process had been going on in other states. Further, the national lecturer had been traveling throughout the length and breadth of the Alliance territory, and lecturers from one state had been invited to campaign in others. Thus the principles which evolved in Texas naturally became identical with those of the Georgia Alliance, as those of

Georgia blended with those of Alabama. In this way during the years 1887–1890 there developed a common basis of agreement which led to the enunciation, in the latter year, of the declaration of principles called the "Ocala Demands."[5]

The significance of the Farmers' Alliance organization for the student of the People's Party, therefore, is clearly to be seen. That order included members of both sexes above the age of sixteen years,[6] and it marshalled them into compact groups which taught them loyalty and patriotism to the cause. It thus fostered the *esprit de corps* among its members, so frequently noted by contemporary observers, which made of the local Alliances such excellent nuclei for the establishment of People's Party clubs in the early nineties. It also provided the means whereby local attitudes and dissensions were harmonized and a state and national declaration of principles arrived at. Both services were of the first magnitude, and if their importance be grasped, the student will have gone far toward explaining the wonderful thoroughness with which the People's Party was organized and put on an effective working basis within the course of a few months from the time when the first call for the party was sounded.[7]

II

The formal organization of the People's Party consisted of an hierarchical system which ran from the local unit up through a maze of higher levels to the state convention and the State Executive Committee. The Populist machinery may be divided for purposes of convenience into three categories: the first includes the basic unit of the party organization; the second, the system of deliberative bodies, the primary meetings and the conventions; and

---

[5]Cyclone Davis outlined this process to the author, though it must be plain to anyone familiar with the Alliance that this is substantially what happened.

[6]There was a separate organization for colored people, a "Colored Farmers' Alliance," which achieved some success in Texas, though it is not clear what size it reached numerically.

[7]The Farmers' Alliance, very strong throughout the farming sections of the State in 1890 and '91, began to decline with the assumption of its program by the People's Party, so that by the middle nineties the order retained but a fraction of its former following. It was dead, except in name, by 1900.

the third, the hierarchy of executive agencies, the committees, which operated at the same levels as the second.

The primary unit was the Populist club which originated during the days when the party itself was in process of development. With the formal launching of the People's Party in the late months of 1891, an occasional Reform club began to be organized, though not much was heard so early of Populist clubs as such. Soon, however, one began to hear of Jeffersonian Democrats, and of Jeffersonian clubs which were nothing more than unit cells of dissatisfied Democrats. It was apparent from the beginning that the newly-formed People's Party and the Jeffersonian Democrats must combine if they would succeed; and when they agreed upon a basis of consolidation in the spring of 1892, the Jeffersonian clubs became, naturally enough, Populist clubs. The movement for organization continued at such a pace that by November 1st of that year there were 3,170 Populist clubs operating in 213 counties of the State,[8] and in 83 per cent of all the voting boxes.[9]

The instant and overwhelming success of the campaign for the organization of Populist clubs may be explained in terms of the background provided by the Farmers' Alliance, and in particular the suballiance. The local Alliance was composed of individuals a large majority of whom were in sympathy with the teachings of Populism, who were determined to cast off the shackles of tradition and vote for the nominees of the Third Party. Thus it was that quite frequently the suballiance became, to all intents and purposes, the local Reform club. The organizer came into a locality and established a club which, since the majority of his converts were Alliance men, resembled closely the suballiance of the community. And the bond often was even closer, for now and again the organizer, being also an Alliance lecturer, would lecture behind closed doors to the local Alliance then throw the doors open to the public and organize a Third Party club. In this case it was a matter of whether the doors were closed or open: if closed, the meeting was that of the Alliance, if open, that of the Populist club, and this frequently was the only practical difference between the two.

---

[8]*The Galveston Daily News*, Nov. 2, 1892.

[9]*The San Antonio Daily Express*, Oct. 16, 1892 (in the Library of The University of Texas, Austin, Texas).

Theoretically, a club was organized in every school district where the strength of the Reform movement seemed to justify it, but actually one might be set up wherever enough Populist sympathizers were found to warrant such a step. Hence clubs were established in communities where they offered the chief means of diversion, and their members came to depend upon them not only for information on public questions, but also for the recreation denied them in their workaday existence. The club was a permanent body, meeting regularly at periodic intervals. Attendance might drop during the off year, and more especially during the winter months, but it continued to meet, and with the coming of spring its members came out in larger numbers once more, to belie the charge that they had lost their faith in the party.

The activities of the Populist club were many and varied, but virtually all hinged on the major functions of disseminating information and fostering incidentally the development of a Populist *esprit de corps*. As elections drew nigh, the procedure took on a tone of formality: speakers were imported from the outside to discuss the issues, and the club became the sponsor for Populist rallies in its locality. Ordinarily, however, the keynote of its activities was informality. Once a week, or less often if circumstances did not favor such frequent meetings, the members came together in the evening and in an atmosphere of good fellowship and perfect unrestraint discussed subjects of interest among themselves. Mayhap a program had been planned, and some local luminary discussed a designated issue, the address of the evening being followed by a general discussion of the subject in which all participated. Or perhaps a debate had been arranged. In the absence of a formal program, however, the members were never at a loss for entertainment. If the evening was a brisk one, they drew their chairs up in a circle and fell into a conversation whose subject almost invariably was "hard times" and proposed remedies, chewing their tobacco meditatively and spitting reflectively from time to time on the sizzling hot stove which provided the rallying point. Or of a spring evening they arranged themselves comfortably about the room, slumping down in their seats or throwing a leg over the chair in front, and continued thus informally their castigation of the party which had brought them to such straits.[10]

It was precisely this system of local clubs which formed the bulwark of Populist strength and which enabled the Third Party to poll a larger vote in each election than the Democratic managers had thought possible. There were, of course, other elements than that of organization entering into the strength of Populism, and within the field of organization the local club was well buttressed by the Populist superstructure which rested upon it. No phase of that structure was more important, however, than the unit cell which provided at the same time an element of continuity by connecting the People's Party with the Alliance and a familiar rallying point for the sympathizers of the Reform movement.

The deliberative machinery of the People's Party may be said to have begun with the precinct primary meeting.[11] To the primary were invited all who professed allegiance to the Populist cause, and no test was used to determine the eligibility of those who offered to participate except the knowledge of the presiding officer. The business of the meeting, which usually was cared for very

---

[10]See the *Dallas Morning News*, Feb. 9, March 2, and March 23, 1895, for accounts of meetings of the Dallas Central Populist Club.

[11]The term *precinct* when used in connection with the Texas county may have any of several meanings. First there is the commissioners' precinct, which serves as both an electoral unit (for the election of county commissioners) and a district for the administration of the county's business. Under the Constitution of the State (Article V, Section 18), each county is divided into four such precincts. Second, there is the justice precinct, which is the district in which operate the justice of peace and the constable. Each county, according to the Constitution (*loc. cit.*), shall have not less than four nor more than eight such precincts. The commissioners' court (the Texas equivalent of the county board) sets up these units, and one finds ordinarily that the maximum number have been provided for. Third, there is the election precinct, which serves as the primary district for the administration of elections. Under the law (see *Revised Civil Statutes of the State of Texas*, 1925, especially Articles 2933 and 2934), each county is divided by the commissioners' court into a "convenient" number of voting precincts, and the word *convenient* has been interpreted to permit the setting up of from four to fifty such districts, the number in any particular county depending largely on considerations of size and population. The typical county has perhaps from fifteen to twenty voting precincts.

The precinct in which the primary met was either the justice or the voting precinct, depending on the county.

expeditiously, consisted occasionally of nominating candidates for the offices of the precinct and always of naming delegates to the county convention.

Above the precinct assembly was the county convention, a delegate body composed of representatives from the various precincts to the number of one for every ten votes or major fraction thereof cast for the Populist candidate for Governor in the preceding election. Its business was of a two-fold nature: first, it selected delegates from the county to the higher conventions of the party, and second, it proceeded, as a usual thing, to the naming of nominees for county offices.[12] In procedure, the county convention offered little or nothing out of the ordinary, resembling in its mode of operation the county delegate assembly of the Democratic and Republican parties.

Between the county and the state conventions were three assemblies which may be passed over with brief mention. The first of these, whose domain was the state representative district, was composed of delegates from the counties comprising the district to the number of one for every twenty-five votes or major fraction thereof polled for the Populist candidate for Governor in the preceding election. Its sole function was to nominate a candidate for the lower house of the State Legislature. The second was a similar convention for the state senatorial district, which, made up of one delegate for every 100 Populist votes, performed the duty of naming a candidate for the State Senate.[13] The third was the congressional district convention, comprising one representative for every 300

---

[12]Occasionally nominations were made by a process which made the convention merely an advisory or a ratifying body, as in Gonzales County in 1896 (*The Gonzales Inquirer*, May 7, 1896). Again, local primary elections sometimes were substituted for the convention system for the naming of nominees, as in Nacogdoches County in 1892 (*Dallas Morning News*, Aug. 3, 1892), Erath County in 1894 (*The Dublin Progress*, June 8, 1894), and Coke County in 1896 (*Coke County Rustler*, July 18, 25, 1896, in the office of the *Rustler*, Robert Lee, Texas).

[13]The basis of representation in the county, the legislative, and the senatorial conventions was specified in the calls thereof; and while it varied from time to time, the figures here used were those on which the assemblies were based in 1896. See *The Weekly Newsboy*, May 13, June 3, 1896 (in the office of the *Newsboy*, Jasper, Texas).

Populist votes in the district and fulfilling the obligation of nominating a candidate for Congress and selecting delegates to the national convention.[14]   In the case of each of these assemblies, the representatives were appointed by the county convention which, therefore, became the keystone of the Populist system of deliberative bodies.

At the apex of the pyramid was the state convention which met every even year in the early summer to consider the matters of defining policies, making nominations for state offices, naming the list of candidates for electors (in presidential election years), and planning the pending campaign and providing for the machinery necessary to its prosecution. It was a body composed of delegates chosen by the county conventions, the number, specified in the call of the executive committee, varying from year to year.[15]   In the heyday of Populism representatives to the number of 1,000 or 1,200 attended the convention from every county of political consequence in the State; they came by railway, and, sometimes from a distance of 200 miles or more, by wagon and surrey, and on horseback.[16] If the truth were told, they came frequently for other purposes than that merely of participating in the proceedings of their party's deliberative assembly: they came for the inspiration

---

[14]*La Grange Journal*, June 2, 1892 (in the office of the *Journal*, La Grange, Texas) ; *The Weekly Newsboy*, May 18, 1898.

[15]The first two state conventions of the party met under unusual circumstances, and their composition was fortuitous. The convention of June, 1892, however, met under a call which invited the selection of delegates by counties on the basis of one for every 300 votes or major fraction thereof cast in the last general election, the total vote being considered and each county being allowed at least one representative. The call of the State Chairman was published in almost all newspapers, large and small, throughout the State, in the spring of the year. See, for example, the *Hempstead Weekly News*, May 19, 1892 (in the Library of The University of Texas, Austin, Texas).

[16]*The Weekly News* (Mexia, Texas) for Aug. 4, 1898 (in the Library of The University of Texas, Austin, Texas) carried an account of a trip by wagon from Limestone County to the state convention of the People's Party at Austin. The party of seven persons traveled in two covered wagons, camping at night and taking several days for the trip. The writer commented to the effect that many other persons in attendance on the convention had traveled the same way, and *The Galveston Daily News* (Aug. 14, 1898) added the information that some of these were women, who brought their children along to enjoy the proceedings. See also the *Dallas Morning News*, Aug. 25, 1898.

and the renewal of faith that would derive from those proceedings, and in this quest they were not disappointed. The outstanding orators of the party were always in attendance, and they gave their best efforts to the business of confirming those present in their preference for Populism.

Operating in conjunction with the conventions were the committees of the party which served as its executive agencies. The local club had its executive committee, chosen by its membership and consisting of a chairman, a secretary, and a treasurer, and the precinct assembly appointed a committee of three called the "central committee," which together with the chairmen of the several clubs within the precinct constituted the executive committee for that area. Similarly, the county convention named a central committee of three, which with the chairmen of the various precincts comprised the county executive committee. The legislative, senatorial, and congressional district committees resembled that of the county. Finally, there was the state committee, composed of the chairmen of the several congressional committees, with a central committee of three selected by the state convention of the party. The executive committee in every case arrived at decisions with regard to matters demanding its attention, and the central committee supervised the work undertaken by the larger body and carried out its instructions. A further difference between the two was to be seen in the fact that the larger committee was designed to serve as an executive committee properly so-called, while the smaller was intended to perform the duties of a campaign committee.[17] The state executive committee operated under the direction of a chairman, selected by the state convention, who served in the capacity of state manager for the party; the central committee served under the supervision of a campaign manager selected by the executive committee, or

---

[17]This was the plan of committee organization adopted by the first state convention of the party. See the *Dallas Morning News*, Aug. 18, 1891. It will be observed that the scheme appears rather complicated, and so it proved in practice. Hence changes were introduced from time to time, but the fundamentals of the system were never altered radically. Thus at a particular time one found, at any level of organization, one committee of some size, which was called usually the executive committee, and another and smaller body which came to be called the campaign committee.

under that of the State Chairman himself who on occasion (as in 1896) served *ex officio* as campaign director.

In the system of primaries, conventions, and committees, then, the People's Party had a logical and complete if somewhat complicated scheme of organization from bottom to top. Beginning with the Populist club, authority graduated inward and upward, until eventually the final decisions were made by the state convention on the one hand and the State Executive Committee on the other.[18] The result was a well-coördinated hierarchy of deliberative and executive bodies which won for the Third Party universal recognition as the best organized political party the State had ever known.

It may prove worth while at this point to compare the People's Party briefly with the Farmers' Alliance as regards organization. If the comparison be pursued from bottom to top in both instances, it will be found that at the two extremes the Third Party resembled closely the body from which it sprang. At the levels between the local unit and the state organization, however, there were important divergences. The People's Party had numerous primaries and conventions, meeting biennially, at the intermediate levels; the parent body had but one of consequence, the county Alliance, which met not biennially but quarterly. The major function of the Populist organs was to attend to the business of the party, while the county Alliance served chiefly as a disseminator of propaganda, keeping up a continuous campaign in behalf of the principles of the order. With respect to county organization, therefore, the Alliance enjoyed an advantage over the People's Party which should have served the Populist managers as a lesson in machinery and methods.[19]

---

[18]The committee was responsible to the convention which was the supreme authority for the party. In practice, however, the executive body was forced to make and execute decisions on its own responsibility, in view of the fact that the convention met regularly only once in two years, whereas the committee convened when it seemed necessary and dealt with such problems as might arise.

[19]The reader may wonder whether the author is not making a distinction here without a difference, in view of the close relationship between the Alliance and the People's Party. It will be remembered (Chapter III) that, in the beginning of Populism, there was a marked similarity between the two in membership, and it may be supposed from that fact that the organization of the Alliance served also the purposes of the Third Party. And so it did, so long as the Alliance enjoyed a healthy existence. The rise of Populism,

A second interesting field for speculation is offered by a comparison of the Populist organization with that of the Democratic Party. The Democrats in 1890 occupied a position of unquestioned security. It had been many years since their hold on state politics had been threatened seriously, and in most sections their control over local politics likewise was unchallenged. In this situation, since politics had become a humdrum matter, little attention was paid to party organization. The dominant party, therefore, had allowed its machinery to disintegrate, with the result that during the early days of the Populist decade it was but ill prepared, from the point of view of party organization, for the desperate conflict that was to follow.[20]

As the People's Party gathered momentum and its adversaries began to perceive something of its strength, they bestirred themselves to devise means to withstand the onslaught. Even so, they did not turn primarily to the building of a strong organization. To be sure occasional Democratic clubs were established, to the number perhaps of several hundred. These unit cells did not compare, however, either in number or in effectiveness with the Populist clubs. Further, the Democrats devised methods of making nominations for elective offices, thus avoiding the division of strength among several candidates which in the early days of Populism often permitted Third Party aspirants to win offices with a minority of the vote.[21] The methods did not differ greatly from those of the People's Party: in the precincts, primaries were held, and in the

however, portended the end of the Alliance, which brought with it the disintegration of the local machinery of that order. The People's Party found an equivalent for the suballiance in the local Populist club, but it failed to find a worthy successor to the county Alliance, which had played an important role in propagating Alliance principles. To that extent, therefore, it yielded to its progenitor in the matter of effectiveness in local organization.

[20]It may be noted in this connection that if the Democrats considered it unnecessary to organize, the Republicans deemed it not worth their while and that the second party of the State was as poorly organized, except in half a dozen of the "negro counties," as the first.

[21]The situation which obtained in the early nineties may be seen by reference to the election records of numerous counties for the year 1892. Those records reveal frequently that for any particular local office there might be as many as three Democratic candidates, whereas the Populists almost always managed to concentrate on one.

counties and the various districts above them, conventions, the
county convention being based on representation from the precinct
and those of the larger districts comprising delegates chosen by
the county convention. At the apex of the structure was the state
convention which usually met biennially and nominated candidates
for state offices and drafted a platform. At each level there was
an executive committee, with a chairman at its head, which served
as a board of directors for the party for its district.[22]

Physically, then, there was considerable similarity between the
organization of the dominant party (when events had demonstrated
to its leaders the necessity of organizing) and that of its young
rival. At bottom, however, the Populists stressed machinery more
and depended more heavily upon it than did the Democrats. They
gave a great deal of time to the matter of organizing local clubs,
whereas the Democratic leaders appeared to be only incidentally
interested in that phase of their activities. Furthermore, the Populist managers were much concerned with the organization of their
party above the local unit and were at some pains to work out a
nice relationship between the various party agencies, while the
Democrats organized only under stern necessity and gave to their
agencies even then a minimum of functions. We may conclude,
therefore, that, whatever the advantages enjoyed by the Democrats,
it was not superior organization which gave the old party the
advantage in its tilts with the advocates of Populism.

III

In the early days of Populism, the strategists of the movement
were content to allow their party to progress by the sheer strength
of its appeal, seeking support solely in the name of the principles
of Reform. Ere long it was recognized, however, that the basis
of their appeal was narrower than need be; hence they turned to a
number of ancillary organizations which indirectly were of some
importance in furthering the cause of Populism.

---

[22]The State Executive Committee of the Democratic Party was twice as
large as that of the People's Party. The Democratic committee was based on
representation from state senatorial districts, of which there were thirty-one,
the Populist on congressional districts, which numbered thirteen.

First among these may be mentioned the glee clubs. People's Party men had learned as members of the Alliance to sing symbolical songs, for in that order vocal music played a large role; and their leaders were quick to sense the benefits to be derived from the continuation of the practice of Populism's progenitor. There was a place, therefore, particularly at the level of the local unit, for the glee club. That place was filled by the occasional organization of such clubs which led the meetings in the singing of songs designed to quicken the pulse and renew the faith of Third Party men.[23]

A second auxiliary organization was found in the "Young People's Reform League of Texas," designed to lay the foundation of Reform principles among prospective voters. It was proposed to organize at every schoolhouse in the State a young people's Reform club which should discuss politics and political issues after the manner of the usual Populist club. Unfortunately, the proposal came at an inopportune time.[24] Thus, while some efforts were made to put the plan into operation, few young people's clubs were organized, and the sub-voters of the State were left largely to their own devices so far as the People's Party was concerned.

A third ancillary organization was the Home Industry Club Association, which was the nineteenth century manifestation of the present day buy-it-made-at-home movement. Home Industry Clubs were established in various parts of the State among both men and women, though apparently the movement localized largely in Dallas County which was the place of its inception. They were not limited in membership to People's Party adherents; on the contrary, they professed to be nonpartisan in character. The sponsorship of the movement by the *Southern Mercury*, however, together with its championship by Barnett Gibbs,[25] served to indicate the

---

[23]*The Dublin Progress*, April 27, 1894; *The Young Populist*, June 7, 1894 (in the Library of The University of Texas, Austin, Texas).

[24]The campaign of 1896 was getting under way even as the suggestion was made, and there was little time for any except straight party work for the next several months. After the election, the editor of *The Southern Mercury*, who had proposed the scheme, found himself so preoccupied with other matters that he never returned to press the Young People's Reform League. See *The Southern Mercury* for April 2, 1896.

[25]Gibbs became the leading advocate of Populism in Texas after 1896.

real nature of the Home Industry Clubs, which assumed actually if not confessedly the character of bodies adjunct to the People's Party organization. That they did not campaign actively for the Populist ticket may be conceded, but that they served the party well by keeping foremost the fundamental principles of reform will hardly be denied.[26]

In the troublous times which beset Populism toward the end of the century, the "old guard" Reformers, unwilling to see the Third Party expire without making heroic efforts to resuscitate it, resorted to proposals for yet another subsidiary organization, a "Direct Legislation League of Texas." Direct legislation and the imperative mandate (the recall) had long been recognized as a means of restoring all power to the people and therefore as being "pure democracy of the Thomas Jefferson kind." Hence by 1899 the editor of the *Mercury*, who had become the real leader of the People's Party in the State, was willing to stake every-thing on a whole-souled sponsorship of the principles on which they rested.[27] The direct legislation league idea did not take hold gen-erally, however, and the editor was forced to be content, instead, with the establishment of random "Reform League Clubs" which served his purpose but poorly.[28]

In these several ways did the managers of the People's Party seek to broaden the basis of its appeal. The Populist glee club, the Young People's Reform League, the Home Industry Club, and the Direct Legislation League—all were designed to add some-thing of method or something of content to the bonafide principles of reform sponsored by the Third Party. Of the four, only the glee club achieved the end sought; the rest either did not progress beyond the stage of proposal, or, being established, did not attain to positions of large influence. We may conclude, then, that the ancillary machinery of the People's Party was almost wholly deficient: gestures were made in the direction of strengthening the party in ways somewhat outside the beaten paths, but the tangible advantages which they brought to Populism were negligible.

---

[26]*The Southern Mercury*, Jan. 21, Feb. 18, May 13, 1897.

[27]See for the development of the Direct Legislation League idea and its fate, *ibid.*, May 4, May 11, May 18, 1899.

[28]*Ibid.*, May 18, July 20, 1899.

IV

Texas in 1890 was filled with the military tradition. Almost every man of middle age or more had participated in the War, and virtually all had returned home proud of the part they had taken in the conflict and eager to live again the stirring days of the campaigns they had known. In such an atmosphere appeared the Third Party, seeking support among those whose fondest thoughts were of the War and whose lives were bound up with the military traditions of the Confederacy. It was but natural that it should seek to appeal to the predilections of these people, for wholly aside from the strength derived always from employment of the jargon and the organization of war, they were especially susceptible to the attractions of military paraphernalia.

Recognition by the leaders of the party of the significance of the martial appeal led to the establishment of two Populist military organizations. The better known of these was the Industrial Legion, a national organization which reached Texas in the summer of 1894. The first call to action in behalf of the Legion indicated the nature of the order. Addressed especially to members of sub-alliances, Populist clubs, labor leagues, and similar workingmen's units, it summoned them to organize locally and petition for a charter and to meet in state session at the same time and place as the state Alliance.[29] Subsequent statements by the commander revealed that the purpose of the Legion was to provide a means for the regimentation of the forces of Reform, and to "guard the ballot box, force an honest count, and combine all the energy of all (Third Party) people in superb missionary work."[30] Its military character was evidenced chiefly by the terminology employed and the methods by which it sought to gain the favorable consideration of laboring men. First, its officers were given military titles, as Commander, Adjutant General, and Quartermaster General.[31] Again, a "simple cavalry and foot drill" was devised for the use of legionnaires, who thus would be able to "present a fine appearance in processions."[32]

---

[29]*Texas Advance*, Aug. 4, 1894.

[30]*The Southern Mercury*, April 25, 1895. See also *ibid.*, April 2, 1896.

[31]The last office, incidentally, was filled by Milton Park, editor of *The Southern Mercury*.

[32]*The Southern Mercury*, Aug. 4, 1894.

Yet again, the purpose of the organization, stressing as it did the need for group coöperation for the defense of the rights of Legion members and conceding openly the possible necessity for armed intervention, emphasized its martial aspects and identified it as a Populist army from which all dissentients might hope for protection.

A more interesting organization had its origin in a secret order which grew up among the protagonists of the Union Labor Party during the late-eighties. At that time the independents in politics, finding themselves facing an impenetrable barrier of party allegiance and boss control, considered it necessary to devise some means whereby they might compete successfully against the alleged evil practices of the old party leaders. Such a means came to hand with the appearance in the State of an organization called the "Videttes," a secret, oath-bound society of reformers who pledged themselves to defend their cause by whatever weapons should prove necessary. The rebels seized upon the society as offering a solution of their difficulties: they adopted its oath and its ritualistic paraphernalia and made of it an organization ancillary to the reform movement, which had not yet become articulate throughout the State.[33]

With the evolution of the People's Party in the early nineties the equivalent of the old Videttes came over into the new party as Gideon's Band, an organization essentially similar to its predecessor. In composition it included only certain picked men and trusted leaders of the People's Party who could be depended upon to do their utmost for Populism. Its motives, in so far as they can be evaluated now, are open to question, though there is general agreement as to its nature. Its members gave the death pledge to secrecy and loyalty; they met quietly on dark nights at prearranged places and engaged in drills and other forms of ritualism; and they agreed by oath among themselves to secure honest elections and fair counts of the vote cast, by pacific methods if possible, by armed force if necessary. They constituted, in short, an organization similar to the later Ku Klux Klan, regarded by its friends as the ultimate

---

[33]*Ibid.*, Oct. 30, Nov. 6, 1888; *The Comanche Vanguard*, Aug. 30, 1913. The daily newspapers of the day also carried reports of the alleged activities of the Videttes. See, for example, the *Fort Worth Daily Gazette* for the month of October, 1888.

manifestation of courage and loyalty and by its enemies as an evil and exceedingly dangerous form of dark-lanternism.[34]

The leaders of the People's Party in these ways attempted to establish organizations which would provide at once a direct appeal to the martial ardor of the people and a means of securing justice by direct action when this should be denied them as a matter of right by their adversaries. The Industrial Legion made a frank appeal for support, coming wholly into the open with its plan and seeking recruits by what amounted to public advertisement. It met with some success, though poverty of leadership caused it to fall far short of the goal of establishing a unit in every community. Gideon's Band, on the other hand, was a secret order, and its public appeal therefore was less than that of the Legion. It had no buttons which its members might wear publicly, nor did it have drill companies in which they might appear to advantage on ceremonial occasions. There were, however, certain compensating factors. After all, it had its oath and its ritual and its passwords, signs, and grips, and it had the advantage of the interest which always attaches to what is unknown. It constituted, therefore, as did the Industrial Legion, an order which appealed to one's spirit of adventure, and the two combined to add to Populism an element of attractiveness for the old soldiers and the young crusaders which otherwise would have been lacking.

Consideration of the Populist organization in all its aspects leads to the conclusion that the People's Party was very efficiently organized in some respects, while in others its machinery was almost wholly deficient. As regards that phase of organization which characterizes all political parties, namely, the clubs, the primaries and conventions, and the committees, there was little to be desired. In one respect only is it apparent that its formal machinery was noticeably weak: there was no agency whose specific business it

---

[34]The author has found few references in writing to Gideon's Band. He has, however, found many who profess a direct acquaintance with the order, and they tell interesting and significant if sometimes conflicting stories of its organization and activities. As to the details relating to the Band there is, as one might suppose, no concensus among these old-timers, but as to the facts of major importance there is general agreement. See Hicks, *op. cit.*, pp. 254–255n.

was to canvass the precinct during the campaign and to get out the vote. These duties were cared for ordinarily by the candidates for local offices themselves or by friends working for them, though in some counties local Populist bosses devised their own peculiar means for organizing the electors and persuading them to vote.[35] In the absence of enthusiastic local leadership the work of canvassing and getting out the vote fell naturally on the shoulders of the local club, which might perform these functions satisfactorily if it should happen to boast an energetic leader or which might ignore its obligations entirely.

In the field of ancillary machinery, however, the party was almost wholly lacking. The Farmers' Alliance troops served as invaluable reinforcements, it is true, but other subsidiary organizations either failed to materialize or, having been set up, failed to fill the place for which they had been designed. Thus the Young People's Reform League, the Home Industry Club Association, and the Direct Legislation League, all directly or indirectly related to the Third Party, were of little or no practical importance in determining the course of development of that party. And the same may be said of the Populist militia. An excellent opportunity was offered, in the case of the Industrial Legion, to organize the Reformers into squads and marshal them under the Populist standard in military array; but the strategists of the party failed to perceive the possibilities offered by the Legion, which therefore was of little consequence as an adjunct of the Reform Party. Gideon's Band, a secret, oath-bound society, was by nature of a distinctly limited appeal. It served some purpose as a specialized piece of Populist machinery, but that purpose was not to attract to the party support which otherwise it would not have won.

Of the numerous plans announced, then, for the establishment of auxiliary societies and associations, few were executed. In truth, it appears that one weakness of the party was the readiness with which such schemes were proposed and then abandoned. Any or all of the various plans might have brought considerable advantages had they been pursued to logical conclusions, for the value of ancillary organizations to the political party is not to be denied.

---

[35]See *supra*, Chap. V; *infra*, Chap. VII.

As it was, however, the appeal of Populism, in so far as organization was concerned, was made exclusively to Reformers as such; and as the People's Party profited from the advantages of a straight party appeal, it suffered also from the limitations imposed by the narrowness of its scope. Strongly organized as a party, it was forced to depend almost wholly upon its own prowess on the field of battle, shorn of the strength which it might have claimed under more favorable conditions.

CHAPTER VII

TECHNIQUE

CONSIDERATION of Populist leadership and organization suggests a number of significant lines of inquiry, most of which eventuate in the important subject of tactics. Populist propaganda and campaign technique involved a variety of factors, among them the Reform press, which may be dismissed here as warranting a separate investigation. Those which remain may be examined from several points of view. First, it is of interest to note the peace time propaganda methods by means of which a background was built for the more intensive appeal of the election period. Secondly, the campaign technique as such demands careful attention. Finally, it will be of advantage to evaluate the campaign itself as a means of ascertaining both the type of conflict which resulted and the efficacy of the methods by which the Populist faith was spread.

I

The keynote of the People's Party peace time propaganda campaign was *education*. Let the voter be informed, the Populist leaders urged, and he must of necessity be converted to the cause of Reform. The genuineness of this faith in enlightenment was attested by the establishment of an occasional Populist educational institution, which was significant as evidence of an interesting attitude if not intrinsically important.[1]

Of the educational weapons available, none surpassed in effectiveness the printed word. From the beginning the leaders of the Third Party recognized the value of printed materials, as was evidenced by their appointment, at the first Populist state convention, of a committee of three on People's Party literature.[2] Almost simultaneously came the establishment of a semi-official though privately

---

[1]The Alliance had set the precedent for such schools by sponsoring the founding of grade and high schools which operated usually under the aegis of a county Alliance.

A "Populist Institute" was established at Rhodesburg, in Van Zandt County, in 1895. See *The Southern Mercury*, Dec. 19, 1895.

[2]*Dallas Morning News*, Aug. 18, 1891.

maintained literary bureau which served as a clearing house for Reform literature. So thoroughly was its work done in the early days of Populism that the bureau was credited in the state convention of June, 1892, with having effected the amalgamation of the Third Party advocates and the Jeffersonian Democrats.[3]

In 1893, the *Texas Advance*, which had become the official Populist state organ, assumed, among others, the functions previously performed by the literary bureau. One of its first acts was to compile a directory of the key men of the Third Party in Texas.[4] A second service consisted in the operation of the *"Texas Advance Reform Library,"* a plan under which the *Advance* undertook to furnish at the lowest price pamphlets and books of interest to Reformers.[5] Now the significant thing about this library service is that Third Party men purchased and read the works suggested and many others besides and so informed themselves on the issues before the country. One might accuse a Populist of many serious shortcomings, but among them would not be a failure to acquaint himself with the Reformer's side of questions of public interest.[6]

Much of the literature recommended was typical of the ephemeral writings characteristic of any period of our history. A great deal was confessedly Reform propaganda, however, and among the titles of this nature was Cyclone Davis' *A Political Revelation*, which set forth the principles of the People's Party and sought to identify it with the party of Thomas Jefferson.[7] The *Advance* insisted that the book would be "a standard work as long as liberty (should

---

[3]*Ibid.*, June 25, 1892. See also *The Galveston Daily News*, Aug. 7, 1892.

[4]*Texas Advance*, Jan. 6, 1894.

[5]*Ibid.*, Oct. 28, 1893. People's Party lecturers and organizers were appointed agents to sell Reform literature, and were given commissions on all sales made. *Ibid.*, Sept. 30, 1893.

[6]In 1894 the Fifth Congressional District Alliance met and voted to establish a congressional district library. The Knights of Labor were invited to coöperate in the enterprise, and a committee was appointed to study the matter. *The Gainesville Signal*, May 16, 1894. If positive action was taken subsequently on the proposed library, no notice of it appeared in the *Signal*.

[7]The Advance Publishing Company printed the book in 1894 and undertook also to find a market for it. As early as May, 1895, the *Mercury* advertised that it had left only 250 copies. The size of the edition is not known. Mr. Davis places it at 20,000 copies, though his memory may be faulty on the point.

endure) in the human heart."[8] In truth, it was purely a propaganda effort in behalf of the Third Party, and its permanent worth is measured by its value as a record of a type of campaign document. A second volume worthy of mention was the *Life Work of Thomas L. Nugent*, published by Mrs. Catharine Nugent after the death of her husband. The book was not primarily a propaganda document; it was rather a bonafide memorial to Judge Nugent. As such it was of some value in spreading the Nugent Tradition, but aside from this incidental service its worth to the cause of Reform was negligible.

The efforts of Populist writers in Texas in the direction of drafting and publishing formal treatises in behalf of Populism were dwarfed by comparison with those of the newspaper writers of the party who kept up a constant bombardment of the Reform editors, beseeching them to publish letters, essays, and poems ranging in length from five lines to ten columns. The foremost leaders of the Third Party were frequent contributors to the columns of the Reform press, and their letters and articles were printed with readiness by the editors and read with avidity by Reformers.[9]

The printed word thus was of first importance in aiding and abetting the growth of the People's Party. Not less important, however, was the spoken word. The party profited from the labors of many speakers, the most prominent of whom were ceaseless in their activities, traveling up and down the State and making from three to twelve speeches a week in their campaign for the cause. Occasionally they congregated at the scenes of important meetings, but for the greater part they traveled alone.[10] From the fortuitous character of the itineraries of these prophets of Populism it is evident that there would be, almost unavoidably, some duplication of effort. Recognizing here a source of weakness to the party,

---

[8]See *Texas Advance*, Nov. 11, 1893, for three notices concerning the book.

The *Mercury* referred to it as "the greatest political educator of the day." *The Southern Mercury*, Jan. 10, 1895.

[9]See *infra*, Chap. VIII.

[10]*The Southern Mercury*, May 28, 1896.

The speakers were paid whatever the local sponsors of their addresses cared to pay them—the state committee of the party made no provision for their reimbursement—and they were fortunate if they received more than they paid out.

State Chairman Ashby created a Populist lecture bureau in the spring of 1895 for the purpose of systematizing the work of oral education.[11] The bureau remained in existence for a year or more but failed except in a very general way to gain the end for which it had been established. Most of the speakers therefore continued to appear when and where they pleased, or where they could get invitations.

Among the Populist speakers there were, of course, men of every type. Some were able to command the attention of crowds of many thousands; others confined their activities to the local club meeting. Whatever their methods and their relative abilities, however, there were few even among the lesser lights of the party who were not experienced in public address and familiar with the issues of the day. They spoke effectively, then, their efforts providing a convincing capstone for the educational campaign inaugurated by the Populist writers.[12]

Quite a different type of peace time propaganda was that which called into play the emotions,[13] and the most effective emotional appeal recognized and played upon the religious preconceptions of the people. Third Party adherents in general, being largely sons of the soil, were God-fearing men. Moreover, many of the Populist leaders had been and some were still ministers of the gospel, and even those who remained free from such a bias recognized readily the value, or the necessity, of the religious appeal. Hence no opportunity was lost to invoke divine aid for Third Party enterprises through the medium of prayer, for the Populist believed firmly that "all things whatsoever ye shall ask in prayer, believing, ye shall receive."[14] Further, the Reform preachers identified Populism with Christianity, finding in Jesus Christ the first Populist; and they substantiated their claims by reference to authority. Thus one People's Party statistician learned by the laborious process of

---

[11]*Ibid.*, June 6, 1895.

[12]*The Dallas Morning News* of July 23, 1892, made some highly complimentary remarks about the abilities of the Populist speakers. See also *ibid.*, Sept. 7, 1894.

[13]The educational appeal, it is true, relied in part upon the predilections of the people and in that sense and to that extent was emotional in character. The chief source of its strength, however, was supposed factual argument.

[14]Matt., XXI, 22. See the *Dallas Morning News*, July 23, 1892.

thumbing through and counting that usury is forbidden 163 times by the Good Book, more than any other sin or crime; yet, he charged scathingly, the Democrats attempt to justify what the Lord has condemned so uniformly![15] Now and again, the scene was enlivened further by the appearance of a confessed minister who selected texts from the Bible and preached bonafide Populist sermons therefrom, introducing and concluding his remarks with a few words of prayer.[16]

The fruits of this process, and indeed of the whole religious paraphernalia of Populism, were that the People's Party came to be regarded by its adherents as the party of righteousness; it came to occupy almost the position of the church and to exact unquestioning allegiance from its partisans as though it were indeed an institution divinely inspired.[17] Thus were religious jargon and practices employed, unconsciously perhaps but nonetheless effectively, to win

---

[15]*The Southern Mercury*, March 16, 1899.

Among the passages cited most frequently in defense of the principles of the People's Party were these:

Nehemiah, V, 3, 10, 11: "*Some* also there were that said, We have mortgaged our lands, vineyards, and houses, that we might buy corn, because of the dearth."

"I likewise *and* my brethren, and my servants, might exact them money and corn: I pray you, let us leave off this usury.

"Restore, I pray you, to them, even this day, their lands, their vineyards, their oliveyards, and their houses, also the hundredth *part* of the money, and of the corn, wine, and the oil, that ye exact of them."

Proverbs, XXII, 22, 23: "Rob not the poor, because he *is* poor: neither oppress the afflicted in the gate;

"For the Lord will plead their cause, and spoil the soul of those that spoiled them."

Luke, XI, 46: "And he said, Woe unto you also, *ye* lawyers! for ye lade men with burdens grievous to be borne, and ye yourselves touch not the burdens with one of your fingers."

[16]Such a preacher delivered a series of three Populist sermons in Dallas, during the course of which he traced every Populist principle directly to the scriptures, even to the subtreasury scheme. *Dallas Morning News*, Sept. 19, 1894.

[17]*Ibid.*, June 25, 1892.

An interesting variation from the usual appeal was to be found in the efforts made to convert the church outright to the cause of Reform. See a letter written for this purpose in *The Southern Mercury*, March 19, 1896.

converts to the cause and to hold them in line after their confession of faith.

Another form of the emotional appeal recognized the popular predilection for song. The committee on literature early recommended *The Alliance Songster*, a collection of songs, parodies usually sung to familiar sacred, sentimental, and popular melodies;[18] and thereafter Populist assemblies did not want for music. Singers were employed now and again to travel with and assist Reform speakers;[19] Populist glee clubs of both male and female voices were organized;[20] an enterprising Texas composer wrote and introduced a "Populist Grand March;"[21] brass bands were employed, though infrequently, to furnish music for largely attended meetings;[22] and the song service became as important a part of Populist meetings as the invocation. Even the state convention yielded to the Populist yearning for song, as for example when Stump Ashby opened the convention of 1894 by leading the delegates in singing "Jesus, Lover of My Soul."[23]

The Third Party's recourse to song was in truth but an implicit recognition of very simple psychological phenomena; namely, first, that people like to entertain themselves, and second, that they like especially to sing, particularly when there are many voices to be heard. The leaders of the People's Party never attempted to explain the place of music in the technical vernacular of the psychologist,

---

[18]The *Dallas Morning News* commented at once on the fact that the People's Party had selected as its official songbook that of the Alliance. Aug. 18, 1891.

Representative titles from the hymn book are illuminating; among them may be noted "The Runaway Banker," "The Farmers Are Coming," "All Hail the Power of Laboring Men," "The Mortgaged Home," and "Greenback's the Money for Me."

Subsequently a second song book was issued and sold for five cents, with the admonition, "Send for them and help sing our party to success." *Texas Advance*, July 14, 1894.

[19]The *Southern Mercury*, May 2, 1895.

[20]The *Dublin Progress*, April 27, 1894; *The Young Populist*, June 7, 1894.

[21]*Dallas Morning News*, June 21, 1894.

[22]The *Southern Mercury*, July 28, 1895.

[23]*Dallas Morning News*, June 21, 1894.

but they were nonetheless aware fully of its nature and its significance.[24]

A third type of appeal which struck at the emotions rather than the reason recognized and took account of the military inclinations of the people. The natural predilection for martial fanfare was made the stronger in Texas during the nineties by memories of the War, which were still fresh in the minds of most Populists. The People's Party drew into its ranks more than its share of older men, comprehending therefore more than its portion of war veterans. Hence it was an easy matter to transform it into the party *par excellence* of the ex-Confederates. Jerome Kearby became the "boy soldier"; the military records of such men as Stump Ashby, Harry Tracy, Marion Martin, and Buck Barry were kept before the public; frequent reference was made to the "kids" who directed the affairs of the Democratic Party; and no opportunity was lost to defend the veterans against supposed unfair treatment at the hands of the adversaries of their party.[25] A Populist militia combined with a martial jargon to complete the illusion of armed conflict.[26] Thus was the People's Party converted into a Populist army, and thus was the military motif employed, along with prayer and song, to strike a responsive chord in the emotions of the people.[27]

The peace time propaganda methods of the Populists were seen at their best in the spectacle called the campmeeting which, originating as a religious festival, was appropriated in turn by the

---

[24]Proof that the importance of Populist song was appreciated at the time may be seen in the following statement, taken from the *Dallas News* of July 23, 1892: "Undoubtedly these songs, sung to lively and familiar airs, are in themselves a strong lever for this movement. They savor strongly of political revolution, though not a revolution of blood."

[25]See a document signed by "A number of ex-Confederate soldiers" in the *Dallas News* of Oct. 22, 1896.

[26]See *supra*, Chap. VI.

[27]Aside from the confessed propaganda methods discussed for the last several pages, the Populist leaders were constantly on the watch for means of lending aid to Third Party men in such a way as to gain converts for the party. Thus for example the *Advance* planned to foster the settlement in Texas of an agricultural colony of thrifty farmers and mechanics from other states and entered into negotiations looking to that end. If anything tangible came of the proposal, however, no record of it has been found. See *Texas Advance*, Dec. 9, 1893.

A REPRESENTATIVE POPULIST SONG

THE PEOPLE'S JUBILEE*

1. Say, workers, have you seen the bosses
   With scared and pallid face;
   Going down the alley sometime this ev'ning,
   To find a hiding place.
   They saw the people cast their ballot,
   And they knew their time had come;
   They spent their boodle to get elected
   But were beaten by the people's men.

   Chorus

   The people laugh, ha, ha!
   The bosses, oh! how blue!
   It must be now the jubilee is coming
   In the year of ninety-two.

2. The bosses got to feeling so big,
   They thought the world was their'n;
   Of the starving people all o'er the land
   They did not care to learn.
   They blowed so much and called themselves leaders,
   And they got so full of sin;
   I 'spec' they try to fool the Almighty,
   But Peter won't let them in.

3. The working people are getting tired
   Of having no home nor land;
   So now, they say, to run this government,
   They are going to try their hand.
   There's gold and silver in the White House cellar,
   And the workers all want some
   For they know it will all be counted out
   When the people's party comes.

4. The election's over and the rings are beaten,
   And the bosses have run away;
   The people's party came out victorious
   And they won election day.
   They cast their votes for truth and freedom,
   Which are always bound to win;
   Up to the polls they walked like freemen,
   And put their ballots in.

---

*From *Songs for the Toiler*, pp. 26–27.

Alliance and the People's Party.[28]   Such meetings usually were held in July and August, by which time the farmer was able to spare a few days for a renewal of his political faith.   The initiative came from a local organization, either Alliance or Populist, which, concluding to sponsor an encampment, set about in a workmanlike manner to make a success of the undertaking.[29]

On the day before the time set for the opening of the encampment the farmers began to arrive, by every available conveyance known, and frequently from great distances.   All through the day and into the night new arrivals came in until on the morning of the opening day the scene resembled that of a great military camp.   There were hundreds and sometimes literally thousands of persons bustling here and there, amid scenes of indescribable confusion though of universal good humor, intent upon arranging their affairs before the invocation which would open the meeting.

Nor had the local committees left anything undone to add to the convenience or enjoyment of those in attendance.   If the guests wished to cook their own food, camp style, there was firewood available; while if they preferred to "dine out," there were restaurants and barbecue pits on the grounds.   For their amusement there were the merry-go-round and the flying jinny, the Punch-and-Judy show, the fat boy, and, if their minds turned to relaxation, the dancing pavilion—set well to one side, for the older people frowned upon so carnal a thing as the dance.   And if they were so minded, they might quench their thirst by the purchase of lemonade and sodapop on the grounds, though if they desired whiskey or beer they must go outside the jurisdiction of the encampment managers, where usually, however, some enterprising person had set up a convenient grogshop.   The whole effect, in short, was that left by the typical carnival scene.[30]

It was not the prospect of a brief vacation, however, which attracted the farmer to the encampment, for despite the atmosphere of carefreeness and good will which prevailed among those present, attendance there involved considerable hardship.   There must, then,

---

[28]*Dallas Morning News,* July 31, 1891.

[29]*The Southern Mercury,* July 25, 1895.

[30]See the *Dallas Morning News,* July 22–23, 1892, for a good description of the campgrounds.

be something offered by the campmeeting besides the prospect of a holiday, and that something was found partly in the spiritual inspiration and hope which the attendant derived from the great revival meeting of his church-party. There the old familiar songs were sung; there also several times daily divine aid was invoked in those fervent prayers of which only a strong evangelist was capable; there again the case of Populism was expounded by the political preachers who had taken the place of the old campmeeting haranguers; there finally all were brothers, addressing each other as "Brother" this and "Brother" that in the approved vernacular of the fraternal order.[31]

But if the farmer attended the campmeeting for the spiritual benefits to be derived therefrom, he attended also to take advantage of the opportunities offered for a political rebirth. Nor was he disappointed in this purpose, for hand in hand with the religious aspects of the meeting went those of a purely political nature. Every Populist leader of consequence always attended the larger meetings, and oftentimes the program committee was able to arrange for out-of-state visitors, as General James B. Weaver, Governor Waite of Colorado, "General" J. S. Coxey, Mrs. Mary E. Lease, and others equally famous.[32] Morning, afternoon, and evening were filled with addresses, interspersed with music, ranging in length from the ten-minute impromptu talk to the three-hour excoriation characteristic of Cyclone Davis. All the while Reform literature was sold from a booth or hawked about the grounds by criers.

The significance of the campmeeting cannot be understood unless one grasps the spirit in which it was conducted. Here were thousands of men, women, and children,[33] many of them come from great distances, who gathered in an atmosphere of good fellowship to imbibe anew the eternal verities of the People's Party. For a whole week they literally lived and breathed Reform: by day and

---

[31]*Ibid.*, June 25, 1892. The *News* was moved on this occasion to remark that "Co-fraternity seems to be one of the aims of the People's Party."

[32]All of these personages and more spoke before encampments in Texas in the summer of 1895. *The Southern Mercury*, July 18, Aug. 1, 1895.

[33]Crowds of from 5,000 to 7,000 were not exceptional, and Mrs. Lease addressed a gathering estimated at 15,000 to 20,000 in Hunt County in 1895. *The Southern Mercury*, Aug. 29, 1895.

by night they sang of Populism, they prayed for Populism, they
read Populist literature and discussed Populist principles with their
brethren in the faith, and they heard Populist orators loose their
destructive thunderbolts in the name of the People's Party. They
found themselves, in short, participants in a magnificent spectacle
which combined educational and emotional appeals in an irresistible
Third Party revival whose vigor stamped the campmeeting as a
brilliant summation of Populist peace time propaganda techniques.[34]

II

It is apparent from the foregoing that the Third Party was the
beneficiary of a constant propaganda campaign of some preten-
sions; so that when the time came for launching the usual election
drive, it was necessary only to accelerate the tempo somewhat to
have going full tilt a vigorous campaign. The speeding up process
was accomplished through the activities of the State Executive Committee, which was assisted for the duration of the conflict by a
special campaign director or committee.[35]

The function of campaign direction involved the Populist headquarters organization in the consideration of a number of problems
of the gravest importance, chief among which was that of finance.
Its managers devised numerous methods of raising money for the
war chest. They depended partly upon voluntary contributions

---

[34]The newspapers of the day were filled with notices of Third Party and
Alliance encampments throughout the length and breadth of the State. For
brief descriptions of the campmeeting, see *The Southern Mercury*, July 18,
1895, and Aug. 8, 1901 (the latter pertains to the last Populist campmeeting
of which mention has been found); the *Dallas Morning News*, July 27, 28,
29, 31, 1891, July 20, 22, 23, 29, 1892, and Aug. 18, 1898; and *The San Antonio
Daily Express*, July 19, 20, 21, 1892.

For a program of a typical campmeeting see *The Dublin Progress*, July 8,
1892.

[35]In 1892, campaign headquarters were established in Dallas under the
direction of State Manager H. L. Bentley. In 1894 and '96, campaign committees of three were appointed. In the latter year at least, however, the
chairman of the State Executive Committee was the actual director of the
campaign. See *The Galveston Daily News*, Aug. 10, 1892; *Texas Advance*,
Aug. 4, 1894; and *The Southern Mercury*, Aug. 13, Dec. 24, 1896.

from individuals,[36] partly upon assistance from the local Populist organizations.[37] Under the urging of repeated requests for aid, the lower levels of the Populist machine pressed their members hard for contributions, and "passing the hat" became a feature of Third Party meetings as much to be expected as the prayer and the song, which were never omitted.

Notwithstanding the variety of the appeals made and the professed willingness of all to help where possible, very little money flowed into the party treasury.[38] In the middle of September, 1892, when the campaign should have been gathering momentum, Manager Bentley announced that to date he had received only ten dollars in contributions and that unless some support was forthcoming he would be compelled to close his office and give up the work of directing the campaign.[39] His plea met with some response, though its limited nature was revealed by the fact that expenditures for the campaign totaled only $1,770.40.[40] In 1896, notwithstanding that year witnessed the warmest campaign ever waged by the party, the director reported voluntary contributions of only $1,119.20,[41] while in 1898 there was no state campaign fund of any description.[42] The party's campaign chest, therefore, was undernourished to the point of starvation; and even if one take into account the personal expenditures of the candidates, which it may be surmised were rather heavy, and possible exaggerations of the poverty of the party by its

---

[36]See the *Fort Worth Daily Gazette*, Sept. 22, 1892; *The Southern Mercury*, June 13, 1895. The latter reference is to an appeal by State Chairman Ashby for financial assistance for J. B. Rayner, the colored orator. See also *The Weekly News*, Sept. 15, 1898.

[37]*Texas Advance*, Oct. 14, 1893.

[38]See *The Galveston Daily News*, Sept. 8, 1894; *Dallas Morning News*, Sept. 7, 1894.

[39]*Fort Worth Daily Gazette*, Sept. 22, 1892.

[40]*Dallas Morning News*, Nov. 29, 1892.

[41]*The Southern Mercury*, Dec. 24, 1896. That the poverty of the party was not illusory was indicated by the nature of some of the expenditures listed. The suite of rooms occupied by the campaign director, for example, was rented for the sum of $15.00 per month and was fitted out with office furniture at a rental of $6.50 per month.

[42]*The Galveston Daily News*, Sept. 25, 1898. The figures quoted here do not include expenditures borne by the candidates personally or by the various local party organizations.

managers, it still must be concluded that the campaign outlay was far too small to provide for anything like an adequate canvass of the State.

The technique employed during the campaign to convert the voter differed chiefly in degree from that commonly used in peace times. Thus, in addition to the books, periodicals, and pamphlets which were kept constantly before the Third Party public, a veritable deluge of new propaganda material appeared with the opening of the campaign. There were, to illustrate, circulars and open letters from the pens of ertswhile Democrats who purported to have had their eyes opened through this or that unsavory incident, and there were also sensational charges made by the Populist leaders and sown broadcast over the State, of which more later. A different type of material was found in the party worker's handbook called the "Populist Compendium,"[43] the book of Reform campaign stories,[44] and the Populist campaign textbook, advertised as "32 pages of red hot Democratic exterminator."[45] Not all of these materials flowed through the party's campaign directors, but that a considerable portion of them did is evidenced by the report for 1896 of the State Chairman, who stated that his office in that year printed and distributed more than 500,000 campaign documents.[46]

In a similar manner the public address of ordinary times was supplemented by a device called the joint debate, which brought a speaker from each party to the same platform under an arrangement for a division of time.[47] Occasionally two opponents would find themselves so agreeably matched that they would arrange for a series of debates throughout the State, though this practice was indulged in more frequently by congressional and county candidates than by those for state offices. The Populist speakers were as able in debate as in oratory, but they were unimpressed by the labors of

---

[43]*Texas Advance*, Aug. 4, 1894.

[44]*The Southern Mercury*, July 2, 1896.

[45]*Ibid.*, Sept. 1, 1898.

[46]*Ibid.*, Dec. 24, 1896.

[47]The usual agreement called for two main speeches of one hour each, two rebuttals of thirty minutes each, and one rejoinder (by the first speaker) of five or ten minutes. The arrangement thus provided an evening's entertainment of three hours, which was not too long a program for the listeners if the debaters did their causes justice.

the campaign committee to coördinate their efforts. Hence the speaking campaign failed to fulfill its promise, due partly to poor planning.

In the realm of procedural tactics, the party pursued policies now and again which merit mention. First among these may be mentioned that which grew out of the firm conviction that a strong local organization was of vital importance to the party and further that such an organization could not endure and remain inactive. Belief in these principles led the Populist strategists to counsel activity above all things and to applaud most those local party authorities who nominated tickets and waged campaigns in their behalf whatever the odds against them.[48] Second may be noted the efforts occasionally made to convert to a temporary espousal of Populism certain dissident groups of non-Populist preferences. To instance, agreements were made more than once whereby the Republican Party supported the Reform candidates. The temporary advantage to the Third Party of "fusion" was not to be denied, though its long-time value as a policy was open to serious question.[49]

The Populist managers, then, were sufficiently energetic in their tactics and varied in their appeals to gain for their state ticket a wide recognition at the hands of the voters. The local campaign launched in the name of the People's Party was, however, of even greater interest than that waged for state offices. At the level of the county there was opportunity for a more thorough canvass than was possible at a higher level, and this meant that the element of personal contact became of first importance, with printed materials playing a correspondingly smaller role. It meant further that a candidate might reveal more individuality than was possible higher

---

[48]The party even entered the field of municipal politics, where, in the case of the larger cities at least, its chances of success were negligible. Thus it nominated a ticket in Houston, where its candidate for mayor ran behind the Democratic candidate by 3,559 votes to 164. *The Galveston Daily News*, April 3, 1894. In Fort Worth its tickets met with somewhat greater success, though there also its candidates were defeated almost uniformly. *Fort Worth Daily Gazette*, Feb. 12, April 5, 1893. In the smaller cities and towns, the party met with a modicum of success. Thus in Holland, a little town of Central Texas, a full Populist ticket was elected. *Ibid.*, April 5, 1894.

[49]The term *fusion* was used to cover any form of coöperation, close or loose, between the People's Party and any other group.
See *infra*, Chap. X, for a discussion of the fusion problem.

up, suiting his technique to the demands of his candidacy, or to his limitations. Again, the conditions under which the local campaign was waged made county politics the field of strategem and direct action, which were attempted only infrequently by the managers of the state campaign. The Populist technique adapted itself without difficulty to the field of local politics.

The workaday local campaign occasionally resembled the election drive sponsored by the state campaign directors. Oftentimes there were barbecues and picnics, with speech-making by the candidates, and rallies, held usually at night, at which those who sought office set forth their claim thereto. Occasionally also there were joint debates, held individually at random over the county or in series by prearrangement between the leaders of the rival parties. The candidates for local offices ordinarily were not noted for their fluency in public address, however, and especially were the Populist spokesmen deficient in that regard. Hence they were frequently forced to adopt one of two alternatives: either they could forswear public appearance and seek out the voter individually, lining him up by personal appeal; or they could agree among themselves to allow their most proficient speaker to bear the chief burden of the campaign.[50] Under the latter arrangement each candidate conducted a still hunt quest for votes under cover, while on public occasions their confessed leader expounded the doctrines of Populism from the stump.

Now and again a local orator of some ability launched the familiar speaking campaign, though the spirit in which the campaign was waged usually was quite different from that found higher up. There was, as an excellent illustration, the contest between W. H. (Wick) Blanton and Tom Morris for the county attorney's office in Wilson County in 1894. Blanton, the Populist candidate, and Morris, the Democratic, were good friends of long standing, and they reached an agreement by the terms of which the campaign was made more pleasant for both. Let the former reveal the spirit of the agreement in words which he used in an interview with the author:

[50]See *supra*, Chap. V.

"I simply went to Morris, whom I had known from boyhood, and said to him, 'Tom, we have got to fight each other in this campaign, but there is no use being nasty about it. I don't want to get out here and tear my pants on barbed wire fences for two months and get bitten by a dozen dogs trying to see every farmer in the county. Let's reach an agreement and be sensible about the matter.'

" 'Very well, Wick,' he replied, 'What's your proposition?'

" 'Simply this,' I answered. 'Let's stump the county in a series of joint debates, announcing our dates ahead of time and meeting the voters at the schoolhouses. Furthermore, there is no reason why we can't travel together. There's no use in having two rigs in constant use: you have one and I have one; let's ride together, using your outfit one week and mine the next. And for that matter, we can also have a common jug, from which both may derive inspiration.'

" 'O. K., Wick,' he agreed. 'Let's set the dates.' "

"And that's the way we campaigned," concluded Mr. Blanton, "and we parted better friends than we were when we started."

In Walker County the Populist candidates for county offices devised a scheme which for economy and expediency was unexcelled. They procured a tent and a mess wagon, which was presided over by a cook, and went on tour over the county. Virtually all the candidates joined the party, which cruised about from one schoolhouse to the next, establishing camp in the late afternoon, holding a rally at night, and moving on the next morning. The efficacy of the plan was attested by its results, which proved to be so satisfactory that the Democrats, it was said, were forced to follow the campaign wagon in order to find audiences for their speakers.

By all odds the most interesting phase of the local campaign was found in those counties which had a large controllable vote. Before passing to a discussion of the campaign in those districts, however, it will prove advantageous to summarize briefly the election laws under which thrived the practices presently to be described. First, it is interesting to note, the statutes provided for no system for the registration of the voters. Instead, any male person who complied with the requirements as to age, residence, and citizenship (or, in the case of an alien, declaration of intention to become a citizen), and who was not disqualified under the law, was eligible to vote.[51]

---

[51]*Revised Civil Statutes of the State of Texas, 1895*, Articles 1730–1736. A system of registration was provided for cities of 10,000 inhabitants and over

Second, in the heyday of Populism there were no corrupt or illegal practices acts.[52] Third, the ballot was privately printed and furnished to the voters by the candidates or the parties, subject to certain rather definite statutory specifications.[53] Finally, while the election machinery seemed adequate to achieve its end of securing honest and fair elections, actually it was under the control of the county commissioners' court and so subject to manipulation in the interest of the dominant local party. Be it noted, in passing, that the judges of election oftentimes were eminently fair in their juggling of the law; for if they permitted questionable tactics by their own partisans, they frequently were no less generous with regard to their adversaries.[54] The election laws of the State therefore were subject to criticism in many respects; and where they

---

(*ibid.*, Articles 1767 *et seq.*), but most of the practices noted below were confined to rural areas and towns of small size. It was not until the passage of the "Terrell Election Law" in 1903 that a scheme of universal registration for voters was adopted, and even then registration was required only by the provision of the law which pertained to the payment of the poll tax; *i.e.*, one who presented himself to vote under that law must present his poll tax receipt or an exemption certificate, and this requirement had the effect of causing the voters to register with the tax collector before election day.

[52]The Legislature passed an act in 1895 relating to direct primary elections, which might be held at the option of the parties, and that act provided for penalties for certain corrupt and illegal practices engaged in during the election. It was not, however, until the adoption of the aforementioned Terrell Law that the State had a definition of illegal acts and penalties that was in any wise adequate.

[53]The essential portion of the law dealing with the ballot follows (*Revised Civil Statutes of the State of Texas, 1895*, Article 1742):

"All ballots shall be written or printed on plain white paper, without any picture, sign, vignette, device or stamp or mark, except the writing or printing, in black ink or black pencil, of the names of the candidates, and the several offices to be filled, and except the name of the political party whose candidates are on the ticket; provided, such ballots may be written or printed on plain white foolscap, legal cap, or letter paper; provided, that all ballots containing the name of any candidate pasted over the name of any other candidate shall not be counted for such candidate whose name is so pasted, and any ticket not in conformity with the above shall not be counted."

[54]Local Populist leaders raised the cry now and again that they had been denied equal rights and privileges with the Democratic managers by the judges of election, and it may be their complaint was justified occasionally. Ordinarily, however, the election officials were guided by rules of "fair play"; it was considered that a boss should be allowed to vote such electors as he was able to

appeared adequate in the matter of machinery, they were in practice too often ignored.

The controllable vote to which reference has been made was found chiefly in the counties of South and East Texas, where the Mexicans and the negroes held the balance of power.[55] The success of a party in those counties was reckoned directly in terms of the ability of its local leaders to round up and bring in the vote on election day. The People's Party failed to place such leaders in the heavily Mexican counties of South Texas, but in certain sections of East Texas it won the support of men who were able to control large groups of negro voters. The methods by which the negroes were "converted" to Populism and voted in the interest of the Third Party were the most interesting of those practiced by its local leaders.

An investigation of those methods reveals three chief modes of procedure which were employed under ordinary circumstances. In the first place, there was the course of action followed where influential negro leaders were found. These leaders, called " 'fluence men," by hook or crook set themselves up as local bosses, wielding such power in many districts that their aid was prerequisite to success.[56] The candidates for office therefore were forced to dicker with them for their support, and to pay for their good will. The standard charge was $25.00 from each candidate for county office; the precinct candidate escaped usually with a $5.00 fee.[57] A skillfully managed campaign, then, brought the 'fluence man a considerable sum of money, mayhap as much as $500.00. With the passing of time, ambitious young negroes who recognized here an opportunity to forge ahead set themselves up as 'fluence men. Thus the

---

control without molestation by the judges, and those worthies as a usual thing accepted this principle without question. See *infra*.

[55]*Supra*, Chap. IV.

[56]If there were " 'fluence men," as the genus is described here, among the whites, the author failed to find trace of them. There were, of course, numerous districts in which influential white citizens controlled many white voters, but only rarely if ever were such local bosses paid for their support.

[57]The 'fluence man was not oblivious to the strategic value of his position, as is evidenced by his frequent acceptance of tribute from candidates of both parties.

cost of election to county office, always high, became prohibitive.[58] Old time politicians have confided to the author that the high price and the uncertainty of negro support were directly responsible for the espousal in many counties of the white primary before the general adoption of that system by state law.[59]

The 'fluence man operated generally over East Texas, though for various reasons it was not deemed expedient always to deal with the negroes through his agency. Further, occasional negro communities recognized no such petty tyrant, and there other methods of dealing with the colored voter must be devised. Among those methods may be mentioned first the "owl meeting," a nocturnal assemblage of the negroes sponsored by the local leaders of the

---

[58]It is hardly to be doubted that some money was spent in bringing out the white vote, though for various reasons so little was said regarding that practice that no information is to be had concerning it. It is known that white voters could rely on the candidates to provide them with "something to drink" occasionally, and especially on and just before election day, but of the outright purchasing of white votes no intimation has been found. It is wholly probable that in the negro counties a very large proportion of the money spent in bringing out the vote went to the lining up and voting of the dusky elector.

[59]The 'fluence man game did not often find its way into the press, though one may learn something of its more obvious phases by referring to the *La Grange Journal* of the issue of Jan. 7, 1897. As in the case of practical methods in politics generally, however, chief reliance must be placed on personal interviews for the actual workings of the system.

Democrats, Republicans, and Populists alike were forced to deal with the 'fluence man, and a recent sheriff of Bastrop County tells some interesting stories concerning his relations with the local negro bosses. One of the most important of these was John Whitley, a big mulatto who controlled more than his share of the negroes. Toward the end of the nineties John fell on evil days, and one of his creditors was forced to repossess his piano for non-payment of installments due on it. As they drove into town with it, another negro sized up the situation and called, "What's the matter, John? Takin' your piano?"

"Yes," replied John, "bad cotton this year has ruined me."

"Bad cotton, hell," jeered the questioner, "it was the Democratic primary that ruined you!"

John grinned wryly and turned to his companion. "You know," he observed, "that's the truth. If it hadn't been for that damn' primary I'd have paid out of debt this election!"

"And," adds the sheriff, "he would have."

People's Party.[60] The time, usually the night before election day, and the place of the meeting were noised about among the negroes beforehand, and in the afternoon of the appointed day they began to appear in squads of half a dozen or ten, some unaccompanied, others under the direction of party lieutenants who had gone out into the country and rounded them up. By dusk the number frequently had reached several hundred.

Meanwhile, the managers of the meeting had not been idle. Since early afternoon they had been busy barbecuing "yearlin's," and the pleasant odor of roasting beef that greeted the arriving guests but whetted their appetites, which were appeased temporarily by tantalizing sips of whisky from the omnipresent jug held in reserve. Eventually, the feast prepared, the negroes set to, carousing the whole night through in a veritable bacchanalian revel of food and drink. Their hosts provided roast beef in unlimited quantities; but they were careful not to be too generous with the jug, for there was yet work to be done.

The sequel of the owl meeting was seen when the revellers of the night before came down to the polling place to vote. They were prepared for the proper exercise of their sovereign right by their hosts, who lined them up before they left the scene of the feast and placed in their hands Populist ballots, folded into odd shapes sometimes to avoid possible confusion. Thus prepared, the colored electors approached the polling place, marching four abreast down the dusty road surrounded by white guards on horseback. Each guard, be it noted, rode with a Winchester across his lap, not so much to keep the negroes in line as to guarantee the company against the ever-present menace of interference by the Democratic leaders. Some distance from the voting place the march was halted. Additional white men appeared, and each took charge of two negroes, leading them to the ballot box. There they found the real "nigger man" of the party,[61] under whose direction the whole transaction had been planned and executed, who seized the proffered ballot, examined it to make certain of its genuineness, returned it

---

[60]The owl meeting was employed by all parties alike, and essentially the same tactics were used by all to gain the ends sought.

[61]A white leader who was adept at managing the colored voters frequently was referred to in conversation as a "nigger man."

to the voter to be deposited in the ballot box or deposited it there himself, and dropped into the outstretched palm the sum agreed upon as the market price of a negro vote, from ten cents to fifty cents, depending upon conditions. The sovereign, having spoken, turned away, his place to be taken by another brought from the constantly diminishing herd outside.[62]

The negro voter, then, demanded and ordinarily received special consideration. The 'fluence man cared for his share of the negro voters; others were rounded up in owl meetings and voted; armed force was resorted to now and again, either as such or as an adjunct of the nocturnal meeting; and for the stragglers who escaped these methods of mass voting individual jugs were planted in convenient brush-heaps near the polling place. There was, to be sure, a continual outcry by members of all parties against such methods, but they must be practiced nevertheless in those days by any who would succeed in the counties of East Texas, where the prosperity of the People's Party, as of all others, was measured directly in terms of the abilities of its local leaders to control the vote of the colored man.

The local and the state campaigns of the People's Party therefore were at variance in several respects. Fundamentally, the two were meant to serve different purposes. The state campaign was designed primarily to convince the voters of the iniquity of the Democrats and the justice of the Populist cause, the local actually to bring them out and cause them to vote for the candidates of the party. Both were highly important functions, the latter not less so than the former. As between the two, the work of the state organization appears to have been done more thoroughly, though it was not without serious limitations. In the field of the local campaign the party usually was forced to yield to the Democrats, though it was

---

[62]The owl meeting and its sequel here described was rather more pretentious than was usually found. Oftentimes, instead of several hundred guests at these meetings, there were no more than twenty or twenty-five. In every instance, however, the tactics were essentially those here described.

As in the case of the 'fluence man, the newspapers were loath to speak openly of the owl meeting and forced voting, though specific references to both may be found in the *Daily Sentinel*, Nov. 2, 7, 1900, and *The Weekly Sentinel*, Nov. 21, 1900 (in the office of the *Sentinel*, Nacogdoches, Texas).

precisely in those districts where it was able to wage intensive campaigns that it achieved its greatest successes.

III

An examination of the propaganda campaign of the People's Party, both peace time and election, reveals several leading themes upon which the spokesmen of the party delighted to dwell. In the first place, they discoursed at every opportunity on the subject of "hard times." As examples of this kind of propaganda, the *Advance* ran a column every week headed "PROSPERITY (?) IN BUSINESS IN TEXAS" in which were listed the business failures recently reported in the State;[63] it featured stories of starvation and suicide caused from lack of employment;[64] it dwelt at length on drouths, five-cent cotton, and other misfortunes of the tiller of the soil—it was, in short, a "calamity howler," and it was joined in its lamentations by virtually every spokesman of Reform in the State. The conclusion was not always definitely stated, but the inference usually was plainly to be seen that the Democratic Party, and more especially "the old beast of Buzzard's Bay,"[65] was responsible for the woes of the people.

Secondly, the Populist managers frequently accused the Democrats of misfeasance or worse outright dishonesty in office. To instance, the junketing trips occasionally taken by the State Legislature laid the dominant party open to criticism even among its own supporters, and the Populists did not fail to capitalize the opportunity offered.[66] Again, it was asserted that in the Mexican counties of South Texas school teachers were hired, not on the basis of their training for their profession, but for their ability to hold the Mexican voters in line with the Democracy. Many of

---

[63]To illustrate, see its issue of Dec. 2, 1893.

[64]See its issue of June 30, 1894.

[65]President Cleveland, so called because of his occasional trips to his home on Buzzard's Bay.

[66]*Dallas Morning News*, March 17, 19, 1895; *The Southern Mercury*, Sept. 1, 1898; *The Weekly News*, Oct. 27, 1898. *The Weekly News* article consists of a letter from a Populist member of the Legislature describing a trip to Galveston by members of that body on which all accommodations, including wine, women, and song, were alleged to be furnished free of charge.

these so-called teachers, it was charged, could not even read and write the English language.[67]   There was no dearth of information and rumor on which to base hundreds of similar charges, and the Populist strategists worked early and late preparing material of this nature for the use of their speakers and their press.

Thirdly, they charged their adversaries with employment of corrupt campaign methods, nor was it difficult to produce evidence which seemed to substantiate the charge.   For example, there was the signed statement issued by Stump Ashby toward the end of the campaign of 1896 to the effect that the Democrats, through their campaign manager, Blake, had offered him $1,000 to withdraw from the race and to assign as his reason a perfidious sell-out by the Reform leaders which made it impossible for him to continue as a candidate of the party.[68]   The Democrats, of course, denied the charge with vehemence.[69]   The relative merits of the Populist and the Democratic stands cannot be assessed accurately on the basis of the information available, but fortunately it is not necessary to evaluate the truth of the charge to note its nature as a theme entering into the campaign propaganda of the People's Party.

Finally may be noted the indictment charging the Democrats with what Cyclone Davis called "fraud, forgery, falsehood, and fiction" in the holding of elections. Something of the alleged evil practices may be seen from the complaints on which Davis and Kearby based their contests for seats in Congress in 1895.[70]   The term "Harrison County methods" came into general use to designate the practices in question, for in that county droves of mules, negroes dead for twenty years, persons whose names were taken from an old city directory of San Antonio, and such notables as Jefferson Davis, Samuel J. Tilden, and Alexander Stephens allegedly were

---

[67]*The Southern Mercury*, Oct. 15, 1896.

[68]See *ibid.*, Oct. 29, 1896.   The elections were held on the Tuesday after the first Monday in November.

[69]The truth of the accusation appeared to be guaranteed by a statement issued by Blake's alleged agent, over the seal of a notary public, in which he confessed to his part in the transaction and by the fact that Ashby did deposit in a Dallas bank to Blake's account the sum of $500 which, as he explained, he had accepted as a tangible evidence of the deal.

[70]*Dallas Morning News*, Jan. 13, 16, 1895.

allowed to vote.[71] Now and again a Democratic partisan rose to refute Populist charges of fraud and corruption, but for the most part they were ignored completely. The simple facts were, the Democratic managers had concluded not to accept defeat in important elections, and the employment of such tactics as seemed necessary to maintain the position of the dominant party was condoned almost universally by its adherents and sympathizers.[72]

Now the men of the Reform Party took their politics seriously. The "gay nineties" of the cities of the North and East were the "starvation nineties" for the Texas farmer who therefore approached the task of alleviating his ills with a grimness which boded ill for any who crossed his path. On the other hand, there was the Democratic Party enjoying a position of confidence and power which, its followers insisted, must be maintained at all costs. In short, both parties were determined to gain their ends, and both were willing to go to almost any extremes to advance their cause.

Under these conditions one might have forecast the situation which developed. The spirit of tolerance, if also of impatience, in which the old guard viewed the incipient Reform movement grew to be one of irritability as the Populist legions returned ever more vigorously to the charge and eventually to one of outright antipathy when that party refused to learn its place and remain in it. Similarly the proponents of Reform, at first doubtful of their proper course, accepted the People's Party in a spirit which progressed from one almost of simple resignation to one which held that party to be the champion of undying principles. When the two parties had reached their respective poles, politics ceased to be bound by the ordinary rules of party warfare. On their part, the Populist professed to have discovered that their non-rural neighbors had presumed to set the "town gang" on a somewhat higher plane than that occupied by themselves. Hence social castes developed, and People's Party

---

[71] *The Southern Mercury,* Oct. 15, 22, 1896.

[72] To illustrate the attitudes alluded to, the author may state that he has interviewed at least a score of old-time politicians of some prominence who were personally acquainted with the contest between Cyclone Davis and David B. ("Old Dave") Culberson for Congress in 1894. Among these men, of whom as many were adherents of the Democratic as of the Third Party, he has not found one Populist to fail to charge questionable practices on the part of Culberson's managers nor one Democrat to deny the charge.

men came to be distinguished by their brothers as something more than fortuitous bedfellows in politics. When they came to town on Saturday, they patronized Populist merchants.[73] They hired Populist school teachers, frequently inquiring into a pedagogue's politics before ascertaining his professional qualifications.[74] In short, Populist principles became a moral code which regulated their every action, and the People's Party, as the defender of those principles, came to be worthy of their best efforts always and especially at campaign time.

The Democrats, naturally enough, answered in kind. The Third Party became in their eyes the place of refuge of political cranks, chronic dissenters, and ne'er-do-wells, and they lost all patience with it. Tiring of the recurrent attacks of Reform speakers, they occasionally lent color to their appearances by egging them from the platform.[75] Populist laborers found it difficult to obtain work in Democratic communities;[76] workmen occasionally were discharged because of their political beliefs;[77] Democratic merchants and wholesalers boycotted Reform mercantile establishments—in short, the spirit of bitterness among Democrats matched that present among Third Partyites, manifesting itself especially at campaign time. The campaign waxed warmer and warmer as the day of election approached, with repeated threats of violence passed between the partisans, and with recourse to direct action that occasionally led to gun-play which first and last claimed the lives of several men from both parties. To such ends did party strife bring the people of Texas during the hectic days of Populism.

---

[73]In Lampasas a People's Party Meat Market was established. *The People's Journal*, Sept. 9, 1892 (in the Library of The University of Texas, Austin, Texas). There were, of course, numerous Alliance stores throughout the State.

[74]*The Palo Pinto County Star*, Aug. 13, 1892.

[75]*The Southern Mercury*, June 18, 1896.

[76]Joseph Weldon Bailey, long a member of Congress from Texas, boycotted Populist laborers on a new home which he built in Gainesville in 1895. When asked about the affair, Bailey readily admitted the truth of the charge, justifying his position on the ground that 90 per cent of the Populists were liars! *The Gainesville Signal*, Sept. 4, 11, 1895.

[77]Prison guards were discharged at the state penitentiaries at Huntsville and Rusk, allegedly because of their affiliations with the People's Party. *Texas Advance*, July 28, 1894; *The Southern Mercury*, April 16, Oct. 1, 1896.

A comparison of the tactics employed by the Third Party with those used by the Democrats reveals that notwithstanding the seeming adequacy of Populist techniques, the old party enjoyed advantages which conspired to give it a very great handicap in the matter of propaganda, as judged by the practical standard of results obtained. First, it is necessary to note the position of dominance occupied by the Democrats, the significance of which cannot easily be overestimated. Psychologically, the Democratic traditions of the State placed the Third Party under a serious disadvantage. In the realm of practical politics continuous control of the Government had secured to the old party control also of the spoils of office, so that the Populist managers were deprived of the assistance of those party "workers," comprising the office-holders and all those who benefit from the régime of the successful party, whose services are so vital a factor in fashioning a winning campaign. Secondly, the Democratic Party enjoyed a decided advantage in the field of finance. The simple fact was that the Democrats commanded large funds for party uses, while the party of Reform found its activities circumscribed on every hand by lack of money. Adherents to Populism would make almost any sacrifice in the way of service to their party, but they would not contribute to its treasury for the reason that they had no money. If this fact be borne in mind, one will have readily at hand a satisfactory explanation for many of the shortcomings of the Populist campaigns—for the glaring error, for example, of conceding without a struggle the Mexican counties of South Texas with their many thousands of votes. Thirdly, the People's Party labored under a heavy handicap in the matter of local leadership. No matter how well planned and executed a campaign of propaganda, its effect is nullified in good part unless there be managers at the level of the county capable of getting out the vote; and while the old party had enough such managers to meet its needs, the new had too few.[78] Finally, the Third Party was kept constantly on the defensive by virtue of the superiority of the Democratic over the Reform press, a factor of the utmost significance presently to be examined.[79] At these points, then, did the

---

[78]See *supra*, Chap. V.

[79]*Infra*, Chap. VIII.

Democrats enjoy advantages which enabled them to cope with the best efforts of the People's Party and to continue in the position of dominance which they had so long occupied.

It appears, from our analysis of the propaganda technique and campaign methods of the People's Party, that the cause of Populism was well attended to in the realm of tactics. In time of peace, the Populist managers fostered an unceasing campaign which stressed educational and emotional appeals in almost equal parts. As an effective summation of this campaign came the campmeeting, which brought the Populist educator and the Reform preacher together as joint directors of a week-long People's Party carnival. In consequence of the vigor and thoroughness of the day-to-day labors of the Populist missionaries, the election campaign entailed no great additional hardships on the party's managers. In their contests for state offices, they had only to accelerate the normal activities of Reform spokesmen to produce an aggressive campaign. In local politics an occasional situation could be met successfully only by recourse to direct action. The Populist directors, driven by what appeared to be necessity, attempted to adapt their methods to the requirements of the occasion, succeeding only to an extent which emphasized the significance of the rôle of the local manager.

The techniques employed gave to the People's Party, considered apart, the appearance of a threatening movement. And indeed, one familiar with Populism as it was practiced by the rank and file of the party will not minimize the spirit of sacrifice and selflessness in which the "forgotten man" of the nineties sought redress through Reform. Rather will he marvel at the methods by which the Third Party was lifted from the level of workaday politics and re-cast to such effect that party became at once social club, fraternal order, and church. What is important in practical politics, however, is not absolute effectiveness but relative strength. Strong in itself, the party of Populism faced an adversary which manifold advantages combined to make stronger and which therefore was able to turn back its attacks in spite of a propaganda and campaign technique in many respects without parallel in the history of the State.

CHAPTER VIII

THE REFORM PRESS

THE REFORM PRESS is properly considered in close relation to the subject of propaganda and campaign technique. It is, indeed, inseparable from a complete study of that phase of Populist activities, for the Reform journal shared responsibilities in the field of propaganda with the speaker and the author. It was not for the press to play a sensational role—that was reserved for such showmen as Cyclone Davis, who drew flaming word pictures of Populism that caught the fancy of the whole nation. Albeit one might expect always to find the Third Party newspaper, a ubiquitous if unassuming little sheet which found its way into thousands of homes and performed there, silently and without display, services of inestimable value to the party.

People's Party journalism may be examined with advantage from two primary points of view. It is of interest to investigate first the Reform papers themselves, with an eye to discovering the part taken by the Third Party in furthering their scope and effectiveness, their nature, and the problems with which they were called upon to deal. The second phase of the subject demands a description of the press campaign and an evaluation of the services performed by the Reform press. But it is necessary, before proceeding to an examination of these matters, to look briefly at the Alliance background of Third Party journalism.

In the field of the press, as in other important directions, the People's Party was the legatee of the Farmers' Alliance. The heart of the Alliance press was the official organ of the order, *The Southern Mercury*, which was published weekly at Dallas under the editorship of Milton Park.[1] The *Mercury* from the beginning was an excellent organ of its kind: it was confessedly a propaganda

---

[1] For some interesting facts concerning the history of the *Mercury* and the method by which it was controlled, see *The Southern Mercury*, April 19, 1888; the *Dallas Morning News*, Aug. 19, 1891.

Sam H. Dixon served as editor of the *Mercury* until 1891, when, choosing the wrong side of the subtreasury quarrel, he was relieved of his duties and Park was appointed in his stead.

journal, but so long as it remained purely the mouthpiece of the Alliance it was able to keep its columns free from the taint of extreme partisanship. Its popularity may be judged from the size of its subscription list which in 1890 contained the names of 26,000 persons scattered throughout the State.[2]

Supporting the *Mercury* was a weekly press which, while not strong in numbers, bade fair to develop into an Alliance bulwark by virtue of. its staunchness and its enthusiasm in the cause. In 1890, there were no more than eight weekly journals devoted to the farmers' fraternity, and they were published in seven different counties concentrated largely in the northern part of the State. All were strong in the faith, however, defending their order with a vigor which seemed to belie the paucity of their numbers.[3] By 1892 the number had increased by more than twice, ten new papers having been added;[4] but thereafter it fell steadily, both from actual deaths among its members and from defections to the Populist press.[5] The Alliance weeklies did not, therefore, at any time constitute a considerable percentage of the total journals of the State, though doubtless they would have increased in numbers had not the Third Party arisen to command their allegiance.[6]

---

[2]*American Newspaper Annual*, 1890 (N. W. Ayer & Son, Philadelphia). In the Texas section of this volume may be found much valuable information pertaining to newspapers of the State for the year indicated. It is not complete in every instance, but the *Annual* nevertheless is the best and most reliable source for a study of such facts relating to newspapers as their date of establishment, political affiliation, and circulation, and frequent reference will be made to it in the pages following.

[3]Numerically their efforts were inconsequential as compared with those of 529 non-Alliance journals of the State. *Loc. cit.*

[4]*Ibid.*, 1892.

[5]In 1895, there were only ten bonafide Alliance newspapers in the State, and by 1901 the number had shrunk to two. *Ibid.*, 1895, 1901.

[6]About the first of the year 1891 an association of Alliance and other independent editors was organized under the name of the National Reform Press Association. *The Southern Mercury*, Jan. 22, 1891; Feb. 27, 1896. The "N.R.P.A." subsequently became an organization of considerable influence and importance. *Infra.*

I

The People's Party from its very birth was deeply interested in the development of the Reform press, whose core it found in the Alliance journals. This interest was manifested early when a committee of five was appointed to "devise ways and means looking to the development and establishment on a permanent and satisfactory basis of the newspaper interests of the party throughout the State of Texas."[7] Thomas Gaines, editor of the *Pioneer Exponent* of Comanche, was named executive head of the committee. Gaines made appointments at once throughout the State to meet those interested locally in Reform newspaper work and discuss with them the possibilities of setting up local Populist journals.[8]

From recognition of the propaganda value of support by an active party press, it was but a step to the conclusion that the welfare of Populism required the founding of a state organ. A preliminary survey seemed to reveal the practicability of the project, and subsequent negotiation resulted in the establishment in Fort Worth of the *Texas Advance*, a confessedly partisan Populist daily.[9] Within the space of a few weeks the *Advance* was beset by serious financial difficulties which soon became so acute that its manager was forced to appeal to the publisher of *The Southern Mercury*, Harry Tracy, to save the journal from suspension of publication. Tracy rose to the occasion, agreeing to move the *Advance* to Dallas and continue it as a weekly Third Party journal.[10] Ere long, however, the early

---

[7] *The People's Journal*, Dec. 16, 1892.

[8] See, for a notice of such a meeting, the *Hempstead Weekly News*, March 9, 1893.

[9] The tireless Tom Gaines had sponsored the launching, early in 1892, of the *Fort Worth Advance*, which he proposed to run in the interest of the People's Party; and when the managers of that party addressed themselves to the task of setting up an official Populist organ, he listened willingly to the suggestion that the *Advance* be converted into that organ. See, for the founding and early history of the *Advance*, the *Dallas Morning News*, May 14, 1892; *Fort Worth Daily Gazette*, March 18, Oct. 5, 1893; *The Palo Pinto County Star*, March 4, 1893; *Texas Advance*, June 30, 1894; and *The Southern Mercury*, Jan. 3, 1895.

[10] The transactions whereby title to the journal passed to the publisher of the *Mercury* were set forth in summary in *Texas Advance*, June 30, 1894. See also *The Galveston Daily News*, Aug. 20, 1893.

history of the paper began to be traced again. The support freely promised failed to materialize; the period of stringency, thought to be temporary, proved permanent; and eventually the new publisher was forced to abandon the enterprise.[11] In the instance of the second failure of the *Advance* the party was fortunate in this respect: there was ready at hand a second journal, the *Southern Mercury,* with which the expiring organ could be amalgamated without much loss of advantage to the cause which it served. For a year the two papers were published side by side; then the *Advance* was eased gently out of the picture, and the *Mercury* became the official organ at once of the Alliance and the People's Party,[12] a position which it retained to the end of the century. Both the *Advance* and the *Mercury* filled excellently the place they were designed to fill as Populist organs. The former never knew a policy which was not strictly partisan, for it was from the beginning designedly a party mouthpiece. The latter, as an Alliance journal, originally was nonpartisan, though never at a loss for vigorous terms in which to couch the desires of its principal. With its succession to the position previously occupied by the *Advance,* it threw off the cloak of nonpartisanship and became as staunchly Populist as it had been Alliance. The cause of Populism, therefore, appears not to have suffered from lack of an effective state organ.

Notwithstanding the failure of the daily *Advance* in 1893 and the excellence of the services performed by the *Mercury* as a Populist weekly, the cry for a People's Party daily was never stilled. In 1895 the matter was raised by semi-official spokesmen of the party, who held a series of conferences to effectuate the founding of such a journal. Harry Tracy, of the *Mercury,* was in no sense enthusiastic over the enterprise, but when his colleagues persisted he submitted a plan to convert his paper into a daily. His offer was accepted, and the initial issue of the *Daily Southern Mercury* was scheduled to appear about February 15, 1896. Even after the negotiations had reached this stage, however, Tracy continued to hold

---

[11]The tale of woe of the publisher may be seen unfolding in the columns of the journal throughout the year 1894. See especially the issues of June 30 and July 7, 1894.

[12]The editorial page of the first issue of the *Mercury* for 1895 reveals its new position as the defender of both causes.

back, in the end refusing, or neglecting, to go through with the agreement.[13] Hence the Populist daily, seemingly assured to the very date set for its first issue, failed to materialize, and the *Mercury* continued to operate as a weekly.

If the enthusiasm of the Populist leaders for the press led to a number of efforts, most of them ill-judged, to establish a state organ, the work of Tom Gaines in the youth of Populism and the repeated advices of the spokesmen of Reform encouraged the local

TABLE XII

TEXAS NEWSPAPERS IN 1895*

	All papers	Farmers' Alliance papers	People's Party papers
Number of counties	245	---	---
Number of counties in which papers were published	192	10	70
Number of towns in which papers were published	368	10	72
Number of towns which were county seats	185	5	48
Number of papers issued daily	59	----	----
Number of papers issued tri-weekly	2	----	----
Number of papers issued semi-weekly	17	---	---
Number of papers issued weekly	621	10	75
Number of papers issued fortnightly	1	----	----
Number of papers issued semi-monthly	3	----	----
Number of papers issued bi-monthly	---	----	----
Number of papers issued quarterly	1	---	---
Total papers all types	704	10	75

*Data from Ayer's *American Newspaper Annual*, 1895.

leaders to set up scores of smaller Reform papers. In 1892, when the party was yet very young, only four weeklies were listed as Populist in their political preferences, though there were seventeen Alliance journals to plead the cause of Reform.[14] The number increased at a remarkable rate during the next few years, however, so that in 1895, when the Third Party movement may be considered to have reached its peak, no less than eighty-five Reform papers were reported, seventy-five of them confessedly Populist and ten standing by the Alliance.[15] They were published in eighty different counties reaching from the Red River south to the Gulf and west

---

[13]See *The Southern Mercury*, Jan. 3, 1895; *Dallas Morning News*, Feb. 20, 26, and March 21, 1895; and *The Galveston Daily News*, Jan. 11, 1896.

[14]*American Newspaper Annual*, 1892.

[15]Compare these numbers with those which measured the strength of the non-Reform press. See Table XII.

to Fisher County. Their nature may be seen from the fact that of the seventy-five out-and-out Populist papers, fifty-five had come into existence since 1892;[16] they were, that is to say, set up for the express purpose of advancing the interests of the Third Party. From 1895 forward the strength of the Reform press decreased steadily. Thus in 1901 there remained thirty-six weekly papers, only two of which were Alliance organs. Of the thirty-four Populist journals, seventeen were in operation in 1895, while a like number had been established since that date.[17] The figures revealed a decline both in the actual strength of the Reform press and in the interest taken by the Third Party men in newspaper work, and they portended the total extinction of the Reform journal at no distant date.

The figures introduced must not be taken as definitive of the strength or nature of the local Reform press. Indeed that press cannot be and could not at the time have been measured with strict accuracy because of its opportunist character. Frequently a paper was set in operation on the initiative of an individual with no training and no financial backing and published until circumstances demanded its suspension. Frequently again an individual undertook the publication of a local paper at the request of friends of Reform who promised to support the venture to the extent of their ability.[18] Yet again there was organized occasionally a joint stock company which proceeded to set up a paper and to retain the services of a publisher and an editor.[19] Finally, Democratic weeklies sometimes granted to the Alliance a column for the news of that order, and once in a great while such a journal carried a two- or three-column section under the heading, "Populist Department."[20] In the instance of the

---

[16]*American Newspaper Annual*, 1895. The twenty remaining had operated in 1892 as Populist, Farmers' Alliance, Democratic, independent, or local papers.
[17]*Ibid.*, 1901.
[18]See, for instances of where local Populist clubs took the initiative in considering the founding of Reform papers, the *Dallas Morning News*, Jan. 20, 1893, and the *Beeville Weekly Picayune*, Dec. 15, 1894 (in the Library of The University of Texas, Austin, Texas).
[19]*The Texas Triangle* (Paris, Texas) was published with the financial support of a joint stock company. See the issue of that paper of Oct. 7, 1898 (in the Library of The University of Texas, Austin, Texas).
[20]A "Populist Department" appeared in the *Hempstead Weekly News* for the duration of the campaign of 1894. It began with the issue of May 17, 1894, and ended with that of Nov. 22.

adoption of any of these plans, the life of the paper was hazardous in the extreme. Now and again a journal was founded for the sole purpose of serving the party during the campaign period, or of performing a special function in behalf of Reform,[21] though the great majority endeavored to place themselves on a permanent footing. The Populist weekly therefore might last for a few weeks or for several years,[22] and its name might be changed three or four times in efforts to give to it a wider appeal or to eliminate unpleasant recollections to which the old title might give rise. In any event, it faced almost certain death eventually, for its editor usually came to the prospect of financial ruin. If he escaped that fate, he found himself in the late nineties groping for a cause to take the place of the People's Party. If the circumstances under which the Populist press labored be kept in mind, it is a matter for no wonder that almost none of the old Reform weeklies have survived to the present day.[23]

In physical appearance the local Reform journal was typical of the usual country newspaper. It contained ordinarily four or eight pages of five, six, or seven columns each; and while the form varied from paper to paper, it might be expected usually, in the case for example of the four-page paper, that the first page would consist of plate material concerning matters of general interest, the second and third would carry "home print" material, the former filled largely with editorials and the latter with local news items, and the fourth would be plate again, with most of the advertisements found there. It appeared usually on Thursday or Friday; its subscription rate was $1.00 per year, occasionally more or less; its circulation rarely reached more than 1,000 weekly, frequently dropping

---

[21]For example, Thomas B. King established a Reform paper, a semi-monthly, at Stephenville (Erath County), devoted exclusively to the cause of direct legislation. *The Southern Mercury*, Nov. 11, 1897.

[22]*The People's Party Herald*, established at Beeville in 1895, lasted for two weekly issues. *Beeville Weekly Picayune*, Nov. 28, Dec. 12, 1895.

The Populist *Corpus Christi Globe*, founded in 1894, enjoyed a somewhat longer life than the *Herald*, but it met a violent end concerning which there was considerable speculation in the Democratic press. *The Beeville Bee*, Oct. 18, 1894.

[23]Notable exceptions are found in *The Dublin Progress*, the *Gainesville Signal*, and the *Hallettsville New Era*, which, vigorous champions of the Third Party forty years ago, continue to enjoy a healthy circulation.

below that figure; and its editor normally served also as publisher, performing all duties connected with the journal, with the aid, occasionally, of an assistant.

The Third Party paper, it may be surmised, traveled a rocky path. The *Advance* and the *Mercury*, set somewhat apart from the typical Reform journal by reason of their size, found themselves confronted on occasion by peculiar difficulties.[24] A majority of the problems attendant upon the Reform press, however, came to the publishers of all such journals alike, whether great or small. Of the problems common to all, the most difficult by all odds involved the question of finance. The Reform paper ordinarily was boycotted by those who purchased advertising space, and its publisher therefore failed to tap the most lucrative source of income available to the press. In vain did the editor of the ostracized paper inveigh against the handicap placed upon him by his political antagonists: he was denied an appreciable income from advertising to the end, which was hastened by virtue of that denial.[25]

A second source of income available to the publisher is found in subscription funds, which are valuable as a supplement to advertising. Thus when advertising failed to produce a living wage for the Reform journal, whether state or local, its publisher now and again launched a subscription campaign to win new readers—and contributors—for the paper.[26] The state journals were especially zealous in their pursuit of new subscribers, and with good reason, for on the one hand their expenses were greater and on the other their income from advertising was less comparatively than in the case of the local weekly. Hence they appointed agents who

---

[24]For example, in 1894 those journals engaged in a controversy with the Dallas Typographical Union over a labor problem which would never have risen to plague the publisher of a smaller paper. See the *Fort Worth Daily Gazette*, June 20, 21, 23, 1894; the *Dallas Morning News*, June 20, 21, 1894; and the *Texas Advance*, June 30, July 14, and Aug. 11, 1894.

An end eventually was put to the matter which satisfied all parties, but not until the quarrel had called down upon the cause of Reform a great deal of unfavorable comment.

[25]The problem of advertising, as it appeared to the Reform journal, was discussed frequently by the *Texas Advance*. See especially its issues of Dec. 9, 1893, and July 7 and Aug. 18, 1894.

[26]See, for example, *The Young Populist*, Sept. 27, 1894.

sought new readers throughout the State; they offered club rates; and they gave premiums for new subscribers ranging in value from a special "Mercury" sewing machine down through shotgun, watch, and corn sheller to such Reform books as *Coin's Financial School*.[27] The state authorities of the party joined in the hue and cry, charging their local representatives to solicit subscriptions to the journals and urging Populists everywhere to lose no opportunity to increase their circulation.[28]

Despite all efforts the Reform journals were faced constantly with the prospect of being forced to suspend because of financial difficulties. On those occasions when subscription obligations were due but unpaid, the publisher ordinarily agreed to carry the debts over for a period, contenting himself with an editorial reminder of the sums due him.[29] Thus over a period of years the paper allowed accounts to accumulate which totaled sometimes several thousands of dollars. Eventually the publisher found it necessary to call for the payment of these obligations, on pain of suspending publication unless considerable sums of money were raised at once. It was then that he learned that his constituency, while willing to acknowledge the debt, was not willing, or able, actually to pay the petty sums of two, three, or four dollars which had accumulated against it during the last several years. He came to realize finally that he was faced with financial ruin, and the most pathetic articles which appeared in his paper were those desperate appeals for aid penned by him in recognition of his plight.[30]

Next in importance to the problem of finance in the life of the Reform journal was that presented by the editor himself.[31] The problem here was confined to the local papers, for the editor of

---

[27]*Texas Advance*, Nov. 4, Nov. 23, 1893; Feb. 24, July 7, 1894; *The Southern Mercury*, Dec. 5, 1895; Sept. 8, 1898.

[28]*Texas Advance*, Sept. 16, Oct. 14, 1893.

[29]Many subscribers, we may surmise, simply had not the funds with which to make good their promises. See *The Southern Mercury*, March 26, 1896.

[30]See, for examples of such editorial appeals for sustenance, the *Texas Advance*, July 7, 1894; the *Gainesville Signal*, Nov. 28, 1894; and *The Weekly News*, May 12, Nov. 10, 1898.

[31]The author endeavors to employ the terms *editor* and *publisher* according as he wishes to emphasize the editorial aspect of newspaper work or the mechanical and business end of that work. Ordinarily these persons were one

the *Advance* and the *Mercury* was a professional newspaper man, and both his reputation as a journalist and his ability were unquestioned. The same might not be said truthfully of the editor of the local weekly, however, for as often as not he was not fitted for his place by capacity, aptitude, training, or inclination. His amateur character and opportunist nature are revealed by a brief examination of the journalistic career of the typical editor. In 1895, there were ninety-four individual names listed as those of editors or publishers of the eighty-five Reform journals. Of that number, only twelve had been in newspaper work (in Texas) for as much as five years, while seventy had enjoyed a professional career of less than three years;[32] only some 12 per cent, or, placing a very liberal interpretation on the term, 25 per cent, might be classified as professional journalists. Nothing serves so well to reveal the itinerant character of the Populist editor, or the ephemeral nature of the Reform press.

There were, of course, exceptions to the general rule, for there were editors in the ranks of the Reformers who were both experienced in newspaper work and interested in the field of journalism as such.[33] These editors formed the nucleus of the Texas Reform Press Association, founded in 1893, an organization which included at its height over 100 Reform newspaper men, though not more than some 30 per cent of these were active in its work. It met annually, and part of the regular business was the hearing of papers and discussions by the members on such subjects as the German Reform press, plate service, advertising problems, circulation, religion and the press, politics and the press, etc., etc. Apart from the program, the Association considered such problems as were raised by its members, providing through this means a clearing house of information and ideas which proved of great value to those

---

and the same man, as is attested by the fact that the *Newspaper Annual* for 1895 lists the names of only ninety-four men as editors and publishers of eighty-five journals.

[32]*American Newspaper Annual*, 1890, 1892, 1895. The figures quoted were arrived at by tracing the name of every man mentioned in 1895 back through the volumes for 1892 and 1890.

[33]See the *Dallas Morning News*, May 10, 1893.

who took part in the meetings.[34] Above the Association, and forming a larger body of which the Texas organization was a section, was the National Reform Press Association, whose annual meetings were largely attended by the active portion of the Texas Association. The National Association performed functions for the Reform press at large similar to those performed in the states by its various sections, and in the later years of the Third Party it continued to provide a spark of life when everything else seemed to point to the early death of the Reform movement.[35]

In spite of this effort to develop among Reform editors a trade-conscious spirit, the fact remains that most of them were opportunists taken from other walks of life. As the president of their association put it, most of them would have been more at home had their editorial weapons been the plow and the hoe instead of the pen.[36] But, he added in the same breath, able or not, they had been forced to take up journalism as a means of defending the workingman and to perform to the best of their ability the tasks imposed upon them. This, in brief, reflected the spirit in which a great majority of the local Reform journals were launched. Circumstances usually conspired to condemn such a journal to a short life, but not for long was it allowed to remain silent. The very fluidity of Populist journalistic talent meant that presently another publisher would appear with sufficient capital, actual or promised, to launch the venture anew, whereupon the cycle would begin again. Thus one paper began where another left off, though as the years passed the resurrections became fewer and further apart until by the end of the century they disappeared entirely.

II

When one turns from an examination of the Reform press as such to a study of the propaganda technique developed by it, one enters

---

[34]The Texas Reform Press Association was mentioned frequently in the pages of the *Advance* and the *Mercury*. See especially the *Advance*, Feb. 3, April 14, June 30, 1894; and the *Mercury*, Jan. 24, April 11, June 6, 1895; April 15, May 20, Nov. 11, 1897; May 26, June 16, 1898; and May 18, 1899.

[35]For notices of the National Reform Press Association, see *The Southern Mercury*, Feb. 7, 28, 1895; Feb. 27, 1896; Feb. 25, March 4, 1897; and May 25, 1899.

[36]*Ibid.*, June 6, 1895.

into a most significant field of investigation. What was the exact extent numerically of the appeal of the press cannot be determined, but it is of interest to recall that, at the height of the Third Party movement, there were more than 100 Reform weeklies in existence.[37] Among these the *Mercury* stood out with its 40,000 subscribers. The local weeklies boasted, on an average, not more than 800 or 1,000 subscribers, which gave them a total weekly circulation of not less than 80,000.[38] It would seem, therefore, that the Reform press at its peak reached some 120,000 readers each week; and if allowance be made for duplications, the figure 75,000 would seem not to be high. This figure assumes additional significance when it is remembered that the total vote cast in the State for Governor in 1894 was only 420,000, and in 1896 some 540,000. Thus it appears that Reform journals combined to reach 15 to 20 per cent of the voters with every issue. It is not too much to say, therefore, that as a medium for reaching the voters frequently and in large numbers the Populist journal was unsurpassed.

The interest early manifested by the strategists of the Third Party in the Reform press led them to take steps to coördinate the Populist weeklies as agents for the propagation of the faith of Reform. Thus the party's newspaper committee was commissioned to arrange with a publishing company to furnish Populist ready prints for the time being, meanwhile proceeding to organize a People's Party newspaper union whose function it would be to print and distribute to the weekly papers political matter, under the direction of a committee of Populist editorial writers.[39] The committee's efforts to

---

[37]*The American Newspaper Annual* for 1895 listed only eighty-five Reform journals, but not every such journal in the State was reported there. The President of the Texas Reform Press Association announced in 1895 that his organization had more than 100 members (*The Southern Mercury*, June 6, 1895), and the *Galveston News* reported that there were more than 125 Populist papers in the State (June 20, 1894). The figure 100 thus appears conservative.

[38]The Reform editor was very reticent concerning the circulation of his paper, but from the few returns made to the *Newspaper Annual* we may surmise that the average circulation was not more than 1,000.

[39]*Fort Worth Daily Gazette*, March 19, 1893; *The Galveston Daily News*, Dec. 31, 1892; Jan. 1, 21, 1893.

"Ready Prints" are found where a central agency, as a publishing firm, undertakes to set up and print a portion of a local paper, as the first and

set up a new company failed completely;[40] but it was able to
perfect an arrangement whereby political material prepared by a
Populist editor was supplied to an established concern, which in
turn contracted with local weeklies to provide a ready print and
boiler plate service.[41]

The value to the People's Party of the arrangement whereby the
political matter which went into the Reform weeklies was written
and distributed by central agencies may readily be seen. It provided a means by which uniformity was introduced into the editorial policies of several scores of journals; in effect, it permitted
one editor, or mayhap a board of editors, chosen by the party and
therefore certified as to political staunchness, to fix the policies of
all the Reform papers subscribing to the service. It was therefore
almost as if the party had published one great newspaper; it was
almost as if the *Southern Mercury* had boasted a circulation of
100,000 instead of 40,000, so well regulated were the editorial
policies of the local journals.

Lest the significance of the editorial be underestimated, it is well
to note something of the type of material upon which the small
Reform newspaper depended to fill its columns. The most interesting fact to be recorded is the scarcity of news material properly

---

last pages, leaving the inside pages to be filled in by the subscriber to the
service with "home print" matter. The paper is shipped to the local editor
each week by express, with half of the editorial work already done.

The Western Newspaper Union, of Dallas, offered by advertisement to print
all of a local Populist paper, under the name chosen by the local publisher,
and to include such editorial and local matter as the editor might wish to
include. By clear implication, all other material necessary to fill the paper
would be furnished by the Union. *Texas Advance,* Nov. 23, 1893.

Under a somewhat different arrangement "boiler plate" material is furnished to the local editor by a central composing and distributing office. Here
the copy is cast into type in "galley" form and shipped by express to the
editor, who cuts it into such lengths as he finds convenient and arranges it
to suit his needs, printing the paper in his own shop.

[40]The Texas Reform Press Association in 1899 perfected plans for the
founding of the Texas Coöperative Printing Company and appointed Harry
Tracy to supervise their execution, but nothing further was heard of the proposed company. *The Southern Mercury,* May 18, 1899.

[41]The National Reform Press Association also appointed annually a ready
print editor whose articles were used widely by the Reform press. *The Southern Mercury,* May 25, 1899.

so-called. No effort was made to follow the course of events in general; the inside pages occasionally recorded items of local interest—there was a "Personal" column, for example, and a random account of an Alliance meeting—but even here the news value of the sheet was small. The historian finds distressingly few adequate comments on matters reckoned today to be of the first importance.

Not that the pages of the Populist weekly were barren of fruit for the reader of that day; on the contrary they were filled with matter considered to be of primary importance. But that matter was written chiefly for propaganda purposes and therefore assumed a distinctly editorial tone. Thus the editorials supplied from the central office assumed a special significance, for they influenced strongly the nature of the local paper. To the leading propaganda article and the column of "Populist Pointers" which appeared weekly through the boiler plate service, the editor added usually some brief editorials, oftentimes in the form of short paragraphs but occasionally of a more pretentious nature, from his own pen. In character, therefore, the editorial dictated the tone of the journal; in quantity it constituted perhaps one-half of all the matter printed there.[42]

Second only to the confessed editorial was the article contributed by the Third Party author. Such articles were submitted frequently, and the editor was always more than ready to print them if it proved feasible. Thus there appeared from time to time in the columns of the Reform journal brief treatises on such subjects as the initiative and referendum, the income tax, and government ownership. These articles might confine themselves to half a column, or they might reach a length of three columns or more. Whatever their length, they were written always with an eye single to their main purpose, namely the propagation of the faith of Reform and the defense of Populist principles.

---

[42]In a random number of the *Texas Herald,* a Populist paper, the author found, exclusive of advertisements, 100 column inches of matter pertaining directly to the People's Party or the Alliance, and much of it was of a confessedly editorial nature. Only thirty-one inches were given to items of general interest.

A random number of *The Weekly News,* a somewhat larger Third Party sheet, contained 141 inches of Populist propaganda and 189 inches of news of general interest.

Oftentimes the monotony was varied by the publication of letters from prominent Populists, which might treat of almost any subject pertaining to Populism. Not infrequently such a letter elicited a reply from one who differed from the views of its writer, who thereupon might consider it his duty to issue a rejoinder in his defense. Thus wordy wars often developed, and the question at hand was aired thoroughly by the partisans, who usually concluded hostilities in an armistice by the terms of which they professed to agree upon the fundamentals of the issue. The letter was much used by the editor of the small weekly, and indeed it served frequently as the vehicle for the article, which was not as much favored in the case of the country paper as in that of the *Advance* and the *Mercury*.

A special type of newspaper propaganda was found in the poem, which originated usually with some local bard whose zeal for the

---

A SPECIMEN OF POPULIST POETRY

POLITICAL DECEPTION*

You may cry protective tariff,
   Till you shout your very hair off,
And conditions will remain about the same;
   For it goes without the axin',
   Justice never comes by taxin',
And tariff tax is just another name.

You may make the laws quite dreary
   With free silver 'til you're weary,
And plutocratic robbery will not stop;
   For if money is not equal,
   No good will be the sequel,
The money grabbers still will be on top.

No use to shout and holler
   For a "sound and honest" dollar,
With a system based on robbery and theft;
   For 'tis gold appreciation
   That has pauperized the nation,
And the masses in the struggle have been left.

Then, voters, don't be fed on
   Bunco, and be led on,
But stop and think before it is too late;
   Give old party hacks a lick on
   The place where Tommy hit the chicken,
And vote the peoples party ticket straight.

---

*From *The Southern Mercury*, June 18, 1896.

cause, we may surmise from his efforts, was more deserving of commendation than the skill with which he put his thoughts into writing. Poems appeared with such regularity that they may be said to have constituted a characteristic feature of the Populist attack. They dealt with a variety of subjects, all having to do directly or indirectly with the Third Party. As works of literature they left much to be desired; but as verses having a purely propaganda purpose they filled a place of some significance in the Reform journal. A second special type of appeal, sharing interest with the poem, was the cartoon. The cartoon usually originated with the plate supply house which presumably retained the services of a cartoonist to produce drawings either on the demand or with the consent of the ready print editor. As contrasted with the poem, which recurred constantly, the cartoon appeared only during the course of the campaign. The two were alike in that both sought to further the interests of Populism by picturing the hopelessness of the current order or the corruption of the old parties or the spirit of service of the Third Party. Neither effected many conversions to the cause, it may be supposed, but both were of some importance in buttressing in pleasing ways the arguments set forth in the serious defenses of Reform principles.

What has been said regarding the propaganda technique of the Reform press has been assumed thus far to be applicable to all Populist journals, large and small alike. The *Advance* and the *Mercury*, however, placed themselves by their policies in a category sufficiently different from that of the small weekly to merit brief mention in their own right. First, they made little use of the plate service and none of the ready print. Instead, their editorials as such were written by or under the direction of their own editor. Secondly, they printed numerous semi-formal articles which sometimes were continued serially through several issues. Again, fewer letters appeared in their columns than in those of their local contemporaries. As regards the poem and the cartoon, the state journals resorted to them quite as frequently as the local, and for the latter they subscribed to the Populist plate service. Despite these differences, the *Advance* and the *Mercury* were substantially similar in

Culberson—I knew there was a storm coming, but didn't think it would amount to a cyclone. Our only safety, boys, is in the cyclone cellar.

From *The Southern Mercury,* June 11, 1896.

policy to the typical Reform journal.[43]   In the matter of staunchness and zeal, they probably were even more wholly partisan than
the smaller Reform papers.   To illustrate the extent of that zeal,
it may be noted that a random number of the *Mercury* for 1896
carried 489 column inches of matter designed directly to benefit the
cause of Reform, and only one three-inch article of a non-political
nature![44] The same issue included among its propaganda materials
one cartoon and three poems.   There was no question, therefore,
concerning the enthusiasm of the state organs for the cause.

It remains now to examine and evaluate the campaign which resulted when the Reform press joined issue with the Democratic
journals.   Let it be understood in the beginning that while there
were numerous professors of non-partisanship among the non-
Reform papers of the State, not more than one in fifty practiced
the principles which they publicly championed.   The Reform press,
of course, was confessedly partisan.   Here, then, were several hundred newspapers divided into two camps, very unequal in strength
but comparable in their zeal for their respective causes.   Let it be
understood in the second place that these were the days in Texas
when men were men and editors were truthful—according to their
lights.   They may not always have printed the things of supposed
advantage to their cause which came to their minds, but so far as
the reader can surmise from their efforts, the omissions were
negligible.   It requires a vivid imagination to envisage a more
partisan policy than these editors were able to devise forty years ago.

In light of these facts one is not surprised at the vigor of the
newspaper campaigns which raged in Texas during the Populist
decade.   The editor, Populist or Democratic, printed the facts as he
saw them, or as he wished to see them (which amounted to the same

---

[43]The *Mercury* did employ a campaign method which appears to have been
unique and which is worthy of comment.   Some four or six weeks before the
date of the elections, it published a special campaign "Hot Shot" edition which
included speeches by the party's leaders, roaring editorials, and damning testi-
monials against Democrats in general and the Democratic candidates in particular.   The publisher agreed to furnish copies of this edition in any number
at one cent each, and Populists were requested to assist in placing large numbers of them where they would serve to the greatest advantage.   *The Southern
Mercury*, Sept. 29, Oct. 13 (Hot Shot Issue), 1898.

[44]The *Mercury*, be it remembered, was a sixteen-page paper.

thing), and then stood by his guns.[45] He might, for example, as he
frequently did, make the bald statement, "My contemporary, the
editor of ————, is a liar." Or he might build an editorial
around the theme that Populists generally were horse thieves (a
charge of uncommon seriousness in Texas in 1890), or, from the
view of the Reform editor, that Democrats were boodlers and grafters
and robbers of food from the mouths of widows and orphans. The
press campaign, in short, always vigorous, frequently became acrimonious in the extreme; the editors dipped their pens in the ink
of vitriol, and the reading public was subjected to a torrent of
abuse, vituperation, scurrility, and recrimination which has not
since been surpassed.[46]

Under such circumstances the Populist editor, and the Democratic
also where he met with active opposition by a local Reform paper,
lived an uncomfortable and uneasy life. At best, he was subjected
to countless unpleasant annoyances; at worst, he was threatened by
his enemies and mayhap even ill-treated on occasion. In Gainesville, for example, the Democratic *Register* demanded at the end of
an unusually warm campaign that the editor of the Populist *Signal*
leave town.[47] In Comanche, where the plant of Thomas Gaines'
Pioneer Exponent was stoned during the course of a Democratic
rally, it was reported that the editor's family was forced to flee his
home for safety.[48] In Sulphur Springs rival journalists fought a

---

[45]*The Comanche Chief*, June 6, 1924 (in the office of the *Chief*, Comanche,
Texas), carries a story relating how its editor dealt with objectors during the
days of Populism. The *Chief* was a Democratic paper unyielding in its allegiance and unsparing in its denunciation of the Populists, and its sallies
frequently gave offense to Third Party men. The rules of the office, however,
were fixed on one point: The editor retracted nothing, and to lend certainty
to his policy he kept a revolver close at hand, to which he resorted when the
occasion demanded.

[46]See, as examples which will indicate something of the nature of the press
campaign, *The Texas Vorwaerts*, Sept. 30, 1892; *The Gonzales Inquirer*, Aug.
2, Oct. 11, 25, and Nov. 1, 1894; *The Weekly Sentinel*, Sept. 26, Oct. 10, 17,
24, 1900, etc., etc.

[47]*Gainesville Signal*, Nov. 7, 1894.

[48]*Dallas Morning News*, Nov. 5, 1892. There were several versions current
of this fracas, some of which denounced the charge as a lie of the whole
cloth. It appears, however, that the accusation was based on truth, though
embellished somewhat for effect.

duel with pistols, the Reform editor being slain and the Democrat wounded.[49] Finally, lest it be supposed that such imbroglios were confined to the hot-heads among the local editors, it may be noted that the *Mercury* itself was sued by W. M. Walton for $10,000 for defamation of character and that its editor confessed judgment in the sum of $500.00.[50] Such instances, by no means uncommon, reveal the bitterness of spirit in which the newspapers participated editorially in the political campaigns of the day.

The matter of assessing the influence of the Reform press with anything approaching accuracy is one presenting many difficulties which, however, may be circumvented partially in so far as general conclusions are concerned. The widespread belief that local Reform journals scattered throughout the State would be of great advantage to the party appears to have been justified, for a casual comparison between the distribution of those journals and that of the Populist vote reveals a positive correlation between the vote cast and the presence of Populist newspapers.[51] Further, it requires no vivid imagination to estimate roughly what must have been the influence of the weekly deluge of Third Party propaganda which permeated the country regularly year in and year out.

The strength of the People's Party press may be measured adequately, however, only in terms of a comparison with the Democratic press; and when such a comparison is made, its relative impotence is apparent. It is true that, in 1895, there were eighty-five Reform journals operating in eighty counties of the State. But it is true also that at the same time there were 619 non-Reform papers, virtually all of them Democratic, that they were published in 192 counties of the State, and that fifty-nine of that number were dailies while some twenty more were issued semi- or tri-weekly.[52] It appears therefore that, whatever the value of the services performed by Third Party papers in the abstract, the ultimate conclusion is inescapable that the Reform press did not compare with the Democratic press, which except in extraordinary circumstances, was able effectively to defend itself and its party against the onslaughts of the Populist journals.

---

[49]*Jacksboro Gazette*, Sept. 24, 1891.

[50]*The Southern Mercury*, Sept. 30, 1897, Feb. 9, 1899.

[51]See also *The Weekly News*, Nov. 17, 1898.

[52]See *supra*, Table XII.

CHAPTER IX

AN ANALYSIS OF POPULIST SUCCESSES

IN THE LAST FIVE CHAPTERS we have examined at length the paraphernalia by means of which the People's Party sought to secure the acceptance of its principles by the voters. Throughout the discussion an attempt has been made to keep in mind the matter of relative efficacies of Democratic and Populist techniques, though no effort has been made to analyze the former except in an incidental way. It remains, however, to pursue the matter to its logical end and to answer the question, with what success did the Third Party meet in its tournaments with the Democracy? The means whereby the party sought to achieve its ends were of the greatest significance; but of wide interest also were the tangible results attained by it, for they serve as a measure of the efficacy of its methods.

The success of a minor party may be gauged by two separate and wholly different yardsticks. First, chief attention may be paid to the election of candidates to office, which is the thing always foremost in the minds of politicians and which is indeed the immediate end of the party. Second, attention may be focussed on the ultimate acceptance of all or part of the party's program by one or mayhap both of the old parties. In evaluating the success of the People's Party it will be necessary to examine both aspects of the matter, for that party was at the same time a political party in the ordinary sense of the term, and so interested vitally in obtaining possession of public office, and a party of principle, whose purpose presumably would be served by the acceptance of its program in any way feasible. It will be advantageous, however, to separate these two phases, stressing for the present the practical results of the Populist campaigns and noting the success achieved by that party as a party. In due course it will prove worth while to note briefly the extent to which the party was able to force the consideration of its principles by the old parties and thus was successful as a party of reform.[1]

----

[1] *Infra*, Chap. XI.

The Third Party nominally waged seven campaigns in Texas from 1892 to 1904, of which only four were of importance. In 1892, '94, and '96, the party constituted a challenge to Democratic supremacy; by 1898, it was definitely on the wane; and after that date its campaigns and the protests of its leaders were of a character which stamped it as a moribund organization. During the heyday of its career, however, it waged campaigns for both state and local office whose effectiveness was attested by the results obtained. Those results may be examined and evaluated as to successes achieved first in state and second in local elections.

I

In the contests for the executive offices of the State the best efforts of the People's Party went for naught. In 1892 and 1894, Judge Nugent ran valiant if hopeless races for Governor against the Democratic nominees; in 1896 Jerome Kearby, with the support of all consequential non-Democratic factions, threatened to overwhelm the old party's candidate; in 1898, the Populist-Republican candidate, Barnett Gibbs, polled a much smaller vote than his predecessor; and thenceforward the party disintegrated rapidly. The Third Party candidate for Governor thus threatened in only one election. Nor were the Reform nominees for other state executive offices more successful than the gubernatorial candidate.

When one turns to the Legislature, however, one finds a somewhat brighter picture, for there the People's Party began with its inception an invasion which continued to the end of the century. With the elections of 1892, held shortly after the amalgamation of the Jeffersonian Democrats with the People's Party men, the Third Party elected eight men to the lower house of the Legislature,[2] and in 1894 the number increased to twenty-two, out of a total membership of 128.[3] Thereafter it dwindled rapidly, only six Populists

---

[2]*Rules of Order of the House of Representatives of the Twenty-Third Legislature* (Austin, 1893). This manual contains a great deal of valuable information pertaining to the Legislature, much of it of a statistical nature and arranged in tabular form.

[3]*Rules, Twenty-Fourth Legislature* (Austin, 1895).

being elected in 1896,[4] four in 1898,[5] and one in 1900.[6] As regards the upper house, the party was not so successful, electing only three senators in the course of the decade under consideration. The first of these served in the Legislature which met in 1893; the other two were elected in 1894, neither being reëlected at the end of his term.[7] The Democratic Party thus found its preserves in the Legislature encroached upon by ambitious Third Party men, though ordinarily the Populist representatives were helpless before the majorities retained by the Democrats.

In personal characteristics the Populist legislator, and particularly the member of the lower house, was set apart from the Democratic law-maker. In the first place, he was older than his Democratic peer. In the Twenty-third Legislature the Populist representatives averaged forty-five years of age; in the Twenty-fourth, almost forty-seven; and in the Twenty-fifth, fifty-two. On the other hand, the 106 Democratic members of the lower house in the Twenty-fourth Legislature, for example, averaged only forty-one and two-tenths years in age, more than five years less than the average of the Populist members. Nor did the difference arise from the presence in the ranks of the Populists of a few patriarchs whose years combined to raise the average of their colleagues; for there was but one Populist representative above sixty years, and he was only sixty-five. On the other hand, there was only one Third Party legislator of less than thirty years, whereas there were fourteen such Democratic law-makers. Thus the Populist representatives were older by several years, on an average, than those elected as Democrats.[8]

A second feature which distinguished Populist and Democratic legislators may be found by comparing their occupations. Of the Populists elected to the lower house in 1892, *every one was a farmer;* of the twenty-two elected in 1894, sixteen, or about 73 per cent,

---

[4]*Texas Legislative Manual for 1897* (Austin, 1897). This handbook corresponds to the *Rules* usually printed.

[5]*The Southern Mercury*, Nov. 17, 1898.

[6]*Manual*, 1901.

[7]*Dallas Morning News*, Feb. 4, 1893; *Rules, Twenty-Fifth Legislature; Manual*, 1901.

[8]The figures used here were taken from the *Rules* and the *Manual* cited above.

were farmers; and of the eight returned in 1896, all but one, or 83 per cent, were tillers of the soil. On the other hand, among the non-Populists in the same body in 1894 only 21.6 per cent were farmers; and in 1896 only 26 per cent. Further, among the Populists serving in the Twenty-third, Twenty-fourth, and Twenty-fifth Legislatures, not one was a lawyer, while of the non-Populist members of the Twenty-fourth Legislature, for example, 47.9 per cent were members of the legal profession.[9] Thus it appeared to the Populist that, although the people of Texas were largely agriculturists, the Government was managed by representatives of other classes, more especially by lawyers; and this sore spot he attempted to remedy by placing men of his own kind in the Legislature.

A third feature which characterized the Populist legislator was his lack of previous training in law-making. Of the eight elected to the Twenty-third Legislature, none had served in that body previously; of the twenty-two chosen in 1894, only two had served before; and of the six elected in 1896, only three. At the same time, in the Twenty-fourth Legislature, 31 per cent of the non-Populists had seen service before, and in the Twenty-fifth, over 30 per cent. These figures reveal first, that the Populist law-maker was a novice and, secondly, that of the Democrats in the House a large percentage were experienced legislators. Further, they complete the picture of an interesting character, a farmer who had but recently left the plow to take his seat among men several years his juniors but who for all his years was lacking almost wholly in legislative experience.

What the Third Party representatives lacked in knowledge of the ways of legislative bodies, however, they threatened to make up in the zealous attention which they bestowed upon problems of party interest. To give those problems adequate consideration they organized a caucus in the House of Representatives. The caucus performed the duties usual to such agents, turning its hand to both

---

[9]The figures on which the percentage calculations were based came from the *Rules* for 1893 and 1895 and the *Manual* for 1897.

legislative and non-legislative problems; and the members stood by
its decisions to a man on party questions.[10]

Populist partisans outside the Legislature were not slow to recognize the opportunity to use their representatives for the advantage
of the party. In the first Legislature of the Populist era there were
too few Reform law-makers to merit attention, but in the Twenty-
fourth there were twenty-two Populist representatives who formed
a bloc important enough to evoke the solicitude of the party managers. In truth, the session was only a few hours old when Cyclone
Davis arrived in Austin. His business was to represent a Populist
in an election contest, but he proceeded at once to meet with the
People's Party caucus, presumably to advise with its members concerning proposed legislation.[11] Again, Judge Nugent took an active
part in defeating a libel bill which would have passed but for the
opposition of the Populists.[12] The daily press, commenting upon
the Populist caucus and the lobbying activities of the Reform
leaders, observed that, experienced or not, the directors of Populism
had learned early and well the lessons of practical politics.

---

[10]The existence of the Populist caucus was known to all, and its proceedings were discussed in the daily press of the day. See, for example, the *Dallas
Morning News*, Jan. 8, 11, Feb. 20, 1895.

In the sessions of 1893, 1895, and 1897 the Populist caucus nominated candidates for Speaker, and each time the vote of the nominee was measured by
the number of his party colleagues in the House. See the *Texas House Journal*
(Austin), *23rd Legislature*, pp. 2–3, *24th Legislature*, p. 2, *25th Legislature*,
p. 2. In 1892 and 1894, Thomas L. Nugent was put in nomination for
United States Senator and each time received the full support of his Populist
followers. *Ibid.*, *23rd Legislature*, p. 134, *24th Legislature*, p. 102.

[11]*Dallas Morning News*, Jan. 8, 1895. Whatever his purpose, Mr. Davis appeared in the several days following to speak with some assurance concerning
the vote of those members, going so far as to suggest to some of the Democratic leaders, in writing, unhappily, that he would undertake, for a consideration, to persuade the Populist legislators to vote *aye* on a certain measure concerning which the Democratic members were divided. His proposition may
have been innocent enough, as he and his party allies insisted it was, but the
"brutal Democratic majority" voted nevertheless to censure him and to deny
him thenceforward the privileges of the House. Thus the first and most powerful confessed Populist lobbyist came to grief.

The whole affair may be found discussed in the columns of the *Dallas News*
of the issues Jan. 24–Feb. 2, 1895. The Populist point of view may be seen
from the *Southern Mercury* for Feb. 7–21, 1895.

[12]*Dallas Morning News*, April 12, 1895.

The situation which obtained in the Legislature during the Populist invasion was unique in the history of that body. The Republican representation was negligible, and the Populists numbered at their greatest strength no more than a score. The Democrats then retained a clear majority always, controlling without question except where almost equally divided among themselves. In light of these circumstances, it is interesting to investigate the question, what consideration was given the Populist interlopers in the organization of the House? In the Twenty-third Legislature, no distinction was made between Populists and Democrats in appointing committees;[13] but a different situation prevailed in the Twenty-fourth, for there the Populists were sufficiently numerous to cause some embarrassment. Hence the Speaker announced that, while he would treat the People's Party men fairly in making committee appointments, he would place the responsibility for legislation squarely on the shoulders of the Democrats where from the preponderance of their numbers it rightfully belonged.[14] His conception of fairness resulted in the appointment of each Populist to 1.8 committee places, while the Democrats averaged 3.5 places.[15] In the Twenty-fifth Legislature, which contained only six Reform representatives, committee appointments were distributed again without regard to party affiliation.[16] It appears therefore that the Speaker, being a Democrat, was magnanimous in perfecting organization in so far as he was able to be so without compromising his party, though he held the weapon of discrimination in readiness to be used when the situation required.

---

[13]*Rules, Twenty-Third Legislature.* Committees were as important in the Texas Legislature as in the typical American legislative body, which is to say that the recommendation of a committee ordinarily was sufficient to determine the fate of a measure. Committee appointments therefore were highly prized, and places on the more important committees were reserved for influential members of the controlling party.

[14]*House Journal, 24th Legislature,* p. 3.

[15]*Rules, Twenty-Fourth Legislature.*

[16]*Manual,* 1897. In the Senate, the two Populists suffered little from the discrimination seen in the lower house in the Twenty-fourth Legislature. In 1897, for example, they were named to sixteen committee places between them, whereas the Democratic senators served on 10.5 committees, on an average. There were, it will be recalled, only two Populist senators in a body of thirty-one members.

A second question pertains to the part actually played by the Populists in the proceedings of the lower house and their policies toward the bills proposed there. An investigation reveals that the Third Party representatives took an active part in debates, though they did not speak as frequently as the Democratic members. Nor did they always speak to good purpose, for occasionally the Democrats refused to hear them and harassed them into temporary subjection.[17] Among their number, however, were a few who in debate commanded the respect of all members,[18] though even they were heard with more of tolerance than of sympathy.

In the matter of tangible results, it may be noted that the Populist legislators supported such bills as seemed to fulfill the needs of their constituents and introduced measures designed to carry out the Third Party program. Among the Populist bills, those of greatest importance may be examined with profit as to their history in the House and the fate accorded them there. It will be worth while further to note also the attitude of the Reform legislators regarding measures of interest to them proposed by Democratic representatives or by the Senate. Populist policies may be discussed conveniently under four headings, according as they related to financial reforms, labor, corporations, and miscellaneous Third Party principles.

The People's Party from the beginning stressed the subject of financial reform, and its candidates adverted constantly to the extravagance of Democratic officeholders and the necessity for retrenchment. Nor did the Populist law-makers forget their platform or their campaign promises. Thus before the session of 1895 was one week old a prominent Reform legislator, mindful of an ancient precept of Populism, introduced a bill to place county officials on salaries, thereby automatically eliminating the fee system.[19] His bill followed one of similar import drafted by a Democratic law-maker, however, and eventually it was dropped in favor of the earlier bill in whose support retrenchment Democrats and Populists

---

[17]See the *Dallas Morning News,* March 7, 1893.

[18]Such a one was J. A. O'Conner of Bexar County, who, more of an independent than a Populist, was universally respected among the members of the House.

[19]*House Journal. 24th Legislature,* p. 41.

combined.[20]   The measure mustered a majority vote at one time, but it ran afoul of a spirited filibuster which secured its defeat despite the united support of its Populist champions to the end.[21]   A second bill in the same session provided that the county commissioners' court should not be empowered to create a county debt of more than $5,000 without approval by a referendum.[22]   The measure received an adverse committee report, and so expired.[23]   A third bill set a limit on the fees which county commissioners might collect as supervisors of public roads.[24]   It reached the Speaker's table through the medium of a substitute measure, but there it died.[25]

As regarded state expenditures, the Populist legislators demanded repeatedly that appropriations be reduced.   For example, early in the session of 1895 one of the leading Third Party spokesmen suggested that the legislators set an example of economy by reducing their own salaries, but his move met with no response.[26]   For example again, a prominent Populist introduced a bill which called for a reduction in the salaries of the railroad commissioners,[27] and another (the original fee bill advocate) suggested a measure designed to reduce the pay of officials for time lost from their respective offices.[28]   In every case the attempt at retrenchment was

[20]*Ibid.*, p. 13.

[21]The legislative history of the fee bill may be followed in the *House Journal*, but more of the actual atmosphere surrounding it may be seen from the columns of the *Dallas News*, especially of the issues of April 18, 21, 22, 23, 24, and 25, 1895.   The *News* was rabidly anti-fee bill in its attitude, and its bias frequently came to the surface in a manner which made it appear ludicrous.   It referred, for example, to the "patriotic minority" which brought about the defeat of the measure, to the "obstructionist majority" which forced its consideration at such length, and to the "assistant Democrats" who joined with the Populists in their unholy war on an ancient institution.

[22]*House Journal, 24th Legislature,* p. 85.   The measure provided further that after such a proposal had been defeated by the people it should not be referred again for a period of one year.

A similar proposal, sponsored by a Populist legislator, had been defeated in the preceding Legislature.   *Dallas Morning News,* March 10. 25, 1893.

[23]*House Journal, ibid.,* pp. 434–435.

[24]*Ibid.*, p. 221.   The bill provided that a commissioner should receive only $1.50 per day for this work and should be paid for only four days each year.

[25]*Ibid.*, p. 300.

[26]*Dallas Morning News,* Jan. 16, 1895.

[27]*House Journal, 24th Legislature,* p. 263.

[28]*Ibid.*, p. 204.

defeated, usually through an adverse committee report. In the
Senate the Populist economists met with some success, though the
reductions effected were negligible.[29] In the Twenty-fifth Legislature, as in the Twenty-fourth, the Third Party men led the fight
for retrenchment; as before, they were soundly beaten.[30] It is apparent, therefore, that the best efforts of the People's Party legislators to effect financial reforms went for naught. Aided by "assistant Democrats," they forced the issue on a few important questions; but for the greater part they were confined to what the *Dallas
News* termed "doodle-bug retrenchment," and even in the field of
the picayune they were so hedged about as to be almost wholly
impotent.

If the Populist law-makers were staunch in their advocacy of retrenchment in public administration, they were not less vigorous in
moving to the defense of labor. Early in the session of 1893 a labor
representative presented a bill calling for the establishment of a
bureau of labor statistics;[31] and though defeated decisively, the
measure commanded the overwhelming support of the Populists.[32]
A second bill of interest to the laboring man was the mechanics'
and laborers' lien bill which was introduced in the same session by
a Populist.[33] The measure was killed by an adverse committee
report. A second bill to the same purpose, introduced in 1895 by
a Reform legislator, was reported favorably from committee but
died on the Speaker's table.[34] A third labor measure, sponsored by
a Populist in the Twenty-fourth Legislature, sought to regulate the
hours of labor of railroad employees. Like the mechanics' lien bill,
it was reported favorably by the committee but was buried on the
Speaker's table.[35] A fourth bill, striking at the system which permitted convict labor to compete with free labor, met the same fate.[36]

[29]*Dallas Morning News*, March 15, 1895. Populist senators and representatives alike opposed the week-end junkets frequently taken by the Legislature,
though they were not able to put a stop to what one prominent Third Party
man called the "weekly drunks." *The Southern Mercury*, March 7, 21, 1895.
[30]*Dallas Morning News*, March 27, 1897.
[31]*House Journal, 23rd Legislature*, p. 128.
[32]*Dallas Morning News*, May 6, 1893.
[33]*House Journal, 23rd Legislature*, p. 66.
[34]*Ibid., 24th Legislature*, pp. 154, 440.
[35]*Ibid.*, pp. 155, 226.
[36]*Ibid.*, pp. 295, 334.

Finally, there was the anti-trust bill which, in its original form, would have prohibited associations of farming and laboring men along with others. The Populist senators insisted successfully on the exemption of such associations.[37] Notwithstanding this small measure of success, the efforts of the Populists in behalf of the laboring man were almost completely unavailing. They gave their wholehearted attention to the problems which arose, but the tangible results obtained were of little consequence.

A third large problem to engage the attention of the Third Party legislators pertained to corporations. The party was unyielding in its opposition to big business enterprises, especially the railroads, and its legislative representatives reflected its attitude. One bill sponsored by a leading Populist provided for a maximum limit for railway freight rates; it came to an end through an adverse committee report.[38] A second, forbidding state officers to serve in the employment of corporations, met the same fate as the first.[39] A third sought to prohibit railroad companies from granting free passes to any state or local officer. Introduced first in the Senate, it was defeated there by a vote of seventeen to twelve, but among the minority were the two Populist senators.[40] These measures, aimed at corporations but more particularly at the railroads, reveal conscious efforts to deal with what the Populist representative conceived to be serious problems.

In addition to the several important measures which we have classified according to subject matter under the headings financial reform, labor, and corporations, the Populist legislators sought constantly to carry into effect other Reform principles. To illustrate, a Democratic representative proposed a constitutional amendment to make citizenship a requirement for voting, confessing that his measure was aimed at the "muddy" vote along the Rio Grande; and though the resolution failed of adoption, the Populists voted for it by an overwhelming majority.[41] To illustrate again, a

[37]*Dallas Morning News*, April 17, 19, 24, 25, 1895.
[38]*House Journal, 24th Legislature*, pp. 263, 946–949.
[39]*Ibid.*, pp. 148, 464.
[40]*Dallas Morning News*, March 23, 1895.
[41]*Ibid.*, Feb. 23, 1895. To be exact, nineteen out of the twenty-two Populists voted for the resolution. The remaining three either were absent or, being present, did not vote.

Third Party leader introduced a bill calling for the appointment of a commissioner for the purpose of providing uniform public school textbooks. The measure went the way of an adverse committee report.[42] Other similar examples might be cited of the unremittent efforts of the Reform legislators to write the program of their party into law, but in so far as tangible results were concerned, they were of no consequence.

The People's Party law-makers, then, supported such Democratic measures as promised to serve their purposes, while sponsoring a number of significant bills on their own account. The efficacy of their tactics may be reckoned from statistics revealing the number and the fate of their proposals for one legislative session in comparison with Democratic measures for the same period. In the Twenty-fourth Legislature, the twenty-two Populist representatives sponsored a total of fifty-eight bills, an average of 2.7 per man, while the non-Populists introduced an average of 6.5 bills each. Of the fifty-eight Populist measures, twenty-eight received adverse committee reports, seventeen died on the Speaker's table, five died in committee, two passed the House but failed to receive the Speaker's signature, two gave way to Democratic measures of like import (of which one passed), one was withdrawn, two became laws without the Governor's signature, and one passed both houses and was approved. Of the four measures sponsored by the Populists which ultimately went into effect, one pertained to the statute of limitations, one to the disposition of surplus artesian water at the state orphans' home, one to the public roads of Parker County, and one to the business of the Delta County court, whose jurisdiction had been taken from it by the Legislature in 1893 for political reasons.[43] The last only may be termed a bonafide **Populist** measure, though if the most favorable interpretation be placed upon the matter only 6.8 per cent of the Third Party bills became law. Further, since one of these was passed as a Democratic measure, the total number of Populist bills passed is reduced to three and the percentage to five. At the same time the House passed 11 per cent of the 687 non-Populist measures introduced before it. The figures

---

[42]*House Journal, 24th Legislature,* pp. 280, 406.
[43]*Infra.*

indicate, therefore, that the Third Party legislators proposed considerably less than half as many bills per man as the Democrats and that the House in turn passed, proportionally, less than half as many Populist measures as Democratic. Nor is it without significance that the so-called Populist legislation which received approval was almost wholly innocuous in character; the measures of real importance to the party were struck down without compunction by the Democratic majority.

It is not to be concluded, however, that the Third Party representation in the Legislature served no purpose. On the contrary, the Populist law-makers exerted an influence far beyond that warranted by their numbers. Particularly was this true of the members of the Twenty-fourth Legislature, who caucused together to determine their course of action then voted their policies to a man. The Democrats, on the contrary, often divided among themselves. There were, in fact, some two score Democratic members of the lower house who were as good Populists as any on many questions, and when they split with the regulars the Third Party men controlled the house. While this occurred infrequently, the Populists occasionally found themselves in control—it was so, for example, with reference to the fee bill. The possibility of the recurrence of this situation was a nightmare to the Democratic managers, who spent much of their time clubbing the Populists and engaging in internecine strife. When they accused the Reform legislators of attempting deliberately to manufacture reputations for themselves and campaign thunder for their party, the daily press joined in the cry, denouncing also those "assistant Democrats" who made possible the strong position of the Populists.[44] The situation resulted in a legislative session which was as hectic as any experienced in the State to that time. The *Austin Statesman* concluded, at the end of the four months of wrangling, that the Democracy had been slaughtered in the house of its friends,[45] and the *Dallas News* agreed, observing that, if "the 24th" was not venal, surely it was imbecile.[46] The latter opinion may have been justified, but the former, as it proved, was that of a

---

[44]*Dallas Morning News*, April 21, 1895.

[45]In its issue of April 1, 1895 (in the Library of The University of Texas, Austin, Texas).

[46]See its issue of May 1, 1895.

partisan delivered in a moment of exasperation. Of the fundamental validity of the hypothesis on which both rested, however, there can be no doubt, for the Populists exerted a strong influence in the Legislature and their presence there created many vexing problems for the Democratic Party.

II

When one leaves the field of state politics proper and comes to the various electoral areas within the State, one finds the People's Party candidates meeting with varying successes. At the level of the congressional district the party usually nominated candidates, occasionally making a strong race behind its nominee,[47] though failing ever to win a place in the national legislative body. Substantially the same story may be told of the campaigns waged for judicial district offices. Populist strategy demanded that candidates be nominated for those offices, but they met with no more success than the Third Party nominees for Congress.

A different situation prevailed, however, in the field of local elections. The county was an important unit in the Populist organization, and as such it enjoyed a distinct advantage over the districts above mentioned. Moreover, it was the locus of operation for a few excellent local leaders who by their personal prowess were able effectively to combine the anti-Democratic forces for the purposes of the county election. Yet again, it offered a compact territory which was more readily adaptable to the purposes of an effective campaign than was the larger district. Finally, it afforded a large number of prizes which made it worth the while of ambitious

---

[47]In 1894, for example, it appeared for a time that Chas. H. Jenkins, the Populist candidate, had beaten C. K. Bell in the Eighth district, and indeed there were many (and they were not all Third Party men) who insisted that, but for some expert counting in Fort Worth's "Hell's Half Acre," he would have won by a comfortable margin. Again, in the same year, Jerome Kearby, the Populist candidate in the Sixth district, trailed the Democratic nominee by only a few votes, and Cyclone Davis pressed hard on the heels of D. B. Culberson in the Fourth. In both of these cases the defeated Third Party candidates contested the elections, only to have the original returns upheld. On other occasions the Populist congressional candidates ran strong races, but none came as close to success as did Jenkins, Kearby, and Davis in the instances noted.

Reformers to bend every effort toward local success for the party ticket. These factors determined the nature of the campaign for county and precinct offices, which frequently was very vigorous.

The effectiveness of the local campaign may be measured by the results which it obtained. In the territory east from Coke County to the Sabine River and north from Frio to the Red River the Third Party at the height of its strength elected scores of county and precinct officers. Now and again it carried into office the whole of its local ticket, though quite frequently each party enjoyed a measure of success. In county politics personal considerations played a large part. Thus strong and popular men often were elected to office even in those instances where their party ticket met general defeat; and the spectacle was presented of a Populist interloper serving along with a number of Democratic officials or of a Democrat retaining his office in the midst of a Third Party landslide.

Whatever the measure of success achieved by the local Populist candidates, the county found all too frequently that its troubles multiplied with the election to office of Third Party men. The Reform official ordinarily was not a politician; that is to say, he was inexperienced in public life. With the characteristics of honesty and forthrightness he usually was abundantly endowed, but his ineptitude equalled his honesty. His administration of office, therefore, if it was free from corruption, also was unleavened by application of the principles whose observance makes for economy and efficiency.[48]

On more than one occasion, indeed, the ignorance or lack of ability of the Third Party official led to charges of incompetence against him. Thus in 1892 the voters of Delta County elected several Populists to office, among them some with doubtful qualifications. The attorney, for example, was not specially equipped to perform the

---

[48]Judge Lyman B. Russell, of Comanche County, relates a story concerning the Populist treasurer of that county which illustrates the incapacity of Third Party officials. A client had commissioned him to pay a debt owed to the county and take up the notes which had been made for the sum. Judge Russell paid the debt, he recounts, but the treasurer refused to surrender the notes, saying that he wished to retain them for his records. Eventually he was persuaded to give them up, after the advice of the Populist county attorney had been added to the importunities of the Judge.

See also *The Weekly Newsboy*, July 22, 29, 1896.

duties of his office; indeed he was not trusted even by his own party.[49] Nor was this difficult to understand, for immediately on assuming office he inaugurated certain practices which betrayed either gross ignorance or willful disregard of the principles of justice—or a keen sense of humor. To illustrate, he issued licenses purporting to permit the holders to play cards, for which he collected $5.00 each, and he signed, or was alleged to have signed, an instrument exempting the holder from prosecution for an "alleged unmentionable offense." The county judge also laid himself open to the charge of incapacity: as an example, he placed civil cases on the criminal docket, presumably being unaware of the difference between the two.[50] In these circumstances the Legislature was asked to remedy the situation by transferring the jurisdiction of the Delta County court to the district court. When a bill for that purpose was introduced, the proponents of the transfer were able to adduce many arguments involving considerations of economy, efficiency, and justice, and the Legislature passed the measure.[51] Some legislators professed to base their vote on a question purely of justice, but most recognized in the bill a measure designed to chastise Delta County, and more particularly the Third Party, for having elected to office allegedly incompetent Populist officials.[52]

---

[49]The official in question, though a Populist, was nominated and elected only by the assistance of the Democrats, who professed to prefer him over other possible nominees. See the *Dallas Morning News*, April 3, 1893.

[50]See *ibid.* for a summary of various aspects of the question, including the charges against the attorney and the judge.

[51]For the nature of the quarrel, see the *Dallas News* for March 26, April 2, 3, 1893; for the progress of the bill through the Legislature, see the *House Journal, 23rd Legislature*, pp. 600, 603, 763, 784, 831, ff., 972, 992, 1007.

The bill became a law without the signature of the Governor.

[52]That the measure was of the nature mentioned is revealed by the fact that in the next session of the Legislature a law was passed repealing the original Delta County act, after the representative introducing the bill had assured the House, in answer to questions asked, that the objectionable attorney of two years before had been replaced by a gentleman "whose legal ability and official integrity was beyond question." *Dallas Morning News*, Feb. 10, April 7, 1895.

The partisan character of the original act may be seen from the vote by which it was passed. Every Populist representative present voted against it.

For a defense of the Populist officers of Delta County, see *The Southern Mercury*, Oct. 10, 1895.

When the method of circumventing Populist incompetence by legislative action proved efficacious, Democrats sought similar action in other instances. The Legislature granted the relief requested more than once. Among others, it abolished the jurisdiction of the Camp and the Morris County courts in order, as the *Dallas News* expressed it, "to castigate (those counties) for electing Populist officers."[53] It was not feasible, however, to punish every county in that manner. Hence, as a usual thing the incompetent Third Party official was allowed to complete his term, when it may be assumed he received his dues from the voters.

From simple ineptitude and incompetence, the Populist office-holder found himself accused of accepting "gifts" for official favors, particularly in the matter of letting contracts. In Gonzales County, for example, the commissioners' court, of which a majority were Populists, contracted for the construction of a new courthouse after dealings which laid it liable to charges of the acceptance, indirectly, of a bribe.[54] A grand jury which investigated the matter reported that while there was not sufficient evidence to warrant an indictment, there were some indications which pointed to crime.[55] A similar situation arose in Grimes County where two Populists voted with two Democratic commissioners to spend $14,000 for a new jail and let a contract for that purpose. It was hinted darkly that somewhere along the route travelled by the contract there had been deposited as graft money $9,000, the difference between the $5,000 estimated to be adequate for the jail and the $14,000 voted for the building. The matter did not reach the stage of preferring formal

---

[53]In its issue of April 26, 1895. It is significant that these acts were repealed in every instance as soon as they had accomplished their purpose.

[54]It was charged that the contractor was paid more than the contract was worth and that he in turn presented to C. K. Walter, the local leader of the Third Party, the sum of $2,500 to be used as a campaign fund by that party. Walter seems to have been the man held chiefly responsible in the alleged deal. See *The Gonzales Inquirer*, Sept. 6, 20, 1894.

[55]*The Gonzales Inquirer*, Aug. 2, 1894. The whole quarrel, as well as the part played by the press in its development, may be seen in the issues of the *Inquirer* of June 28, Aug. 2, 30, Sept. 6, 13, 20, 1894.

It is interesting to note that the Democratic candidate for county attorney defeated Walter, who stood for election to that office as a Populist in 1894. *Ibid.*, Nov. 1, *Supplement*, 1894.

charges.[56] In other sections of the State accusations were made on occasion which sought to convict Populist officials of profiting from the spoils of office. Many of these, it may be assumed, were mere campaign stories, though an occasional charge appeared to have some basis in fact.

Yet a third accusation lodged against Populist officials rested on charges of peculation in office. Such charges, which came to light in various portions of the State, concerned personal misfeasance ranging from official neglect to embezzlement. As an example of negligence, there was the case of the officer in Wilson County whose accounts were so irregular and so loosely kept that he was indicted after a grand jury investigation. He was never brought to trial, for it was recognized generally that his only offense was an indifference born of poor health. Of more serious consequence were the cases arising in Jones County which entangled the treasurer, the judge, and two commissioners in the toils of the law and led to the removal of the first on charges of false entry, collusion in the purchase of land for a county poor farm, and misapplication of funds.[57] The treasurer was indicted but was never brought to trial. Those familiar with the facts who survive today

---

[56]The lead in pressing the accusations seems to have been taken by disillusioned Populists who were interested chiefly in the fact that, although the Third Party platform demanded the referendum of proposed bond issues to the people, the commissioners' court, the two Populists concurring, agreed to undertake the jail project without ordering such a vote. The charge of graft appears to have been of secondary importance. See *The Patriot* (Navasota, Texas) for Aug. 19, Sept. 2, 9, 1897 (in the Library of The University of Texas, Austin, Texas).

[57]The pertinent facts concerning the chief charge against the treasurer follow. That official had placed some $3,000 of the county's money on deposit in the Bank of Anson, which was forced to close its doors. He was responsible for the loss, but instead of causing him to forfeit his bond to cover it, the commissioners' court entered into a deal whereby 200 acres of land were purchased from the owner of the defunct bank for a county poor farm. The court paid to the erstwhile banker $1,500 for the land in county scrip; he turned the paper over to the treasurer, who passed it on to the court; and that body cancelled it and gave the treasurer credit for half of the sum due the county, allowing him to pay the other half part in cash and part in promises, the latter secured by notes. See *Bland* vs. *State*, 36 *Southwestern Reporter*, p. 914 (1896), and 38 *ibid.*, p. 252 (1896) ; and *Bland et al.* vs. *Orr, County Judge*, 39 *ibid.*, p. 558 (1897).

agree that, while the treasurer and the commissioners' court were indiscreet, the transaction to which exception was taken was honestly conceived. More serious yet were the cases involving the tax collector of Comanche County and the treasurer of San Augustine in charges of embezzling county funds. The former escaped conviction by the court, but the latter was convicted and sentenced to a term in prison, which he served. It is apparent, therefore, that regardless of the partisan motives which often prompted the complainant, the charges of peculation were serious in their consequences for both official and party.

It appears, then, that the Populist office-holder quite frequently placed himself and his party in an embarrassing position by reason of his inexperience and incompetence, his willingness to profit from the spoils of office, and his failure on occasion to observe the accepted principles of financial management or, less frequently, the rules of simple honesty. Some reflection, however, will lead to the conclusion that the dishonest Third Party officer was not typical, and there were notable exceptions to the general rule of ineptitude. In Erath County, for example, the Populist sheriff was regarded as one of the best peace officers the county ever had, and in Lampasas County the Populist sheriff served with such success that he had no opponent in his campaign for reëlection.[58] It is significant that both of these highly satisfactory officers served as sheriff, an office demanding more of firmness and strength of character than of training and technical ability. Where the latter requirements were prerequisite to the satisfactory discharge of official duties, competent candidates could not always be found. Hence untrained and mayhap unlettered men sometimes were elected to office, with the result that the Populist official soon gained a wide reputation as an incompetent and inefficient servant. The reputation frequently was merited, though it must be added that he was honest in the main and desirous of performing satisfactorily the duties of his office.

The query which arises now is, how did the Populist holder of local office compare with the Democratic official in the matters of ability and integrity? As regards ability, the scales appear to indicate an appreciable advantage in favor of the Democrat, and

[58]See the *Lampasas Leader*, Oct. 24, Nov. 4, 1898.

for apparent reasons. First, the old party, as has been noted, retained the allegiance of practically all members of the bar, so that it had every advantage in respect of men qualified for the important offices of county judge and attorney. Secondly, the advocates of Reform set little store by technical training and knowledge, accepting generally the old Jacksonian idea that every man has an equal right to serve the government and further that all men are equally competent to fulfill the duties of public office. Firm in this belief, they paid more attention to such matters as staunchness in Populism and the balancing of the ticket than to training and ability, with the inevitable result that inferior men frequently found places on their tickets. Finally, a Democratic officer might be wholly innocent of knowledge of the duties or the procedure of an office when elected yet might develop a real expertness through repeated reëlection and long experience. The Populist officer, on the other hand, usually not only was new at the game but failed of reëlection. He was compared, therefore, novice that he was, with experienced officers of the opposing political faith and quite naturally was found wanting in ability.

As regards integrity, it is somewhat more difficult to express a reasoned opinion. It is clear that, during the Populist decade, more Reform officers were called to task for questionable acts than Democratic, considering the total number of local officials from each party. That fact may, however, be explained in a variety of terms. It is undoubtedly true, for example, that Third Party officials, being unversed in the ways of politics, often committed blunders which a cleverer manipulator would have avoided and that on his part the Democratic office-holder was able to couch in harmless phraseology or to conceal entirely "deals" which would have brought a Populist to grief. It is true further that the Democrats watched the People's Party officers with the vigilance of a hawk, that they allowed no unguarded act to pass unnoticed, that they possessed the means (money, press, and influence) by which to pursue investigations and to prosecute, and that they could count on a state-wide audience which was anxious to hear of the discomfiture of the Populists and to "see justice done." Thus while it appears that the Democrats enjoyed an advantage in regard to integrity as in respect of ability, a conclusion to that effect is not justified.

A more charitable conclusion, and probably a more accurate one as well, is that they were merely more adroit and more discreet, and not more conscientious.

It was the announced policy of the People's Party to nominate candidates for every office filled by popular election. Thus from the time when the party first became a factor in the State to the time when it polled only a negligible vote a full ticket for state executive offices was nominated; and while the nominees threatened to win only in 1896, they furnished the dominant party with more competition than it had known for twenty years. The Reform Party enjoyed some little success in its contests for places in the Legislature, electing in the banner year of 1894 some 6.4 per cent of the Senate and 17 per cent of the Lower House. The Populist legislators were not able, by reason of their numerical weakness, to procure the passage of legislation advocated by their party, but their numbers were sufficient to enable them to force the consideration of many bills by the Democratic majority. If the measures proposed were defeated by the Democrats, the Populists at any rate had caused them to take a stand on the principles which the proposals involved. In the various electoral districts within the State the attacks of the People's Party were repulsed by the Democrats with negligible losses, though its candidates for Congress more than once narrowly missed election. In county and precinct elections, however, the Third Party enjoyed considerable success, sweeping to complete triumph in some counties and compelling the Democrats to share offices with it in many others. The Reform officials elected were but indifferently successful in the administration of their offices, though their shortcomings resulted ordinarily from lack of training and experience and not from malice or dishonesty.

The successes of the Third Party thus were confined to the conquest of several legislative seats and many counties. They were sufficiently numerous and widespread, however, to give the State a real taste of Populism, and the people, with the unselfish assistance of the Democratic leaders and the press, concluded from the sample that they were better off under exclusively Democratic rule. Many factors .entered into this decision, not least among which was the fact that the Populist legislators appeared or were made by their adversaries to appear impotent, vindictive, and sometimes ludicrous, and the county officials, unlearned and inefficient at best and at worst actually venal and corrupt. It is not necessary to agree with the staunchest of the Democrats to conclude that the Populist office-holders made a disappointing showing and that they contributed little or nothing of a lasting nature to the cause of Reform.

CHAPTER X

DEMOCRATIC REPRISALS: THE END OF THE

PEOPLE'S PARTY

ONE FAMILIAR with the temper of the Democratic leaders will understand that there was no disposition on their part to allow the Third Party to carry its candidates into office and its program into effect by default. If their adversaries were stalwarts in their advocacy of Reform, they were no less staunch in their adherence to the traditional party; and if the Third Party managers were ready to employ any methods necessary to gain the ear of the people, they were willing to fight fire with fire and sword with sword. Hence the struggle between the two parties became a hammer-and-tongs combat before the downfall of the challenger. The initial phase of the quarrel, seen in the campaign of 1892, portended little of the intensity of the contests to follow, for the Democratic directors must set their own house in order before attacking seriously the Populist interlopers. That task was completed, however, with the union of the Hogg and the Clark forces under Culberson in 1894 when the dominant party once more was able to present a united front against its enemies. The campaigns of '94 and '96, therefore, saw the hapless State embroiled in campaigns which for vigor and spirit had not been equalled since Reconstruction. They also saw the culmination of the Reform movement and the disintegration of the Third Party. How the Democrats met the attacks of the Reformers and how the People's Party crumbled before the counter charges of the old party constitute a most significant phase of Third Party politics.

I

When the Third Party movement became articulate in 1891, its leaders found that the Democratic directors were not disposed to take them seriously. Further, they learned shortly that such sporadic efforts as were launched against them might be expected to be ill-timed and ill-conceived, if indeed not actually of some advantage to their cause.[1] Thus as the campaign of 1892 approached, the Democrats found themselves in a difficult position. Populism had spread like wildfire since the summer of the preceding year, while the old party was never in poorer condition to undertake an important campaign. In the first place, a fratricidal conflict threatened its complete disruption; and in the second, a long period of unchallenged dominance had lulled its leaders into such a sense of security that they had allowed its organization, and more especially its local machinery, to fall into decay.

Under the circumstances there was no alternative for the managers of the dominant party but to concentrate on settling their domestic difficulties and make light of the new party giant. Hence they adopted consciously the policy of belittling the Populists, filling the air with stories, anecdotes, and other devices designed to make of the People's Party an object of opprobrium, scorn, and ridicule. To illustrate, a troublesome and persistent cattle horn fly was dubbed promptly the "Third Party fly," and it became known far and wide by that name. Again, the alleged folly of the Reformer was pointed out frequently: an ingenious editor, to instance, contrived a letter from one John Henry Damphool, who complained that because of the expenses of Populism in days lost from work, time and trouble in attending Third Party encampments, boarding Populist speakers, subscribing to Reform newspapers, and buying Reform literature, he had failed to pay out of debt the preceding fall for the first time in seven years.[2] Thus did the Democrats seek to deal with the Third Party by ridicule, a method which was especially favored in the early days of that party.

If the Democratic leaders purposed to laugh the People's Party out of existence, however, they were doomed to disappointment. The surprising showing of the Reform candidates in 1892 served as a warning to the managers of the old party, who prepared to give to the contest of 1894 their undivided attention. They encouraged their local aides to organize Democratic cells, especially in districts of strategic importance; and as the campaign came on, they entered

---

[1] *Supra*, Chap. II.
[2] *The Palo Pinto County Star*, Feb. 25, 1893.

the field with speakers who toured the State in the interest of the party. They resorted also to written propaganda. In short, they employed the usual techniques of campaigning, revealing in the use of those tactics no marked superiority over the Populist managers. The Democrats indeed would have experienced rough sledding had they depended primarily upon the hand-to-hand combat of the stump, for the People's Party boasted speakers second to none in effectiveness.[3] The directors of the old party, however, recognizing the potency of the Populist haranguers, turned to other methods, among which strategy was of primary importance.

The strategy of the Democratic generals called first for charges against their adversaries which either embroiled them in arduous campaigns of denial or impaled them on embarrassing confessions. There was, first, the accusation which reflected on the character or motives of the Populist leaders. It was alleged, for example, that some, as Nugent and Francisco, were religious cranks, while others, as Gibbs and Kearby, were infidels.[4] It was charged further that many were downright dishonest: those connected with the Alliance Exchange, for example, were characterized in some quarters as swindlers and embezzlers,[5] and even Barnett Gibbs was pointed to as a tax-dodger.[6] Again, all were characterized as political misfits, ne'er-do-wells, opportunists, and chronic dissenters. These charges and many others like them came in a steady flow, directly or indirectly, from Democratic sources, in what today would be called a "whispering campaign."

A second indictment sought to identify the People's Party with every odious organization which came to the attention of the Democratic managers. To illustrate, when the party was linked in gossip with a mysterious "dark lantern" military band, it was charged that

---

[3]*Supra*, Chaps. V, VII.

[4]Nugent was constrained to defend himself on this score (*Texas Advance*, June 2, 1894), as was Gibbs (*The Southern Mercury*, Sept. 8, 1898). The latter, with his unfailing good humor, insisted that he was a candidate for the gubernatorial office, and not for heaven, and that as such his record would stand comparison with that of his Democratic rival.

[5]The Alliance Exchange, a great Alliance wholesale farmers' supply house located in Dallas, had gone bankrupt in the late eighties at a loss of thousands of dollars to its stockholders.

[6]*The Southern Mercury*, Sept. 8, 1898.

its directors were contemplating its complete militarization.[7] Again, the party was stigmatized as the sponsor of the American Protective Association, and spokesmen of the Mexican, German, and Bohemian elements responded in a way which indicated that the dart had found its mark.[8]

Yet a third charge pertained to alleged defections from the party by prominent members. To illustrate, rumors were rife during the campaign of 1894 that Judge Nugent had withdrawn or would withdraw as the Populist candidate for Governor, and the known poor health of the nominee made credible the baseless report. On occasions of bonafide withdrawals by prominent Populists, the Democratic press outdid itself in broadcasting the news.[9] For the greater part, however, the rumors of defections were unfounded, a fact probably recognized by the Democratic strategists who set them circulating.

A fourth accusation connected the Third Party with the Republican in a cry of fusion, heard on every hand during the days immediately preceding an election. In the campaign of 1896, to take the best known instance. the Democratic managers produced and circulated widely two letters, one written by a Republican leader and the other by a Populist, which set forth in detail the provisions of a fusion agreement between the two minor parties.[10] The

---

[7]*The People's Journal*, Dec. 30, 1892.

[8]The press was filled with the A.P.A. question in 1894, and some mention was made of it in 1896. See, for example, *Texas Advance*, Feb. 3, March 17, 24, 1894; *The Galveston Daily News*, Nov. 25, 1893, March 9, May 30, Aug. 26, 1894, March 22, May 15, 1896; *Dallas Morning News*, May 6, June 3, Aug. 24, 25, 1894; *Fort Worth Daily Gazette*, May 6, 1894; *The San Antonio Daily Express*, June 14, 21, July 1, Oct. 15, 1896.

The Populist press, of course, denied the charge with vehemence.

[9]See notices in journals as widely scattered as *The Weekly Newsboy* (Oct. 10, 1894, Oct. 28, 1896), the *La Grange Journal* (Oct. 15, 1896), *The Beeville Bee* (Oct. 9, 1896), and the *Pecan Valley News* (Oct. 10, 1894, Oct. 14, 1896— in the Library of Howard Payne College, Brownwood, Texas). The references to the year 1896 pertain to the withdrawal of W. M. (Buck) Walton, the Populist candidate for Attorney-General.

Note that in every case the announcement was released by the press only a short while before the day of election, so that it was impossible for the Populists effectively to refute it..

[10]See *The Beeville Bee*, Oct. 2, 1896, and *The Jacksonville Banner*, Oct. 23, 1896.

effectiveness of the charge may be reckoned from the large number of confessed Populist backsliders, as estimated from letters printed in the newspapers, Populist as well as Democratic.

A fifth charge brought against the People's Party played upon the prejudices growing out of the War. It seemed advantageous, for example, to identify the Third Party as a product of the North and to accuse it of being too friendly toward the negro. In the latter direction, the Democrats found that evidence accumulated almost without effort. It was a simple matter, therefore, to prove that Populist leaders had held out special inducements to the negroes, that they had fraternized with them,[11] and that they had promised them certain concessions, as, for example, to be called for jury service.[12] With regard to most of these charges, the Populists could do naught but confess their truth, though the confession admittedly alienated large blocks of white voters.

A second type of Democratic strategy involved the deliverance of a deft stroke which either compromised the Populist managers or galled them almost beyond endurance. For example, when the Third Party people scheduled a great campmeeting at Greenville for the spring of 1896, Democratic sympathizers promptly spread a rumor of a smallpox epidemic in that vicinity. Again, the Democrats conceived a brilliant stroke now and again with regard to the negro vote. As an example, in Sabine County a local Democratic leader represented himself, in correspondence with Republican State Chairman Grant, as one deeply interested in the welfare of the Republican Party, and he furnished the chairman with the names of prominent negroes of the county who began shortly to receive quantities of Republican literature. In these, and in many other ways which might be noted, did the Democrats harass the Third Party managers. The steps taken frequently were little more than scurvy tricks of a petty nature, though they made a definite contribution to the technique of the major party's campaign.[13]

---

[11]In Nacogdoches County a charge by the Democrats that a prominent Populist had shaken hands with a negro leader almost led to serious trouble.

[12]In the same county the Populist sheriff attempted to carry the promise into effect, with none but evil consequences for his party. See *The Jacksonville Banner*, Nov. 2, 1894.

[13]One may find repeated references to such practices in any Populist journal. *The Southern Mercury*, for example, was filled with complaints against them.

A third bit of Democratic strategy consisted of a system of rewards and punishments which were visited upon the citizen according to his merits. The Third Party adherent found himself out of a job now and then, for example, by reason of his political beliefs, and in some sections he was even barred from jury service.[14] The rewards were not wholly negative in nature, however, as is evidenced by the concession allegedly granted to the Populist chairman of Cass County. That individual quit his post and his party, and two weeks thereafter, it was charged, his brother returned home from the penitentiary with a full pardon from a life term. Of what avail, Third Party men asked plaintively, to compete against adversaries of so little principle?[15]

A final type of strategy pressed into use against the Populists took into account the element of human nature, which was frequently ignored in the heat of partisan battle. It is found exemplified best in the campaign waged for Congress by S. W. T. Lanham in 1896. The usual contest was a hammer-and-tongs affair characterized chiefly by vigorous denunciation on the part of both candidates. But Lanham would have none of that. Instead, he approached his audiences in a sentimental, teary-eyed, friends-of-my-boyhood manner, pleading with his listeners in a husky voice to forget their petty differences and unite again in the party of their first love. A few weeks of such campaigning literally broke the resistance of the Third Party in one of its strongholds: People's Party men returned to the Democratic fold in numbers, and a race which in the beginning had looked very unpromising ended in a handsome victory for the candidate of the Democrats.[16]

---

[14]*The Southern Mercury*, June 6, 1895. The reference is to a letter from a Populist in Rusk County who charged that the Democratic district judge stacked the jury commission, so that no Populists were summoned for service.

[15]*The Dublin Progress*, Oct. 16, 1896.

[16]*Pecan Valley News*, June 3, Aug. 12, 1896; *The Dublin Progress*, Aug. 28, Sept. 4, 1896.

The present editor of *The Goldthwaite Eagle*, who is a veteran newspaper man of his section of the State, vouched for the efficacy of Lanham's methods in an interview with the author and confessed that his own newspaper tirades against Populism had had the sole effect of making the Third Party people more obstinate in their adherence to Populism.

The leaders of the Democracy thus depended in good part upon strategy for the effectiveness of their campaigns. Frequently, however, it developed that skill in maneuvering alone would not suffice. In particular, in the Mexican and negro counties the purchaseable vote often necessitated recourse to direct action, and occasionally to force. In the Mexican counties of South Texas, where the Reform movement did not threaten the supremacy of the dominant party, it is enough to note that the Democratic managers manipulated the Mexican vote as their interests required.

A different story must be told of the negro districts, however, for there the apostles of Populism championed the faith of Reform to such effect that the leaders of the old party were hard put to retain control. The result was the old methods of direct action, long unused, were resurrected and brought to bear once more. The owl meeting, for example, and the strong arm tactics which accompanied it were pressed into use.[17] In one large respect the Democratic methods differed from those of the Third Party: in eight or nine strongly negro counties the old line leaders sponsored the organization of a White Man's Party which combined all white voters into an association against the negro and those accustomed to profit by his manipulation. While the White Man's Party ordinarily did not affect the People's Party, it was utilized in Grimes County to oust the Populist sheriff, whose dominance depended upon his control of the negro vote.[18] The White Man's union, in so far as Populism was concerned, served the purpose chiefly of indicating the length to which the old party managers would go to maintain white (Democratic) supremacy in the negro strongholds. If the weapons of direct action did not avail to gain the end sought, they employed other means;[19] and finally if it became necessary, they

---

[17]*Supra*, Chap. VII.

[18]One who is willing to undergo the hardships involved may learn many interesting things concerning the White Man's Party from those who have a first hand knowledge of the organization. Practically nothing, however, has been written on the subject.

[19]To illustrate the means available, it may be noted that in Walker County the precinct lines were changed in such a way as to throw the voters of a negro community into a precinct whose voting place was located across a large river, with the result that the number of votes cast by the members of the community decreased appreciably.

counted out their opponents and made returns which revealed the results desired. It was, therefore, very difficult to defeat the candidates of the established party in the negro districts. Despite the best efforts of the Democrats, despite the machinations of their strategists and strong men, the Populist nominees for both local offices and legislative seats frequently were elected. In these instances the Democratic managers deemed it necessary to make the situation as unpleasant as possible for the intruders. With regard to Populist local officials, they charged inefficiency and incompetence; they prevailed upon the Legislature to pass special laws taking away their powers; they brought suit against them charging a variety of offenses—in short, they sought to hound them out of office and point out to the voters their error in having elected them. With respect to Third Party legislators they pursued the same course, holding their victims up to ridicule, magnifying trivial incidents into mountainous indictments against the Reformers, and pointing out constantly the alleged inefficacy of their tactics.[20] In short, the battle continued unabated until the last Populist had been harried from office, either through removal or resignation or, more generally, through failure to obtain reëlection.

The Democrats, then, were tireless in their efforts to accomplish the defeat of the Third Party. The Populists, however, were a hardy race, returning repeatedly to the charge with unabated enthusiasm. More than once their candidates pressed close upon those of the old party whose leaders thereupon prepared to administer the *coup de grace* to Populism. The final blow was reserved to the last possible moment, for if it insured the death of Populism it also implied the justice of Reform principles. It involved, in brief, the absorption of the People's Party by the Democratic through the adoption, in whole or in part, of the fundamentals of the Populist program. Neither Democrat nor Populist was content to make an end to the quarrel in this fashion, and both lived in constant dread, the former lest it should be necessary that it adopt the principles of Reform, the latter lest that be an inevitable consequence of the issue. In point of fact, these fears proved to be well founded, for

---

[20]*Supra,* Chap. IX.

the Democratic Party ultimately deemed it expedient to seize the leading principles of Populism for its own.[21]

In these several ways, therefore, did the Democratic directors wage defensive and offensive drives against the Populist pretenders to power. Beginning with a campaign which made use of the stock methods, they varied their attack by recourse to strategy. The deft stroke did not always avail, however, for there were large groups of voters who were unable or unwilling to grasp the significance of the strategem. For these, direct action with its corollary, force, was reserved. Notwithstanding these devious devices, Third Party candidates frequently obtained possession of office, and this necessitated a never-ending campaign until the forces of Reform had been utterly routed. Finally, when every alternative had been exhausted and the Populists continued to return to the charge, the Democrats yet had one last recourse, namely the adoption of the Reform program and the absorption of the Third Party, to which they were forced eventually to resort.

II

For five years and three vigorous campaigns the Third Party stood up under the constant bombardment of the Democrats, apparently with nothing more than a few surface scars to indicate the severity of the conflict. The Populists indeed seemed actually to thrive on adversities, for they returned to the field of battle after each rebuff with renewed vigor and redoubled strength; and at the beginning of the year 1896 there was apparently nothing to foreshadow aught but continued growth and perhaps ultimate success for the People's Party.

To one accustomed to reading the signs of the times in politics, however, all might not have seemed so favorable to the Third Party. In Texas, it is true, there was little of a discouraging nature, but Populism, as a national movement, must take into account the whole field of national politics. For some years prior to 1896 the so-called national issues had not been of a type to embarrass the advocates of Reform. As the presidential election year approached, however, a cloud began to gather on the Populist horizon, for the

---

[21]*Infra*, Chap. XI.

question of free silver, long associated with the demand for more money, was discussed with ever greater seriousness; and it began to appear that one of the old parties, probably the Democratic, might make the white metal an issue in 1896.

The national leaders of the People's Party viewed the possibility of such a campaign with conflicting emotions. A national campaign for free silver under the Democratic standard seemed to offer a definite hope for the acceptance of the foremost of Populist demands, but at the same time it would contain a serious menace to the Third Party, threatening it with the possibility of total extinction. It was not given to the Reform leaders, however, to indicate conclusively whether they would like to see the issue so raised; instead they must determine the course of their party concerning free silver in whatever position it might find itself during the campaign. Suppose neither of the old parties should espouse the cause of silver, they asked themselves. In that case the way would be plain, for the People's Party then would need only to follow the natural course and pronounce for silver money. But suppose one should accept the challenge and force a fight on the issue? In that event, the party would have an alternative: it might, in the first place, maintain its organization and wage a separate campaign, standing behind its own nominees "in the middle of the road," or it might, in the second place, "fuse" with the party friendly to free silver and wage a joint campaign in the common cause. There was little disagreement among the Populists as to the course they should pursue in the event that free silver should go begging for a champion, but discord prevailed among them concerning the tactics to be adopted in case one of the old parties should pronounce for silver.

As the time for the national conventions approached, the Populist tacticians concluded to employ a bit of strategy: they would call their convention to meet after those of the old parties, thus securing to it the advantage of the last and final voice in the matter of platform. The decision was not reached without considerable debate. It was perceived that the espousal of free silver by an earlier convention might undermine Populism; but the game was thought to be worth the risk, for it was hoped that both of the old parties would either ignore that issue or deal with it so equivocally that the way would be left open for its championship by the Populists.

Those who accepted this view could not, of course, foresee the brilliant eloquence of Bryan, whose "cross of gold" speech at one stroke brought him the Democratic nomination for the Presidency on a free silver platform and wrecked completely the plans of the Third Party men. They had hoped to wage a vigorous campaign for free silver in their own right against both of the old parties; they had now to consider the policy to be pursued by the Reform Party in a campaign in which the Democrats would support a "Popocratic" candidate on a Populist platform! In this unceremonious fashion was the course of the Third Party changed for the campaign of 1896, and, as it proved, for all time.

All the while, the leaders of the Third Party in Texas viewed the national situation with naught but misgivings. In 1895 a large majority of them were staunch middle-of-the-road men,[22] nor did their attitude change with the advent of the presidential election year. Hence they regretted the decision which called the Populist national convention to meet after those of the other two parties; a better plan, they believed, would be to "jump the gun" by seizing the silver issue and forcing the other parties to wrestle with the *fait accompli* in subsequent conventions. Once the convention was called, however, they had no option but to accept the decision and, if possible, force the nomination of a straight Third Party ticket. The latter they sought to insure by sending 103 delegates to the convention who were mid-roaders to a man.

As the date for the Populist national convention drew near, it became evident that the proceedings were likely to be marked by anything but harmony, for the fusion-midroad quarrel grew ever more bitter. Thus when the convention met on July 22, the party was divided nationally into two irreconcilable camps, each suspicious and intolerant of the views of the other. The battle which ensued resulted in a fusionist victory, for while the convention was prevented from endorsing the Democratic candidates for both President and Vice President, as some few Populist leaders wished to do, it nevertheless was prevailed upon to nominate Bryan for the Presidency and Tom Watson of Georgia, a staunch Populist, for the Vice Presidency. At the same time a request was made that

---

[22]For evidence of their staunchness consult the columns of the *Mercury* for the issues of Sept. 12 to Oct. 10, 1895.

the Democrats withdraw Sewall, their candidate for Vice President, in favor of Watson, thus completing the fusion deal and making it a reciprocal rather than a unilateral arrangement.

In the negotiations which led to the nomination of the fusion ticket the Texas delegation had no part. On the contrary, they remained true to mid-roadism, attempting to block the fusionists and force the nomination of straight Populist candidates. In the achievement of this purpose they failed, though the valor of the "immortal 103" delegates from Texas was granted by all; and having failed, they accepted the decision, though with ill grace, and returned home to work with whatever zeal they could muster for the combination ticket.[23]

Few Texas Populists, then, liked the ticket agreed upon, and all insisted that the Democrats must withdraw the name of Sewall and substitute that of Watson. Sewall nevertheless continued to stand. Moreover, Bryan failed formally to accept the nomination of the People's Party. As time wore on, it became apparent that the Democrats did not intend to carry out their part of what the Populist leaders considered to be an implied bargain. The plight of the Third Party therefore became desperate: it must establish its right to a separate place in the campaign for free silver or concede that the Democratic Party had become the party of Populism and reconcile itself to an early death. And the Democrats, far from recognizing Populism's claim to a condominium in free silver, demanded as the price of admission to the bandwagon

---

[23]As was to be expected, partisan strife grew extremely bitter during the course of the convention, and charges of perfidy and treachery were heard on every hand. Whatever the attitude of the fusionists at the close of the meeting, the mid-roaders felt very definitely that they had been "railroaded." They charged, for example, that strong mid-road delegations, as those of Texas and California, had been seated in such a way as to preclude their coöperating on the floor of the convention; that the chairman had manipulated the meeting to suit the ends of the fusionists, regardless of the wishes of the mid-roaders who, it was insisted, were in the majority; and that the lighting system had proved very capricious, the lights failing on one occasion at the precise moment when the fusionists would have been routed utterly but for the untimely forced adjournment. These charges, repeated to the author by more than one of the surviving "103" from Texas, reveal the depth of the feeling engendered by the fusion-midroad quarrel.

unconditional surrender. Thus uncompromisingly did the Democratic Party become that of Populism, very neatly absorbing the Third Party and blotting it from the national canvas.

In Texas the People's Party made the best of the sorry situation, continuing to consider Bryan the nominee of the Reformers but upbraiding the Democrats for their refusal to accept Watson. On the side of practical politics, the Populist campaign committee proposed to the Democratic state convention that the two parties divide the electoral ticket, the Democrats naming eight electors and the Populists seven.[24] When the Democrats refused to entertain this proposal, the Third Party named a list of Populist electors which in the final count carried for Bryan and Watson only Sabine County.[25] Thus the People's Party in Texas found itself facing the same situation as that which confronted the national organization.[26]

Even in these difficult circumstances, the People's Party of Texas might have weathered the storm with some success if the portion of its platform susceptible of achievement by state action had been more convincing and if its Democratic rival had left it to pursue its way in peace. The last was not to be for the apparent reason that, when the demand for a measure became sufficiently widespread, the dominant party seized and took action on it. The leading Populist state issues thus became those of the Democratic Party. Its secondary demands, as for example those pertaining to direct legislation and the recall, the proposed "cornbread and bacon" railway, and the projected maritime college, proved unequal to the task of bearing up alone the weight of a separate political party. The People's Party, in truth, rested essentially on important issues of an economic nature, and once those issues had received attention it found itself robbed of its *raison d'être*. Nationally, it was forced into bankruptcy by the free silver campaign; locally, the party found its well-being so inextricably interwoven with that issue that

---

[24]*The Southern Mercury*, Aug. 27, 1896.

[25]The columns of the *Mercury* for the year 1896 were filled with the quarrel here discussed, charges and counter-charges, accusations and denials appearing with almost every issue.

[26]Professor Hicks, in his *Populist Revolt*, Chapter XIII, presents clearly and concisely an analysis of the events of 1896 from the point of view of the People's Party.

it was only a question of time until it would be forced to follow the national organization into oblivion.

The Third Party, then, declined rapidly after 1896, principally because of the course of national politics. Within the State, however, there were certain factors which contributed not a little to the process of disintegration, among them the relationship between Populism and Republicanism. When the place which free silver was to occupy in the campaign of 1896 had come generally to be understood, when the air was filled with the cry of perfidy and treason, the Republican managers came to the Populist leaders with a fusion proposal: vote for our national ticket, they proposed, and we will support your state ticket. Thus, they argued, all will profit; mayhap we will poll a winning vote for President and you will carry the State and so be avenged of the Democrats.[27] History does not record the Populist answer, but it does reveal that there was a considerable interchange of vote between the two parties.[28] Dr. John Grant, State Chairman of the Republican Party, came out actively in support of the Third Party ticket,[29] instructing the local Republican managers to work for the Populist candidates. One factor only had the fusionists overlooked, and that was the wishes of a colored gentleman of renown, one William ("Gooseneck Bill") McDonald. McDonald refused to abide by the agreement made but on the contrary stumped the State for the Democratic candidates, speaking to large colored audiences throughout East Texas. That his work was

---

[27]The newspapers of the day printed columns of charges concerning this alleged trade. See, for example, *The Beeville Bee*, Aug. 21, 1896 (in the Library of The University of Texas, Austin, Texas).

[28]The following table, while it furnishes no basis for a mathematically accurate estimate of the number of votes interchanged, gives rise to some interesting general conclusions of unquestionable validity.

The Election of 1896 in Texas

	Candidate for Governor	Presidential Electoral Ticket
Democrat	298,643	284,000
Republican		158,650
Populist	238,325	76,750
Total Vote Cast	536,968	519,400

[29]*The Southern Mercury*, Oct. 1, 1896; *The Beeville Bee*, Oct. 2, 1896.

an important factor in the defeat of the fusion ticket no one questioned; indeed, he was credited in many quarters with having turned the tide for the Democracy.[30] Again in 1898 a similar combination was effected, but in 1900 the Republican managers refused a proposal made by the Populists for fusion, choosing to nominate a straight ticket.[31]

The effect of fusion with the Republicans could have been naught but adverse for the People's Party. The Republican Party enjoyed an unsavory reputation in Texas by reason of its activities during Reconstruction, hence the efficacy of fusion with it was measured by success at the polls. The Populist-Republican alliance failed to achieve success. Fusion therefore proved of no advantage to the Third Party. On the contrary, the Democrats were quick to seize upon the combination and with the aid of renegade Populists and recalcitrant Republicans to broadcast the "deal" throughout the State. The tangible results of this campaign are to be seen in the hordes of Reformers who left the People's Party in 1896, many of them announcing through the press that the reason for their apostasy was the fusion agreement with the Republicans.

A second factor within the State which hastened the disintegration of the People's Party was the lack of harmony, after 1896, among its leaders. In an important sense the innumerable conflicts which sprang up may be considered as little more than a manifold continuation of the quarrels growing out of the old issue of fusion *versus* middle-of-the-road. After the Democratic *coup* of 1896, the leaders of the Third Party had two practicable alternatives. First, they might either admit dismal failure or claim complete success— and they had an option here—and allow their party to go into voluntary dissolution. Many of them, believing this to be the proper course, returned forthwith to the Democratic Party. Or secondly, they might insist on the maintenance of a party organization, which was the alternative favored by a large majority of the Populist managers.

If substantial agreement appeared on the general course of party action, however, there were at least two large differences of opinion

---

[30]*The Southern Mercury*, Oct. 6, Dec. 10, 1896; *Dallas Morning News*, Dec. 10, 1896.

[31]*The Southern Mercury*, Sept. 20, 1900.

SO NEAR AND YET SO FAR.
Or Why Bill McDonald Fused With the Democrats.

McDonald—Say Gubner doan you hoal dat bait sech a distance in de future.
Çulberson—That 's all right Bill. All you have to do is to whoop up the colored vote for the democratic ticket and all will be well.

—Illustration from Texas Siftet.

From *The Southern Mercury*, Oct. 22, 1896.

A Populist explanation of "Gooseneck Bill" McDonald's position in the campaign of 1896.

as to the methods to be pursued. There were those first who believed that the Third Party should retain its separate organization and nominate candidates on its own responsibility. The adherents of this doctrine, the middle-of-the-road men, were in the majority almost to the end of the century. Their spokesman locally was Editor Milton Park, of the *Southern Mercury*, whose attitude was marked by courage and steadfastness, if also by obstinacy and poor judgment. On the other hand, there were those who insisted that the party could serve no useful purpose by nominating candidates and waging hopeless campaigns. Let us therefore pursue an opportunist policy, they urged, driving bargains with any who will assist us in carrying our program into effect. The proponents of this policy, called fusionists (sometimes made to read con-fusionists by the mid-roaders), were in a distinct minority in the beginning; but they were ably led by Cyclone Davis, and their numbers increased yearly.

Here then was the germ of the quarrel which hastened the disintegration of the People's Party in the years following 1896. Park, if the truth be told, placed the welfare of the party first: perceiving that there was no place for a political party which had neither fundamental principles nor the urge to elect its candidates, he spent his days in zealous labor for the party to which, as editor of its official journal, he had become so devoted. On the other hand, in the person of Cyclone Davis the fusionists boasted a champion second to none. Davis had travelled widely in the interest of Reform, associating in his labors afield with such national leaders as Weaver, Butler, and Taubeneck, all able advocates of fusion. His contacts and his ability to see Populism in a detached light convinced him of the futility of straight party contests, and he became a confirmed proponent of fusion, thereby placing principle above party. He became at the same time, in the eyes of Park, one with that most odious of persons, the Populist who would sacrifice his party for a modicum of success by combination.

The rift between the two giants of Populism, minimized or ignored in its incipiency, grew ever wider. It came, indeed, to symbolize the chief problem before the party. Men who had worked together for a decade in behalf of Reform followed Park and Davis into opposing camps and became bitter enemies. Davis and his followers dealt directly with the national committee of the party, which was controlled by fusionists. Park and his colleagues, failing to convince the national committee of the error of its way, called a mid-road national conference and caused to be set up there a "national organization committee" which was, in effect, the national committee of a new political party, the mid-road Populist party.[32] Park himself was named to head the committee.

During the campaign of 1898 the fusion issue was relegated to the background, but with the approach of the presidential campaign of 1900 the quarrel broke out afresh. Park in truth found himself standing almost alone, with the support of none but Jerome Kearby. Of the remaining leaders, the four outstanding men, Davis, Tracy, Bradley, and Bentley, had become confirmed fusionists. The strife became ever more bitter; the fusionists defended their cause vigorously against the mid-roaders, who were untiring in their attacks.[33] A feeble effort was made in the late spring to reconcile the two forces, but the conferences called for that purpose found the task too great. The end came when Tracy, finding the state conference of May, 1900, in control of the mid-roaders, led the fusionists in bolting.[34] Thereafter little attempt was made to dissemble. The fusionists acted independently, and soon they ceased to act at all; the mid-roaders continued as the People's Party, though their efforts were half-hearted and their party indeed but a shadow of the old Third Party of the first half of the decade.[35]

The effect of the fusion quarrel on the rank and file of the party and on the morale of the leaders can be readily imagined. Petty bickerings, which sometimes assumed the character of serious quarrels, supplanted the seeming mutual trust and confidence which formerly had prevailed. In such an atmosphere the ordinary member of the party was lost completely: the men whose directions he had been wont to follow implicitly no longer served him as guiding lights illuminating all the same clear path, and he knew not where to turn. In his extremity he turned frequently to the Democratic

---

[32]*Ibid.*, April 22, June 10, July 8, 1897.

[33]The approach of the breaking point may be seen in the columns of the *Mercury* during the winter and early spring of 1900. See especially the issues of Jan. 4, 18, 25, and Feb. 1, 8, 1900.

[34]*Ibid.*, May 10, 1900.

[35]See Hicks' *Populist Revolt*, Chapter XIV, for an account of the fusion-midroad quarrel throughout the country and the decay of the People's Party.

Party, though often he found solace in the espousal of another cause, or in the adoption of a passive attitude with regard to public questions.

While the state leaders of Populism were about the business of speeding the end of their party by their ceaseless quarrelling, the cancerous infection of disharmony spread into many localities. To instance, a serious quarrel developed as early as 1894 in Frio County, where the editor of the Populist *Vindicator* persisted in printing uncomplimentary opinions concerning the Third Party sheriff. That individual tolerated the editorial attacks for some months, then exacted satisfaction by shooting and killing the of-fending critic.[36] Two years later a series of disputes arose involv-ing several prominent Populists of Erath County, not all of whom accepted with good graces the settlements of the questions which were agreed upon.[37] Again, in Nacogdoches County in 1900 a dis-illusioned old man, formerly a trusted spokesman of Reform, dis-covered that he had spent ten years of his life and considerable sums of money in a chase for a will-o'-the-wisp which had netted him nothing; and, concluding that he had been wronged by the managers of the party, he raised the hue and cry of ingratitude and robbery, attacking his former associates in a series of savage let-ters to the press.[38] Instances of a like nature might be multiplied almost indefinitely, but it suffices to say that the situations sketched were typical of those which arose in many sections of the State during the decade of the People's Party, but more especially from 1896 on.

Further evidence of the decline of the Third Party may be found in a factor which was at the same time both cause and effect, namely the marked deterioration in the personnel of Populist leadership. The Populist tickets for the early campaigns have the names of Nugent, Davis, McCulloch, Ashby, Jones, Kearby, and a host of other men of abilities comparable to those of the foremost Demo-cratic leaders. In later years, however, the tickets indicate that the party fell eventually into the hands of lesser lights, for among

---

[36]*Texas Advance*, July 28, 1894.

[37]*The Dublin Progress*, June 19, July 3, 10, 17, 24, 31, 1896; May 28, Nov. 26, 1897.

[38]*The Weekly Sentinel*, Sept. 26, Oct. 10, 17, 24, Nov. 2, 1900.

the nominees there appears the name of not one of its former trusted leaders. The speakers of the party, as listed in the *Mercury* for, let us say, 1893 and 1900, reveal the same unmistakable tendency. The conclusion therefore is so clear as to be almost self-substantiating that the People's Party, ably led in the beginning, was taken over in its later years by men who were qualified by neither ability nor experience for the tasks they assumed.

The reasons for this deterioration are not difficult to ascertain. Among them, the chief perhaps is that half a dozen of the ablest men in the party were claimed by death during the course of the decade.[39] In the second place, some of the foremost men of the party left the State, removing to other sections of the country.[40] In the third, many of those remaining, concluding that their efforts in the cause of Reform were fruitless of benefits, withdrew to private life without show or display.[41] In the fourth place, a few returned to the Democratic Party, which they had renounced to become Reformers. In the fifth, considerable numbers of the chief advisers of Populism went into the camp of the fusionists, thus becoming inactive in the latter day proceedings of the party. By these devious routes did the founders of the Third Party desert their creation and, by depriving it of able leadership, hasten its ultimate downfall.

The interest taken by the directors of the People's Party in its welfare was the measure, in general, of the spirit of the rank and file of the party. For so long as Populist organizers roamed over the hills and prairies of the State, for so long as stump speakers

---

[39]Among these were Thomas Gaines, H. E. McCulloch, Thomas L. Nugent, and Evan Jones.

The regularity with which the leaders of the party passed on in the early nineties led to the suspicion, entertained in some quarters, that not all of the deaths were natural, and there were occasional dark hints concerning "the small bottle" in the hands of Democratic henchmen.

[40]The *Comanche Chief*, in an issue of the year 1902, remarked that most of the Populist leaders had emigrated to the Indian Territory. Presumably the *Chief* alluded to local leaders, though it is true that some well known Populists, among them Stump Ashby and Thomas P. Gore, removed to Oklahoma after the heyday of the Populist movement and entered politics there.

[41]Such a one, for example, was Stump Ashby, who for some unaccountable reason disappeared from public notice for a period during the late nineties.

went among the people and harangued them on the virtues of Populism, for so long as campmeetings were held for the revivification of the Reform spirit—for just so long did the citizen listen to the alluring story of the promise of Populism.[42] The time came, however, when the old prophets ceased to appear as usual and when a doctrine of defeatism took the place of the former unrivalled confidence evident on every hand. When that time arrived, the common man of the party followed the lead of its acknowledged directors and arranged for a new disposal of his political allegiance according to his preferences. There is no better evidence of the significance of leadership in the career of the People's Party than that provided by a study of the relationship between that factor and the loyalty and enthusiasm of the rank and file of the party.

In these terms, then, may the fall of the Third Party in Texas be explained. First, and overshadowing all, was the nomination of Bryan for the Presidency by the Democratic Party on a free silver platform in 1896. Attendant upon this event, as an explanation of the party's failure to survive in the State even though attacked vitally as a national organization, was the fact that the Populist state platform was not sufficiently strong to justify the existence of a separate political party, especially in view of the frequent usurpation of Reform principles by the Democrats. Again, the policy which dictated combination with the Republicans brought little or no advantage and much grief to the Third Party. Yet again, the state leaders of Populism fell into conflict among themselves, principally over the problem of fusion, and their quarrels found a counterpart in the strife which too frequently developed in the county, to the undoubted detriment of the Reform movement. Finally, the old and trusted leaders of the party disappeared, carrying with them the vigor which had marked the early campaigns and the spirit and enthusiasm with which the party had been supported by the masses of its members. The party, in short, fell upon

---

[42]Of interest in this connection, and of some importance also, was the decline of the Farmers' Alliance. That order had done yeoman service in the youth of Populism by furnishing issues, leaders, and strength of organization to the young Third Party, but it had been allowed to deteriorate steadily until, by the middle nineties, it was innocuous as a factor of statewide consequence. There can be little doubt that there was a distinct relation between the decline of the Alliance and the subsequent collapse of the People's Party.

evil days; it grew querulous as it grew older, and finally it came
to that point of sterility which presaged its early death. Only by
courtesy was it called a political party during the last several
years of its existence.

During the campaigns of the early nineties, the party which for
so long had governed the State as it had pleased found its position
threatened seriously for the first time since Reconstruction. Its
reaction was a perfectly natural one: it tolerated the Third Party
until it was no longer safe to do so, then it fell to and harried the
Populists out of the land by methods which led to campaigns as
bitter as they were intense. The Reform lines withstood the Democratic charges temporarily, then broke in a retreat which soon became a rout. There was one, however, who refused to admit defeat.
Ever zealous in the cause in the halcyon days of Populism, he
suffered no diminution of faith after the turn of the tide. Even the
editor of the *Mercury* eventually must recognize the inevitable, however, and this he did in a series of despairing editorials at the end
of the year 1898. Three thousand men, he complained, will walk
ten miles through the snow to see a prize fight, yet those same men
would not walk ten steps to hear the best Reform speech ever delivered.[43] "This," he observed, "is the kind of cattle reformers
have to deal with in Texas."[44] He soon recovered his equanimity,
however, returning to defend his party against what he considered
to be the insidious attacks of the traitorous fusionists. And here
we find him at the end of the century, attempting now to reconcile
Populism and Socialism, now to effect a new combination of all
reform forces, but laboring always to save the remnant of the party
which except in name had been dead for four years.

[43]*The Southern Mercury*, Dec. 8, 1898. The allusion is to the fight between
Corbett and Sharkey of Nov. 22, 1898.
[44]*Ibid.*, Nov. 17, 1898. In this editorial, the writer inveighed chiefly against
the lethargy of the voter.

CHAPTER XI

SUMMARY AND CONCLUSIONS

THE FOREGOING eleven chapters complete a detailed analysis of the People's Party in Texas. It remains now for us to summarize briefly on the findings and to make certain observations which appear to be warranted by the study.

I

It is necessary to note, by way of background, that Texas in 1890 presented certain features which must be borne in mind when this State is considered as a field of action for political parties. First, it was a one-party state, with the Democratic Party in a position of dominance; second, it was essentially an agricultural empire. Its preference for Democracy and its agrarian nature must be grasped by one who would understand any important phase of local politics during the last decade of the nineteenth century.

A further consideration of importance grows from the grievances nursed by the farmer from the time of the Civil War on. First, there were certain conditions in the field of politics which were not to his liking. Again, there were many phases of the agricultural problem which demanded adjustment, as for example those pertaining to prices obtained for farm products and to the marketing system. Further, in the field of transportation conditions were equally unsatisfactory. The railroads, of course, were the chief object of the citizen's wrath, or solicitude, in this direction. Finally, there was much that might be subjected to criticism in the domain of public finance: in the sphere of the Federal Government, it was apparent (to the farmer) there was too little money, while in that of the State the system of taxation seemed unfair and unjust.

Thus dissatisfied, it is not strange that the farmer sought relief by organization during the last quarter of the century. The Grange, the first nation-wide post-War movement among the farmers, early revealed serious shortcomings, and its place, in a sense, soon was taken by the Greenback Party, which came to the front for a brief period to advocate politically the financial views of the farmer. Followed the Farmers' Alliance, which in turn gave way to the

People's Party, as had the Grange to the Greenback Party. The Grange, the Greenback Party, and the Alliance, all strong in Texas in their day, served to flat-break the ground for Populism, which followed in due time.

When Governor Hogg assumed office in 1890, he found himself in a most difficult position. The discontented elements, temporarily quieted by the new Governor's vigorous championship of the railroad commission, soon became active again; and ere long their leaders and the Governor were again at loggerheads. Eventually an issue was named on which battle was joined. It was found in the subtreasury plan of the Alliance, which, espoused by the malcontents, was rejected by the Governor and his party advisers. Cut to the quick by the action of the Democratic spokesmen, which virtually ostracized them from that party, the subtreasury men segregated themselves in a group called the "subtreasury" or "Jeffersonian" Democrats. Meanwhile a new political party, the People's Party, had come into being. Some investigation revealed that the new party and the Alliance were not greatly different in the important respects of leadership and program. There seemed, then, little reason for maintaining separate organizations for Jeffersonians and Populists, and the two groups fused, in April, 1892, to form the People's Party of Texas.

The program of the new party offered little that was new. Resting basically on the old Jeffersonian idea that all men were created free and equal, it insisted on adjustments in the fields of land, which under its theory ought to be preserved against the large and more especially the alien landholders; transportation, in which domain the railroads demanded strict regulation; and money, of which, as every Populist knew, there was too little in circulation. To these major demands were added some, as for example those relating to tax reform and trust regulation, of an auxiliary though important nature. Of a piece with the demand for fiat equality in the world of economics were the suggestions in the field of politics for the popular election of officers, short terms, limitations on reëlections, low salaries for public officials, direct legislation and the recall, and proportional representation. All or virtually all of these proposals grew logically from Populist adherence to the theory that all men are equal in rights and that the government therefore must guarantee them substantial economic equality and grant them equality in public rights and privileges.

Socially and economically, the new party depended largely on the support of the poor, small farmer for its voting strength, which fact stamped it as preponderantly a rural party. Its vote among the farmers was greatly increased by the support of the Farmers' Alliance, which came over into the Populist camp bag and baggage in the early days of the party. In addition to the poor farmers, the People's Party drew on the sheep ranchmen for support, and upon workingmen in general. Among merchants and professional classes it was all but ignored.

In the field of politics, the Third Party grew historically out of the old Greenback movement whose chief dogmas it accepted as its own. Its adherents, nevertheless, were whilom Democrats for the greater part. Now and then the Republicans came to its assistance, and throughout the decade the Socialists and the Prohibitionists supported its candidates with a large percentage of their voting strength. The party therefore drew on divers sources in the world of politics, though it was regarded rightly as a malcontent organization comprising chiefly renegade Democrats.

The People's Party was, however, something more than an ordinary political party, for it partook strongly of the nature of a religious order. Its leaders were for the most part staunch believers, as were the rank and file, and the Bible was referred to frequently as the final authority for the Populist creed. The Reformers were Protestants almost to a man, and their zeal made it easy enough for their political adversaries to stigmatize them as anti-Catholics, though apparently there was little justice in the charge.

In the matter of racial distribution, the People's Party drew largely upon whites who were native-born of native-born parentage, who comprised some 63 per cent of the State's total population. In the colored districts, whose population equalled 22 per cent of the State's total, the Third Party was forced usually to yield to the Democratic Party and frequently also to the Republican. Among the "foreign" population (*i.e.*, the population either foreign-born or native-born of foreign-born parents), which comprised 15 per cent of the State's total population, the party made few converts. In the Mexican counties of South Texas the strength of Populism was negligible, as it was also in the German districts of Central

Texas. Among the minor racial groups, the Czechs, the Poles, and the Swedes, the Reform Party likewise was almost wholly impotent. Hence it may be concluded that it was very largely a party of white, 100 per cent natives, with some little support among the negroes but none of consequence among the so-called foreign elements.

As regards the important element of leadership, the Third Party appeared at first blush to be well fortified. Particularly in the field of state leadership did its position seem strong, for it boasted the adherence of leaders who symbolized the Populist myth of justness and honor, who were very effective as speakers, and who possessed considerable ability as organizers. Some reflection will reveal, however, that the state leaders were not as strong in every respect as they at first appeared, for by important standards by which the qualities of political leadership may be judged they betrayed certain grave if not fatal weaknesses. In the domain of local politics, the party of Reform profited in certain counties from the allegiance of some very able leaders whose significance to Populism is demonstrable. In most sections, however, the Democratic Party maintained a distinct superiority in leadership at the lower level, and the conclusion is warranted that the Third Party, not overly strong in state leadership, was much weaker in the county.

In organization the People's Party, springing as it did from the Farmers' Alliance, profited directly from the machinery of the parent order. On its own account, it devised an hierarchy of primaries and conventions which paralleled the Alliance scheme rather closely. Like its progenitor, the Third Party boasted active units called Populist clubs which were found by the thousands during the heyday of Populism. Above the club was the primary, a precinct assembly of Populists; and above the primary, the county convention which met biennially for the nomination of local candidates and the selection of delegates to the higher conventions. Above the county were the representative, senatorial, and congressional district conventions, and finally the state convention. At each level was found also an executive committee, and usually a separate campaign committee. The former was subject to the convention from which it derived its authority, the latter to the executive committee.

Aside from the formal machinery, numerous auxiliary organizations were projected; indeed, some few systems of clubs with Populist predilections were set in operation, though these latter did not attain the importance which might have been theirs under more favorable conditions.

The propaganda techniques of the People's Party may be divided into two classes. First there were the methods employed for converting non-believers and strengthening the spirit of the faithful in times of peace. Among those methods was the educational campaign, pursued unceasingly through the agencies of printed appeals and Reform speakers. Ably abetting the educational campaign was a type of appeal which took into account the emotional weaknesses of the people. A brilliant summation of the Populist peace time propaganda methods was found in the campmeeting, an adaptation of the old religious festival known familiarly by the same name, where educational and emotional appeals were combined into a powerful weapon for Populism.

A second and frequently entirely different type of technique was that found in connection with the campaign proper. Here the leaders of the party appointed a state campaign committee or a campaign manager, under whose direction a vigorous battle, both in words and in writing, was waged with the opposing forces. Hand in hand with the campaign waged throughout the State were the battles fought at the level of the county under the direction of the local Populist chieftains. By far the most interesting phases of the local campaign were to be seen in those sections where some degree of bossism developed, as in the negro districts of Central and East Texas. There the Populist manager was forced frequently to resort to direct action, barter with the negro " 'fluence men," and organize "owl meetings" after the fashion of the times. The campaign which resulted, both state and local, often was bitter and acrimonious in the extreme. The Democrats stood their ground, and feelings were aroused which long out-lived the campaign which gave them birth.

Properly considered along with the subject of Populist propaganda and campaign techniques is the Reform press which played an important part in both peace time and election campaigns. The leaders of the Third Party from the first encouraged the growth of Reform journals, and the weekly *Advance* and later the weekly *Mercury*, which served the party in turn as state organs, were established in response to their demand. Populist weeklies also were set up throughout most of the State to the number, at the height of Populism, of about 100. Reform newspapers operated under severe limitations but were able nevertheless, through the medium of editorials, articles by loyal authors, letters from sympathizers, poems, and cartoons, to perform valuable services for the party. Their vigor and enthusiasm, however, were more than offset by their lack of numerical strength, for as compared with the Democratic press that of the People's Party was very weak.

The equipment and techniques thus far considered brought to the Third Party only a modicum of success at the polls. In state elections the executive offices remained free from Populist encroachments, though a few Reform candidates were elected to the Legislature. There they introduced, spoke for, and voted almost unanimously for bills designed to carry into effect the demands of their party. Since the Democratic majority refused to listen to their suggestions, few bills sponsored by them were passed, though they were able to make their presence felt by combining with the retrenchment Democrats. Even so, however, the practical significance of their vote was not great. Locally, a number of counties fell wholly or partly into the hands of the Populists. In those instances it seems fair to conclude that, notwithstanding the many charges of inefficiency and even dishonesty, some of which undoubtedly were justified, the Reform officers served usually as satisfactorily as had their Democratic predecessors.

It was too much to expect that the Democratic Party would submit to the indignities heaped upon it by the advocates of Populism without rising to the defense of its name, its platform, and its spokesmen. In the beginning, it is true, the managers of the old party, being engaged in domestic house-cleaning, were inclined to ignore the People's Party. In time, however, they recognized the seriousness of the situation and evolved a defense more than adequate to withstand the charges of their adversaries. Employing all the strategy at their command, and resorting to "strong arm" tactics when the occasion demanded, they literally overwhelmed the Populists in a merciless counter-campaign. The party of Reform, evincing surprising stamina, approached its third campaign with considerable confidence. Meanwhile, however, darkening clouds were gathering on the horizon. The free silver agitation had reached such proportions that the national Democracy was constrained to espouse the cause of the white metal, and with its decision was sounded the death knell of Populism. Numerous factors contributed to the decline of the People's Party, which, active and robust in 1896, had lost all semblance of its former strength by the end of the century.

II

It is in order now to offer certain observations concerning the People's Party and the study here made of it. The nature of these observations may be indicated by a number of questions, a discussion of which will bring out the points which appear to deserve emphasis. First, in what terms may the rise of the People's Party be explained? Second, what are the obstacles which confront a minor party, and how did these difficulties operate on the Third Party in Texas? Third, what are the services which a minor party may be expected to perform? In what manner did the People's Party, particularly in this State, execute the functions which might legitimately have been expected of it? Fourth, what is the significance of such a study as is here made of third party politics?

Of the various acceptable explanations of the phenomenon called Populism none is more attractive than that which characterizes the movement as a child of the Frontier. The late Professor Frederick Jackson Turner has pointed out how the staunch individualism of the pioneer shades off gradually into a demand for protection and assistance by the government; how the rugged equality originally enforced by the conditions of frontier life thus becomes a legal equality guaranteed by law; and how the changed attitude is evidenced by agitation for free silver and greenback money, trust regulation, popular election and short terms for all officials, direct legislation and the recall, and other dogmas too numerous to record.

This authority indeed has gone further: he has analyzed the ideology of Populism and has so correlated it with the geographical distribution of Populist strength as to leave little doubt of the fundamental correctness of his conclusions.[1] Nor do they suffer when applied to the People's Party in Texas. There is much to be said for the proposition that this State in the nineties was yet frontier territory. Without pressing that point, there is no question but that its western and west-central portions were in the frontier stage of development. And, supporting Professor Turner's thesis, it was precisely in the west-central counties that Populism had its greatest vogue in Texas. It was those counties which furnished the staunchest leaders of the Third Party; it was there that men talked most about equality, that they revolted first, fought hardest, and surrendered last. The Populist movement, in Texas and elsewhere, was a complex of many forces, not least among which were the conditions and the state of mind bred of frontier life.

A second explanation of the People's Party (which in no way conflicts with the first) takes into account sectional interests. Professors Merriam and Gosnell have said that the political party is "one of the great agencies through which social interests express and execute themselves,"[2] and Professor Holcombe has adapted and elaborated the idea in detail.[3] From this point of view, a party consists of those who, from their interests, cannot afford not to coöperate, who expect to receive some direct benefit from their adherence to the cause. A new party therefore arises when shifting interests demand a partial or complete realignment of loyalties. Thus the People's Party becomes a mouthpiece for the farmers of the Mid-West, the silver men of the Mountain area, and the farmers of the South, who combine on a program of manifold demands, chief and most potent among which is that for free silver. It requires no great erudition to see what is the value of this explanation of the national parties, nor is its merit appreciably diminished when

[1] See his volume entitled *The Frontier in American History* (New York, 1921), especially at pp. 32, 147–148, 238–239, 246, 276–277, 305–306, and 327.

[2] Charles E. Merriam and Harold F. Gosnell, *The American Party System* (New York, 1929), p. 435.

[3] In his *Political Parties of Today*. See also M. Ostrogorski's *Democracy and the Organization of Political Parties* (New York, 1902), II, 457–458.

applied to the State. It is clear at once that the People's Party in Texas existed chiefly to give voice to the demands of the impoverished farmers and that, while its leaders locally made an earnest effort to command the support of other interest groups, it remained largely an agency through which the agrarians made known their desires.

A third thesis of demonstrable validity recognizes that there are times when the old parties are content to wage sham battles over traditional issues, so that interests which require attention must command a new champion. To illustrate, the national major parties in 1890 had grown fat and lazy in their contests over issues of twenty years' standing, and in 1912 they again were coming rapidly to a similar point of sterility. In the first instance, the People's Party rose to put an end to the knightly tournaments of the traditional combatants; in the second, the Progressive movement injected a new vigor into national politics.[4] Minor parties come to the front, then, when political campaigns degenerate into a species of shadow boxing. In these terms may be explained in part the rise of the People's Party in Texas. In 1890, the Democratic Party of Texas had not had its mettle tested seriously in fifteen years. Consequently its helmsmen had learned to steer a serene middle course which encouraged, nay made necessary, the defection of those who desired action. Hence the People's Party came into being in part because of the refusal of the dominant party to deal with the issues of the day.

A final explanation of Populism rests on the idea that on occasion the leaders of the old party or parties will become so tyrannical in their actions as to foment rebellion in the ranks. The idea doubtless is somewhat far-fetched as a plausible explanation of the rise of new national parties, though local situations which might give rise to revolt can readily be imagined. In Texas in 1890 such a situation existed. It appeared, for example, that a definite line of succession to the Governorship had been established, with the Attorney General advancing as a matter of right to the higher office after the traditional two terms of service. Further, there was considerable dissatisfaction at the domination of the Democratic Party

[4]See Edward McChesney Sait, *American Parties and Elections* (New York, 1927), p. 198. See also Ostrogorski, *op. cit.*, p. 359.

by the "Tyler Gang." The Governor, James Stephen Hogg, was from Tyler (in Smith County); the Chairman of the State Executive Committee, N. W. Finley, was from Tyler; and when in 1891 the Governor appointed to fill a vacancy in the United States Senate his life-long friend and associate, Horace Chilton, of Tyler, it was almost too much for the voter to bear. Murmurings of discontent swelled rapidly into a chorus of charges of boss rule, and the People's Party of Texas sprang to the defense of the voter against the alleged clique.

The Third Party in Texas therefore may be understood only in the light of consideration of various forces. If it was in part a movement growing from the frontier spirit of equality translated into a demand for government protection and aid, it was also, and quite logically, a movement which rested on sectional social and economic interests; if it sprang in part from the refusal of the major parties (or, in Texas, the major party) to deal with significant issues, it was likewise in some sense a rebellion against the tyranny of the Democratic leaders. It was, then, of manifold sources and motives.

A minor party, whatever its character, labors under certain handicaps which obstruct its road to success. It must, if it wishes to maintain itself as a semi-permanent force in politics, hold out to its supporters some tangible hope of capturing the government offices at the level at which it seeks to operate; it must, in brief, promise to become a major party in order to establish itself as a serious threat to the existing parties. Notwithstanding the positive need, or at any rate the acknowledged utility, of a definite hope for success at the polls, it is an extremely difficult task for third party leaders to achieve any considerable electoral successes, for reasons which may be examined briefly, with special reference to the People's Party in Texas.

To begin with, the new party which aspires to national prominence finds that many accepted practices in politics, some constitutional or legal and others customary, block its path. To illustrate, consider the method by which the President is elected. Designed to secure nonpartisanship in selection, the method in fact has been turned to serve the ends and purposes of political parties, with the consequence that the presidential election has become the supreme test of party strength. A majority vote in the electoral college is required to elect a President, but such a vote results ordinarily only from the sustained efforts of a well-organized, well-financed, national political party. In short, the method of choice of the chief executive officer militates against the development of minor parties, guaranteeing as it does that no such party, under ordinary conditions, can hope to win.[5] The significance of this item for the student of the People's Party in Texas will appear from a recollection of the fact that that party was but the local manifestation of a national movement whose chief demand called for action by the National Government and whose leaders actually hoped, until the acceptance of free silver by the Democrats, to elect their candidate for President in 1896.

A second difficulty faced by minor parties relates with equal weight to state and national politics. It pertains to the drafting of a program which will be acceptable to all dissident elements. The problem is intensified by the fact that the more congenial factions presumably are arrayed already into the opposing camps of the major parties, so that the third party leader is confronted with the task of adjusting the differences of mutually antagonistic and frequently irreconcilable elements whose only bond oftentimes is their discontent.[6] The difficulty of reconciling these malcontents, apparent in the case of the national People's Party, may be seen also in that of the Third Party of Texas. Here there were disillusioned Democrats, Republicans, Greenbackers, Socialists, and Prohibitionists who demanded to be recognized in the party's program, and "postoak" Americans, Negroes, Germans, Mexicans, and other racial groups which ought likewise to be recognized. Along with the consideration of the diversity of available materials from which a minor party may be coined goes the factor of sectionalism. It may be, as has been said, that sectionalism is hateful to the American mind,[7] but this does not obviate the fact that parties are and seemingly must be based upon sectional interests.[8] It is, however, a

---

[5]Professor Holcombe has discussed this factor, and certain others in addition, in a careful and dispassionate manner in *op. cit.*, pp. 315 ff.

[6]Professor Holcombe takes a different view of this matter, holding that "the minor parties . . . are ordinarily more homogeneous and hence more harmonious than the major parties can possibly be." *Op. cit.*, pp. 343–344.

[7]James Bryce, *The American Commonwealth* (New York, 1895), II, 48 ff.

[8]Holcombe, *op. cit.*

matter of extreme difficulty for a minor party to put together enough strength in the various sections of the country to carry the day nationally. Locally also the appeal to special interests frequently goes awry. Thus in Texas the Populist appeal to the native white American farmer was very strong, so strong indeed that it served in part to alienate other social and economic and racial groups that might otherwise have professed Populism. The minor party then has a delicate course to steer, for it must at once appeal to and beware of special interests and localism; and by its ability properly to balance its policy regarding these factors is determined in part, and perhaps in large part, its success.

A third handicap confronting minor parties, both nationally and locally, arises from the need for and the difficulty of procuring adequate financial backing. Money almost always comes slowly into the coffers of the third party, for strong financial interests usually are too firmly entrenched in the existing parties to deem it advantageous to contribute to the chest of a new and untried organization. Further, the People's Party occupied a particularly unfortunate position in that its very existence rested on an anti-corporation, anti-wealth, cheap money program. Hence it is not strange that its national campaigns were poorly financed or that locally it was cramped by its limited resources. The poverty of the party in Texas, a matter of common knowledge, was the subject of unceasing complaint by its managers.

Again, new parties often take the field under leaders who lack both reputation and experience in politics. The Popocrats of 1896, it is true, found an inspiring leader in the person of Bryan, while the Progressives in 1912 commanded the services of the talismanic Roosevelt. The People's Party as such, however, numbered among its leaders no such prophets but was forced to rely on lesser lights for guidance. In Texas the party won the adherence of some prominent men of personal repute and ability, among them a few of political experience, but the foremost politicians of the State eschewed Populism as it were a plague. The truth is, political leaders are thoroughly familiar with the dangers of revolt. Further, they "know the ropes" under the existing setup; and if at any particular time they do not occupy places of influence, they entertain the eternal hope that things will take a turn for the better and they will be placed in power. They are concerned, then, with the maintenance of the existing alignment; they turn a deaf ear to the importunities of reformers. Minor parties therefore are forced to look among the less skilled, the less heroic, and mayhap the less able for their leaders.[9] It was so of the national People's Party, and it was no less so of the People's Party of Texas.

A different sort of obstacle has been found by some authorities of eminence in the character of the American people. The voters of this country, it has been said, are very fond of association and very sensitive to charges of disloyalty. Further, they have a considerable faith in and regard for order and the established authority, with the net result that they have become a well disciplined army.[10] Nor are they content to pursue their manifold ways in peace: the orthodoxy of the Puritans has transferred itself from the church into other fields, carrying with it unreasoning loyalty to institutions long established and contempt for and fear of those of recent origin or those beyond the pale.[11]

In politics this state of mind has made for a traditionalism which has been the wonder of foreign observers and the subject of caustic comment by American writers. The party provides a place of refuge for those who need social and group intercourse; its dogmas come to be accepted as revealed gospel; a creed of conformity envelops the voter, demanding above all things party loyalty and regularity.[12] Party fetishism thus takes the place of volitional action until in many quarters if not in most the voter has no option but to "vote the ticket": as Brand Whitlock has put it, adherence to one party or the other becomes a matter, not of intellectual choice, but of biological selection.[13] Once this attitude has been created, the notorious inertia of the electorate takes care of the matter of consistency and continuity. Bryce has recognized something of that

---

[9]Bryce, *loc. cit.* See also Robert Michels' penetrating study of the oligarchical tendencies of party leadership in his *Political Parties.*

[10]See Bryce, *loc. cit.* and p. 256.

[11]Ostrogorski advanced this idea in explanation of the "formalism" of American party life. *Op. cit.*, p. 587.

[12]See *ibid.*, pp. 353 ff, and pp. 588 ff.

[13]Quoted in Sait, *op. cit.*, p. 167. There was a story told some years ago of a small Texas town where, when two Republican votes were cast, the postmaster was seized and charged with repeating.

inertia in a telling phrase, "The Fatalism of the Multitude," which characterizes it in a manner which cannot be here improved.[14]

The significance of the above-described attitude for the student of minor parties should be at once and compellingly apparent. With special reference to the People's Party in Texas, it may be recalled in briefest fashion that Texas in 1890 was traditionally a one-party state; that the Republican Party had been of little consequence and less repute since Reconstruction, sharing with the negro, in the popular mind, the odium for having brought the State to the verge of chaos; and that the Democratic Party had risen as the saviour of Texas, bearing that title with such grace that its position as "the party" had become impregnable. Whole counties there were which boasted not a single white Republican.[15] The people, overwhelmingly Democratic in their sympathies, were of no mind to be converted to heresies.[16]

Minor parties, then, encounter innumerable obstacles in their march toward success, and the wonder is, not that so many have failed, but that so many have succeeded, in the common acceptance of the word succeed. If the national People's Party was heir to all the ills of minor party politics, the Third Party of Texas found its path likewise beset by what proved to be insuperable difficulties. The Populists, in sum, fought valiantly, but the odds against them were too great.

The People's Party therefore failed most miserably, if as the criterion of success one accepts the idea that the purpose of a political party is to gain control of the government by electing its candidates to office. Indeed, in this sense, if our national history points the way, a minor party may expect to succeed wholly and

---

[14]In *op. cit.*, Chap. LXXXV.

[15]The writer distinctly remembers the day not many years ago when, in a county in East Texas, his grandfather pointed out to him a citizen who looked like other men but who was set apart by virtue of his political beliefs. He was a Republican, the only white one in that part of the county.

[16]It is worthy of observation here that the Populist party suffered for some of the sins of its forbears and its contemporaries in minor party politics. Greenbackism, Union Laborism, Prohibitionism, and like panaceas had made the voter wary of third party "isms" and had rendered it necessary for a minor party to prove first of all that it was not harebrained. See Ostrogorski, *op. cit.*, p. 458.

so become a major party, as did the Republican Party, or to fail completely and pass off the scene, as have most minor parties; for apparently there is no place in our system for a permanent or semi-permanent third party. But if our history records the failure in one sense of the People's Party, it also suggests a different yardstick for the calculation of the successes of minor parties, a yardstick which by comparison makes the first criterion seem rather crude. Third parties, it has been pointed out repeatedly, ordinarily are parties of principle, and their very existence serves usually to indicate the presence of issues either ignored or avoided by the old parties. A more just criterion for judging of the success and worth of a third party may, therefore, be found in the answer to the question, what were the effects of the party upon political issues and the tone of public life?

Judged by this criterion, the People's Party presents an entirely different aspect. In the field of national politics, it forced the Democratic Party to the drastic step of accepting its cardinal demand and nominating Bryan on a free silver platform. Thus it virtually re-cast that party, causing it to renounce the leadership of Cleveland and become, in effect, a new party whose nature is revealed by the appellation, "the Popocratic party," with which it was endowed by the gold standard men. In Texas the Democrats early began the process of absorption of Reform principles which has not ended to the present day. In 1894 they wrote into their platform the Populist demand regarding convict labor;[17] in 1896 they approved the national Populist planks calling for free silver, the non-retirement of legal tender notes, the abolition of the national banks as banks of issue, the election of United States Senators by popular vote, and the income tax, and the state planks demanding a reform in the fee system and a mechanics' and laborers' lien law;[18] in 1898 they appropriated the Third Party protest against the indiscriminate issuance by the railroads of free passes.[19] In view of the fact that a railroad commission amendment and an alien land law had been carried earlier, the seizure of these planks by the Democrats left the Populists few issues regarded by them

---

[17]Winkler, *op. cit.*, p. 341.

[18]*Ibid.*, pp. 372–374, and 385–388.

[19]*Ibid.*, p. 404.

as vital. They had succeeded, then, beyond their wildest dreams, for in an important sense they had converted the Democratic Party to Populism.

But the services of the People's Party did not end with the championship of new issues. The old parties, state and national, in 1890 had allowed their zest of youth to degenerate into the complacency of middle age, their ideals into the familiar party traditions. Politics thus had become a workaday business, with little to disturb its serenity. It remained for the People's Party, bursting rudely in upon the placid scene, to revivify our political life by its espousal of principles once known but long forgotten by the major parties. "Restore the government to the people!" was the cry which resounded from the lips of Populists the country over, whether fusionists of Nebraska or mid-roaders of Texas, and its echo came back with redoubled volume years later from the lips of Roosevelt's Progressives. The spirit of idealism implicit in Populism, if somewhat removed from the realm of achievement, was genuine; its value, if intangible, was real.

The Third Party therefore may be said to have discharged satisfactorily the functions incumbent upon it as a minor party and thus to have achieved a large measure of success. In resumé, it may be noted, with particular reference to the People's Party of Texas, that it liberalized public thought and sentiment, making it safe if not popular to voice one's honest opinions on the issues of the day; it served, through its speakers and its press, as an educator of the populace of no mean influence; it struck lusty blows at, though it was not able to change markedly, the state of mind separating the South from the North; it kept up a steady bombardment against extravagance and profligacy in public expenditures and against corruption in public office, thereby participating in the (supposed) mitigation of those evils; and, most importantly, it brought forward issues which long had been side-stepped or ignored by the dominant party and urged them to such purpose that that party was forced to take action, frequently along the lines recommended by the Populists, in self-defense.[20] The action taken had the ultimate

---

[20]Jerome Kearby seems to have understood more clearly the functions of minor parties than most of his colleagues. In a letter by him to the *Southern Mercury* (Feb. 1, 1900) are found these words: "I care but little for party

effect of despatching the Third Party, which thus gave its very life to the cause in whose behalf it had been conceived, the victim of its own effectiveness.

In conclusion, attention may be called again to the necessity for bearing in mind the relation between the People's Party of Texas and the national People's Party. The Third Party in this State was not an entity in itself, but an integral part of the national organization, as is evidenced by the collapse of the local movement along with the national with the appropriation by the Democrats of the free silver issue. Nor should the local nature of this study be allowed to obscure that relationship. A larger study might have been made of the national People's Party, but such a study could not have been conducted satisfactorily because of the lack of adequate materials. Among the data indispensable for a reasoned analysis of a national third party movement are numerous detailed analyses of the party in various smaller units, as the states. The investigator of a large problem stands no less in need of definite and concrete facts than that of a small one, though quite frequently it is a physical impossibility for him to procure adequate data by first-hand investigation. Hence he must rely in part on studies made by other students who have so circumscribed their problem by limitations of time and space as to enable them to conduct a thorough examination of all available sources. In the field of politics, no satisfactory analysis of third parties in the United States has been made, nor will such an analysis be made, it is believed, until a number of local studies of minor parties have been completed. The study here brought to a close, together with others like it, should make possible the effective execution of larger and broader works; and if it serves in that capacity, it will have performed perhaps its greatest function. Meanwhile, the relation between the subject investigated and the larger problem should be kept prominently in mind.

---

success. If we can force a recognition of our policies and secure for them a practical operation, I am content. I want good government, pure politics, faithful administration of the laws, economy in high and low places. I care not who makes the law, so it is just, or who administers it, so it is impartial."

BIBLIOGRAPHY

In the pages which follow the author has made no effort to note every work, large and small, which has appeared on the People's Party in the last half-century. Instead he has attempted first to indicate only a few references which are of assistance in constructing a background, both general and local, for an understanding of the Populist party. The results of this effort are to be seen largely in Sections I and II below. If a more extensive bibliography is desired, an exhaustive one may be found in Professor John D. Hicks' book, *The Populist Revolt* (Minneapolis, 1931), pp. 447–464. A second aim has been to list the sources on the basis of which the foregoing study was made. Those sources, which are largely primary in nature, are found chiefly in Sections III, IV, V, and, to a less important extent, VI.

I. BOOKS AND MONOGRAPHS

Allen, E. A., *The Life and Public Services of James Baird Weaver* (Cincinnati, 1892).

Arnett, Alex Mathews, *The Populist Movement in Georgia,* in *Columbia University Studies in History, Economics, and Public Law,* V. 104 (New York, 1922).

Barker, Wharton, *The Great Issues* (Philadelphia, 1902).

Biesele, Rudolph Leopold, *The History of the German Settlements in Texas, 1831–1861* (Austin, 1930).

Brown, John Henry, *History of Texas,* 2 v. (St. Louis, 1893).

Bryce, James, *The American Commonwealth* (New York, 1895), Vol. II.

Buck, Solon Justus, *The Agrarian Crusade* (New Haven, 1920); *The Granger Movement* (Cambridge, 1913).

Chamberlain, H. R., *The Farmers' Alliance* (New York, 1891).

Clark, John B., *Populism in Alabama* (Auburn, 1927).

Davis, Jas. H. (Cyclone), *A Political Revelation* (Dallas, 1894).

Dunning, Nelson A. (Editor), *Farmers' Alliance History and Agricultural Digest* (Washington, 1891).

Haynes, Fred E., *Third Party Movements Since the Civil War, with Special Reference to Iowa* (Iowa City, 1916).

Hicks, John D., *The Populist Revolt* (Minneapolis, 1931).

History of Texas, Together with a Biographical History, etc. (Chicago, 1892, 1893, and 1895).

Holcombe, Arthur N., *Political Parties of Today* (New York, 1924).

Johnson, Frank W., *A History of Texas and Texans,* 5 v. (Chicago and New York, 1914).

Loughery, E. G., *Texas State Government* (Austin, 1897).

McVey, Frank L., *The Populist Movement* (American Economic Studies, V. 1, No. 3).

Merriam, Chas. E., *American Political Ideas* (Macmillan, 1920) ; *Four American Party Leaders* (New York, 1926) ; *New Aspects of Politics* (Chicago, 1925).

Merriam, Chas. E., and Gosnell, Harold F., *The American Party System*, Revised (New York, 1929).

Michels, Robert, *Political Parties* (New York, 1915).

Morgan, W. Scott, *History of the Wheel and Alliance and the Impending Revolution* (Fort Scott, 1889).

Nugent, Mrs. Catharine, *Life Work of Thomas L. Nugent* (Stephenville, Texas, 1896).

Ostrogorski, M., *Democracy and the Organization of Political Parties* (New York, 1902), Vol. II.

Peffer, W. A., *The Farmers' Side* (New York, 1891).

Porter, Kirk H., *National Party Platforms* (New York, 1924).

Potts, Chas. S., *Railroad Transportation in Texas* (Austin, 1909).

Ramsdell, Chas. W., *Reconstruction in Texas* (New York, 1910).

Sait, Edward McChesney, *American Parties and Elections* (New York, 1927).

Thrall, H. S., *A History of Texas* (New York, 1885).

Turner, Frederick Jackson, *The Frontier in American History* (New York, 1921).

Watson, Thos. E., *Political and Economic Handbook* (Atlanta, 1908).

Woodburn, Jas. A., *Political Parties and Party Problems in the United States*, 2nd edition (New York, 1914).

Wooten, Dudley G., *A Comprehensive History of Texas*, 2 v. (Dallas, 1898).

Weaver, Jas. B., *A Call to Action* (Des Moines, 1892).

II. ARTICLES

Allen, Wm. V., "The Populist Program," in 52 *Independent*, 475–6.

Barker, Wharton, "The People's Party," in 52 *Independent*, 2192–4.

Barnhart, John D., "Rainfall and the Populist Party in Nebraska," in 19 *American Political Science Review*, 527–540.

Butler, Marion, "The People's Party," in 28 *Forum*, 658–662.

Canfield, J. H., "Is the West Discontented?   A Local Study of Facts," in 18 *Forum*, 449.

Clayton, Ben F., "Politics and the Farmer," in 160 *North American Review*, 166–171.

Haynes, Fred E., "The New Sectionalism," in 10 *Quarterly Journal of Economics*, 269.

Keasbey, Lindley M., "The New Sectionalism: A Western Warning to the East," in 16 *Forum*, 578.

Macy, Jesse, "The Farmer in American Politics," in 3 *Yale Review*, 369.

Martin, Roscoe C., "The Grange as a Political Factor in Texas," in 6 *Southwestern Political and Social Science Quarterly*, 363–384; "The Greenback Party in Texas," in 30 *Southwestern Historical Quarterly*, 161–178.

Nation (editorial comment), "The Discontented Farmer," 71: 66–67.

Peffer, W. A., "The Passing of the People's Party," in 166 *N. A. R.*, 12–23; "The Mission of the Populist Party," in 157 *N. A. R.*, 665–678; "The Trust in Politics," in 170 *N. A. R.*, 244–252; "The Cure for a Vicious Monetary System," in 22 *Forum*, 722.

Roach, Hannah Grace, "Sectionalism in Congress, 1870–1890," in 19 *American Political Science Review*, 500–526.

Stahl, John M., "Are the Farmers Populists?" in 163 *N. A. R.*, 266–275; "Free Coinage and Farmers," in 22 *Forum*, 146.

Tracy, F. B., "Rise and Doom of the Populist Party," in 16 *Forum*, 240.

Vaile, Joel F., "Colorado's Experiment with Populism," in 18 *Forum*, 714.

Walker, C. S., "The Farmers' Movement," in *American Academy of Political Science*, IV.

Watson, Thos. E., "The People's Party Appeal," in 57 *Independent*, 829–832; 65 *Independent*, 882–886.

III. PUBLIC DOCUMENTS, RECORDS, AND REPORTS

Records of Election Returns (County), 1888–1906 (for the general elections). These records were examined in the offices of the county clerks of the following counties: Angelina, Bandera, Bastrop, Blanco, Brazoria, Brown, Coke, Comal, Comanche, Cooke, Delta, Erath, Fayette, Freestone, Gillespie, Goliad, Gonzales, Grimes, Guadalupe, Hood, Kendall, Lampasas, Marion, Matagorda, Medina, Mills, Montgomery, Nacogdoches, Navarro, Palo Pinto, Robertson, San Augustine, Somervell, Stephens, Walker, Wharton, Williamson, and Wilson.

Register of State and County Officers, 1888–1906 (in the office of the Secretary of State, Austin).

Report of the Commissioner of the General Land Office (of Texas), 1928–1930 (Austin, 1930).

Revised Civil Statutes of the State of Texas, 1895 (Austin, 1895).

Revised Civil Statutes of the State of Texas, 1925 (Austin, 1925).

Rules of Order of the House of Representatives of the Twenty-Third Legislature (Austin, 1893).

Rules of the Twenty-fourth Legislature (Austin, 1895).

Southwestern Reporter, Vols. 36, 38, 39.

Texas House Journal, Twenty-third, Twenty-fourth, Twenty-fifth, and Twenty-sixth Legislatures (Austin).

Texas Legislative Manual, 1897, 1901 (Austin, 1897, 1901).

The Constitution of Texas.

United States Census Reports, Eighth, Ninth, Tenth, Eleventh, Twelfth, and Thirteenth Census.

IV. NEWSPAPERS

A. Daily Newspapers

Dallas Morning News (Published at Dallas, Texas).

Fort Worth Daily Gazette (Fort Worth, Texas).

Houston Daily Telegraph (Houston, Texas).

The American (Philadelphia, Pennsylvania).
The Austin Statesman (Austin, Texas).
The Galveston Daily News (Galveston, Texas).
The San Antonio Daily Express (San Antonio, Texas).

B. Weekly Newspapers

Beeville Weekly Picayune (Published at Beeville, Texas).
Coke County Rustler (Robert Lee, Texas).
Columbia Gazette (Lake City, Florida).
Gainesville Signal (Gainesville, Texas).
Hempstead Weekly News (Hempstead, Texas).
Jacksboro Gazette (Jacksboro, Texas).
La Grange Journal (La Grange, Texas).
Lampasas Leader (Lampasas, Texas).
Nacogdoches Plaindealer (Nacogdoches, Texas).
North Texas Farmer (Paris, Texas).
Pecan Valley News (Brownwood, Texas).
Svoboda (La Grange, Texas).
Texas Advance (Dallas, Texas).
Texas Farmer (Dallas, Texas).
The Beeville Bee (Beeville, Texas).
The Champion-Press (Center, Texas).
The Comanche Chief (Comanche, Texas).
The Comanche Vanguard (Comanche, Texas).
The Daily Sentinel (Nacogdoches, Texas).
The Dublin Progress (Dublin, Texas).
The Goldthwaite Eagle (Goldthwaite, Texas).
The Gonzales Inquirer (Gonzales, Texas).
The Jacksonville Banner (Jacksonville, Texas).
The Palo Pinto County Star (Palo Pinto, Texas).
The Patriot (Navasota, Texas).
The People's Cause (Cooper, Texas).
The People's Journal (Lampasas, Texas).
The Pioneer Exponent (Comanche, Texas).
The Rusk County News (Henderson, Texas).
The Southern Mercury (Dallas, Texas).
The Texas Capital (Austin, Texas).
The Texas Herald (Paris, Texas).
The Texas Triangle (Paris, Texas).
The Texas Vorwaerts (Austin, Texas).
The Truth (Corsicana, Texas).
The Weekly News (Mexia, Texas).
The Weekly News-Boy (Jasper, Texas).
The Weekly Sentinel (Nacogdoches, Texas).
The Young Populist (Paris, Texas).

V. INTERVIEWS

The author has engaged in conversation with no less than 500 persons whom he has had reason to believe would have some information on the subject at hand and has solicited and received considerable data by correspondence in addition. Of the conversations, some 250 have been sufficiently valuable as sources to warrant their being classed as personal interviews. The writer has drawn heavily upon these interviews for interpretation and understanding, and often also for specific data. He has not, however, referred to them as sources, for the reason that most of them were granted only after he had pledged himself to treat the information given as confidential, or in any event not to divulge the name of the person interviewed.

VI. MISCELLANEOUS MATERIALS

Almanacs

The Houston Post Almanac.

The Texas Almanac (published by the *Dallas Morning News*).

American Newspaper Annual (Philadelphia, 1890, 1892, 1895, 1901).

Constitution of the Farmers' State Alliance of Texas (Dallas, 1890).

Macune, C. W., *The Farmers' Alliance* (mss. of the memoirs of Dr. Macune).

Masters' Theses (The University of Texas), unpublished.

Budd, H., *The Negro in Politics in Texas, 1867–1898* (1925).

Cox, A. B., *Economic History of Texas During the Period of Reconstruction* (1914).

McKay, S. S., *Texas During the Régime of E. J. Davis* (1919).

Pamphlets

Forney, John W., *What I Saw in Texas.*

Lang, W. W., *Texas and Her Capabilities.*

Letters to the Alliance Men of Texas.

Minor Chronicles of the Goodly Land of Texas.

Sansom, John W., *Battle of Nueces River* (San Antonio, 1905).

Speeches of Judge G. N. Aldredge (delivered at Sherman in 1894 and at Washington in 1896).

Private collections of letters, papers, and documents, made by

Biard, Jas. W. (Paris, Texas).

Clark, Dr. Pat B. (Clarksville, Texas).

Davis, J. W. H. (Navasota, Texas).

Rayner, J. B. (Calvert, Texas).

Skillern, W. A. (Nacogdoches, Texas).

Young, W. P. (Blossom, Texas).

(These collections were made available for the use of the author in each case either by the original collector or by a member of his immediate family.)

Proceedings of the Farmers' State Alliance of Texas.

Proceedings of the Texas State Grange.

Reports of the Texas Co-operative Association.

Songs for the Toiler.

The Holy Bible.

Type of Farming Areas in Texas (Bulletin No. 427, Texas Agricultural Experiment Station, May, 1931).

Winkler, Ernest William, *Platforms of Political Parties in Texas* (Austin, 1916).

INDEX